Publish and be damned
www.pabd.com

Travels in the Galaxy

Dave Horth

Publish and be damned
www.pabd.com

First published in Great Britain 2005 Dave Horth.
The moral right of Dave Horth to be identified as the author of this work has been asserted.

Designed in London, Great Britain, by Adlibbed Limited.
Printed and bound in the UK.

ISBN: 1-905225-15-6

Dedication

This book is dedicated to our families both past, present and future.

Thanks especially to Eliza for her total support.

Introduction

Eliza and I started living together in 1990. Ever since, we had wanted to go off travelling, but life being what it is kept getting in the way. Careers, studying and children were the main three (all exceptionally valid) reasons for staying, living and working in and around London.

In 2001 events came to a head which finally pushed us to go. September 11th made us slightly paranoid and fearful for our very future. Georgia, our eldest, was in her penultimate year at primary school – once in secondary school, the ability to take her out for a significant period would be removed and, at 18 would she want to go with us? By then, Indigo our youngest, would be in the same situation. Eliza was made redundant from her job and I was more than bored in mine.

We decided to jump at the opportunity and take an elongated trip, but where?

If it was just the two of us, I am sure that we would have gone further afield, but with two young girls, my paranoia about the state of the world and perceived risks overseas made us settle for somewhere nearer to home where there was easily an escape route available if things went badly. Focusing on one country rather than random wanderings was the right thing for us. We had known Italy for many years, but had not gone anywhere further south together than Turin or Milan. So we would go to Sicily and wend our way north. My brother Paul said "Christ, Dave, why do you have to go somewhere as dangerous as Sicily?" "Paul," I replied, "Chechnya is dangerous, Sicily is not."

The trip would be more complicated with children. I felt it was important to ensure that we saw and did things on most days as it would be very easy to slip into a do-nothing-but-lie-around-on-the-beach holiday. This proved to be a lot harder work than I expected, keeping up enthusiasm for visits over such a long period was hard work. There were definitely times when we suffered from tourist fatigue.

Georgia – who prefers to be called George – got the blessing of her primary school headmistress to miss the summer term. She promised to write a journal of her travels as part of her homework. I too took up journal writing and this book is the result. George managed to write on most days, but gave up in the last couple of weeks. The book shows the same events through the different perspective of first daughter then father.

Travels in the Galaxy

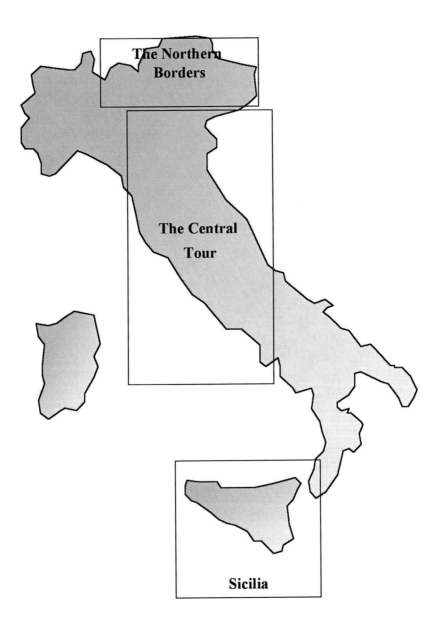

The Northern Borders

The Central Tour

Sicilia

Part 1: Sicilia

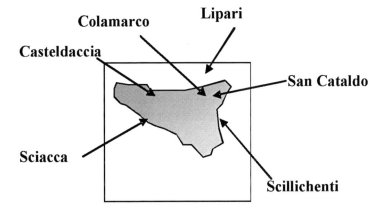

The Journey South
Day 1
Mileage 0
Wednesday 24th April 2002
The Road To Freedom

Mum woke me up at 4:20am! I was about to moan at my mum when I remembered that my adventure was just beginning. Sitting bolt upright and mum said "I've never seen you move so quickly!" After a couple of minutes I got out of bed and got dressed. We left at about 4:30 am and we were on our way to Dover and Italy. After an hour or so drive we reached Dover. The boat that took us from Dover to Calais which took about an hour and a half. Now the time (in French) was about 9:30 am (in England it was about 8:30am) At about four o'clock we stopped at a playground just before we left I spotted a key and brought into the car. We finaly stopped at an old French hotel called Les Negociants, the beds were very comfortable. We had dinner at a place called Chez blanc. For dinner me and Indigo had stake and chips which I enjoyed. After that I had a headache. The ice creams looked advertising (appetising) but they were coffee rather than chocolate.

*

We were up bright and early at four am. Except it wasn't bright, it was still dark. As usual, on the night before early starts, I had woken up several times worried that I had slept through my alarm. So I had a very disturbed night. Our farewell curry was thankfully lying dormant. The moon was almost full, and its light glared down at me through our windows most of the night.

We packed the very last bits and I wondered how we would manage to continually cram everything into the Galaxy as we went around Italy. Our luggage was bound to expand. Eliza woke the children and got them up and dressed. Both were keen, excited and got up with good grace. After saying goodbye to our cat and her four kittens it was time to go. It was ten to five and we were on our way.

How many miles were we going to do? Eliza thought about 3,000. I thought nearer five. We would see.

Even at this time of day, we were surprised at just how much traffic there was already on the move. Driving over the bridge at Dartford gave us our last view of the Thames and in the distance London, lying there grey in the early dawn light. We were on the 7am Seafrance boat from Dover to Calais. The boat itself was so peaceful – going mid-week, out of season and early. Normally, even at seven, the boats are busy, but today it was all quiet. It was very misty and calm and we took some time to see we were actually moving. Breakfast was a soothing time. George drank vast quantities (for George at any rate) of orange juice. And then we were in France!

I felt an increasing sense of unbridled release and unadulterated joy throughout the day. Somehow, inexplicably we had managed to free ourselves from the constraints of career and the cage of the daily commute. For us this was truly our road to freedom, even if it was only for a few short months.

We weren't sure how far to go today, but decided to stop in Bourg-en-Bresse. We drove into the town and seemed to go round in ever decreasing circles as we tracked down the tourist office. We went straight past it as there was nowhere to park… and then we were sucked into more one-way systems and pedestrian areas.

We parked, at last, at half past five. Nearly twelve hours on the road from home. Then, trying my broken French, I had to get my first ever euro coins for the parking meters.

On the way back to the tourist office we spotted a Logis sign and so decided to try our luck there, but it turned out to be the Logis office – and it was closed – and not a hotel.

I went on to the tourist office while George and Indigo went to play in the park with Eliza sitting on the bench watching. It was lovely. Warm sunshine was bathing our bodies.

In the tourist office, they found a hotel for us in the centre (Les Negociants). We all sat outside and had a drink. The town centre was very old with lots of eighteenth and nineteenth century buildings. Magnificent facades with decaying elegance surrounded us. The atmosphere was very relaxed, the French seemed content to be French at home.

We found our hotel after navigating in ever increasing circles around the town only to be directed from the front door of the hotel to the garage entrance via yet another convoluted route.

The old lady at reception who looked a bag of bones and a centenarian, but was probably only old enough to get a free bus pass, had great difficulties standing, finding her balance and getting her legs to work. I'm so glad I haven't got any sign of my dad's arthritis (yet). The interior of the hotel was a mixture of the old and the very old. Even some of the light bulbs looked like Edison originals. There were a set of wonderful looking cupboard doors on the ground and first floor hallways, but we couldn't work out how deep they could be. When we opened them for a peek inside there was no Narnia like depth to them only a solid brick wall. How very disappointing.

The local guide book gave information about local restaurants graded from 4 * down to zero star down to fast food. We decided to look at the zero star restaurants doing local/regional cuisine. We picked one in Place Bernard. This square seemed like one of the old centres of the town at the end of a long boulevard and with a fountain in its middle. The fountain had faces of men and lions around it and was about thirty feet tall. Unfortunately it was not working.

The restaurant, Chez Blanc, was attached to a Best Western Hotel which slightly put us off. I'm very glad it didn't. The food was wonderful. It may have been chicken and rice, chicken and mash and steak and chips, but not like anything you would get in England. Poulet de Bresse is a speciality of the region. The chicken is fed on special grass and herbs to give it excellent flavour. They were delicious. Soup and terrine as starters with wonderful French desserts simple made the meal.

We ended the day completely stress free and we reflected on our extremely good fortune to be here at the beginning of our travels. It was wonderful.

Day 2
Mileage 541
Thursday 25th April 2002
To The Med

Mum woke me up again this morning At 8:00 we went down for breckfast and had hot chocolate, bread, butter, strawberry jam and orange juice. After breckfast we got back in the car to Genova. We tried to get to Portofino (which is a place in Genova which my granddad recommended) but we couldn't get to Portofino because it was liberation day, so we turned around and drove to the port of Genova. We arrived at about seven o'clock. I was starting a picture of a building when the boat to Palermo started to load so I had to get back in the car. The boat didn't leave until 10 pm! For tea I had a bread roll. Our cabin was small, but it fitted all four of us in perfectly. Even though the boat didn't leave the port until ten, me and Indigo did not go to bed until 11:45.

*

All quiet in the hotel until the workers began their day. There was much banging and drilling going on as the hotel was undergoing refurbishment. It appeared that they were bringing it up to 1950's standard.

Le petit dejeuner was in the bar: French bread, croissants and brioche, hot chocolate, tea and coffee. For us this was a real treat.

Then off toward the Mont Blanc tunnel.

Near Geneva we encountered an anti-fascist demonstration. They had stopped the motorway traffic and were protesting against Le Pen who had just won the second place in the first round of the French Presidential election. People were suddenly worried and were waking up to the prospect that he may even be elected!

The motorway views were magnificent with great bridges and viaducts, tunnels and mountains.

The Mont Blanc tunnel had recently been re-opened to traffic after a horrific fire had closed it two years ago when nearly 40 people had died. The locals had got used to having their quiet valleys back without the noise and the pollution associated with the through traffic. Now the tunnel was opened to cars and trucks under 19 tons as a compromise.

We got to the tunnel about noon. There was not much traffic on the French side, but it still seemed to take forever to pay the toll and go through the tunnel. On the way out on the Italian side there were long queues. The queue went on for over four miles. Everyone in Italy appeared to be wanting to leave. What was it about April 25th? It must be an Italian bank holiday.

Once past the immediate vicinity of the Mont Blanc tunnel, past the Aosta Valley, all the roads were empty in both directions as we drove on to Genova.

In the last 10 miles before Genova however, the roads again became really busy. Everyone seemed to want to go along the coast. We found our way to the ferry terminal and then decided to go to Portofino – a place recommended to us by Mike, Eliza's father. This is about 30kms east of Genova, through industrial areas and built up areas. There were flats, both small and large, old and new, decorated in pastels: yellow, ochre, green, pink and so on. Old towers and new office blocks with clashing architectural styles were both standing proudly shoulder to shoulder. Roads twisted along at ground level and fairly flew along stretching flyovers. The full gamut of Italian mish-mash of style was laid out around for our viewing pleasure. The town owed much of its wealth to the port and everything else had grown up around it organically and chaotically. Eliza manfully drove towards Portofino through all of this. It was extremely busy and was very similar to the Como lakeside drive except much more built up. We arrived at Santa Margherita and tried to drive to Portofino. The queue just to drive around the coast did not seem to be moving. And when it did, it was from cars giving up and turning around. After a while we gave up too, turned around and parked on the beach. We walked along the promenade back to Santa Margherita watching the Italians still in the queue quietly fuming with an amazing calm resignation. We had our first Italian ice cream of the trip and Eliza was ecstatic as they had soya ice cream. Was this the Italian equivalent of a bank holiday Monday in Brighton? Yes and no. We found out that it was liberation day to celebrate the ousting of the Germans, so they had a reason to celebrate and remember. Our bank holidays seem to either have a religious connection or have no real significance in the history of Britain and it is therefore difficult to engender a sense of occasion.

We went back to Genova and down to the dock and the awaiting boat – Il Excellente. We had our own cabin and the girls were excited to be sleeping on board a ship. Indigo insisted on putting on her sparkling fireworks dress before we took a turn around the boat. There were some ghastly singers desperate to entertain. A piano bar and cocktails. The restaurant was full, so we settled for a serve yourself meal which really was probably all that the children could face. We stayed around for a while, Indigo really wanted to watch the lady singing. It certainly wasn't my cup of tea and I suddenly remembered why "luxury cruises" would drive me to drink. Indigo seemed to be happy watching and taking it all in so that was just fine.

Day 3
Mileage 880
Friday 26th April 2002
Mediterranean Journey

We woke up on the boat and found ourselves in the middle of the Mediterranean Sea, with no land in sight. By now we had been sailing for about 10 hours. I was famished I still had eyes bigger than my belly. I chose two bread rolls (with honey and jam), a hard boiled egg (I didn't eat this I thought it was soft boiled), a croissant, orange juice and hot chocolate. I painted a waterfall and an island that I could see from the boat. At ten there was a really "boring" fire drill. We got off the boat at 6:00pm. At the port of Palermo we had to get out and fast. We settled down in a hotel called Villaggio agli Androni, which is near the airport of Palermo.

*

Wake up at sea.

It was all very quiet and tranquil. Unlike sailing on the North Sea, there is practically no sensation. The sky is crystal clear blue and the sea is very flat. It looks just a little crinkly, like flattened out silver paper from a chocolate bar.

The day is also flat with very little to do to pass the time apart from eating and drinking.

We had an emergency drill at 10 o'clock. This was a "multimedia event". There was a video recording of a very old set of cartoons of the emergency procedures. The camera zoomed around this cartoon strip showing incomprehensible pictures. We were then treated to seeing a filmed evacuation practice. It looked as if no one had ever done it before… and of course there were no passengers involved…. It filled me full of confidence.

The English was very much "Allo, Allo" style.

"In an emergencia go to a mustard station and use the roots showered on you by the crow"

Mind you this was understandable. I imagine that my Italian version of this would be woefully misunderstood.

In the end, it worked out very well. The Italians showed how to put on a show. The electric curtains closed without a hitch around the projector, the lights came back up and the background musak gently increased in volume, but just enough to make you comfortable. I was surprised there was no spontaneous applause at this.

After lunch, George and Indigo and I went onto the sky deck to do some watercolour painting. George's is coming along very well and Indigo's coordination and hand control is getting better by the day.

I went to wake Eliza as we were passing Isola di Uscita. I was gone for less than five minutes, but when we got back George and Indigo were covered in blue paint!

We had to empty our cabins and prepare for docking. I played cribbage with George and suddenly realised why all the Italians had been playing cards either nestled round a few tables by the (closed and empty) swimming pool or outside on the deck. I thought they were been stoical for Italians, sitting in the fresh air while wrapped up in pullovers and anoraks, but no they were avoiding cheating. No, sorry, avoiding being cheated against. All the tables in the lounges had mirrored surfaces; so trying not to look at George's hand while we dealt was not easy.

Drifting into Palermo was glorious. The sight of the Sicilian landscape was awesome. Amazing cliffs and rocky outposts arrayed themselves in a wonderfully clear blue backdrop. Everywhere had razor sharp jagged edges. Docking seemed to take forever as though they had never done it before (although I am sure that they had). Then there was the usual scrum for the exits. (Not too bad today as the boat was probably only 25% full). The stairs down to the lower garages were very treacherous, steep and slippery with only the occasional handhold. The girls and the luggage were allowed to disembowel~~ark~~ at the dockside while I descended the depths for the Galaxy.

Eliza decided it was safer to let me navigate and took to the wheel. Straight in at the deep end. The exit from the docks was through a set of cast iron gates straight into the Palermo rush hour. Five lanes of bustling traffic with no lights to help ease us in. Luckily we wanted to turn right so it was a matter of putting your foot down and hoping that the timing was right. Palermo drivers made Northern Italian drivers look quite sane. You know, the ones that overtake around a blind bend going up-hill into a tunnel with road works having had too much to drink and using one hand to cover up one eye to avoid double vision. Well Palermo drivers also use three lanes for every two that are marked, don't stop at red traffic lights, go both ways down one way streets, have cars with dents and scratches worn with pride, machismo pride in never giving way under any circumstance…but they did do a double take at us: A right hand drive, British car with no dents *and* a woman driver. Trying to catch *my* eye when waiting for us to blink simply didn't work… and after Eliza found the horn… she was away.

We drove off to our destination in Terrasini. The directions were, to say the least vague. The whole route out of Palermo towards the airport was obviously a popular summer destination, but in typical Italian style, the buildings had a Shantytown feel about them. Most did not look finished and those that were, were built against the power of the sun in the summer. We drove past the airport, which was situated, strangely I thought, at the bottom of a set of cliffs. No overshooting allowed there then.

The road to Terrasini rapidly went from autostrada to white road. Potholes are definitely fashionable down here. We went straight through Terrasini without any sign of the hotel we had booked, but then signs appeared for the Villaggio agli Androni. "The village of brothers?" I asked. "No, the Village of Men". We both had visions of a very gay night. Following the signs became very tedious as the road became thinner and whiter until suddenly we were there.

The gardens were great, the rooms were primitive but clean and adequate. We had arrived in the middle of a school trip with 3 coaches of children between 11 and 13. We were worried about parking and leaving all our possessions in the Galaxy overnight, but not overly so from the children, because they seemed to me more concerned with showing off in front of each other or trying to catch the eye of a girl or a boy.

We went to the restaurant, which, of course, was heaving. They managed to give us a table out of the way upstairs. We had what the children had: pasta with tomato and basil and roast chicken and potatoes. Not haute cuisine, but it was really flavourful and a perfect end to the long trip down.

The sunset over the water and the views were tremendous. The sky's colour ever changing from sky blue to orange, red turquoise, green, indigo, deep blue and finally night black. Three planets were visible, Venus, Saturn and Jupiter. And later there was a full moon.

We had local grown oranges - juicy and unrivalled flavour. The man from Del Monte would have been pleased. Even pealing the pith off was a pleasure.

Both George and Indigo wanted to sleep in the same room as Eliza. So I went to sleep on my own.

Day 4
Mileage 902
Saturday 27ᵗʰ April 2002
Settling Down At Last

I woke up today and I started to read some of "Five on A Treasure Island." Which was very exciting. When dad came through he and mum had a bath, while they were in the bath I got dressed. When dad had got dressed he took me and Indigo to a lemur and a parrot. When I got my digital camera out the lemur started to pose for the camera, even though I didn't get any pictures of him (I ran out of space in my camera.)

19

For lunch I had spaghetti alle vongole, but I didn't like the vongole because it had to much chilles on the top of it. After lunch dad had ice cream – in a BUN! He got messer than me and Indigo! Then we went to the Casetta Rosa which is our next stop we are staying here for a week.

*

I woke up at 1 a.m. with the sound of mosquitoes in my ear and with itching hands, face and arms. I went to look at myself in the mirror to check if I had any signs of a rash, but no.

I woke up again at 5 a.m. to the sound of a car alarm going off. "Oh no," I thought and got dressed. Eliza met me at the door and gave me a knowing look. I went off to find the car, but found we were locked in to the hotel. Great. I snuck back into bed and managed some dozing sleep for an hour or so. I got up again and went down to the car. Everything was fine. We were being more paranoid than was absolutely necessary, but actually paranoid enough for our first night. Nothing would be worse than losing everything on our first night in Sicily.

It was such a glorious morning that I went for a walk to try and find my way down to the seafront, but all the paths and roads petered out into nothingness and fences.

By the time we got everyone up for breakfast, all three coach loads of children had gone off leaving a devastated but quiet breakfast room. We had a chance to admire some of the décor including model boats, wooden carvings of mediaeval war scenes with some gruesome head chopping in full view, a couple of painted Sicilian carts, various pots and pans, beautiful glass wine making/tasting devices and a fish tank.

Outside, there was a cage with a monkey in it. Very pretty, but quite sad looking.

We drove off in search of Villa Cefala in Santa Flavia where we were booked for a week. The autostradas have some interesting slip roads: both coming on and going off. They looked as if they were built by simply crashing through the crash barriers. After that they appeared to have been formalised via tarmacing around potholes. This time, driving around Palermo was less frenetic, or, more likely; we were more adjusted to the local driving conditions.

Sicilians do things on a grand scale. There was a rubbish dump by the side of the motorway. A pile of mangled, squashed and crushed cars neatly piled up would satisfy most places. This one also dealt with aircraft. Two enormous aeroplane noses and cabins peaked over the top of all the other accumulated metal, peering down at the passing motorway traffic.

We found our way to Santa Flavia and then came to a halt. I hadn't printed off the directions to the Villa Cefala and the save I had done of the web page turned out to be just the short cut. Isn't technology wonderful? We made some phone calls in broken Italian and eventually managed to find someone whose broken English was far superior to our broken Italian. Easy enough to find if only we knew where to look.

The main Villa was rather grand with a large double marble laid staircase out the front in very traditional style. Giovanni met us and showed us the way to Casetta Rosa where we were staying. We had to drive through the orange and lemon groves – what a wonderful whiff in the air. The Galaxy was brushed on both sides and the top by overhanging branches.... And then we were there. I had a momentary panic trying to work out how I was going to reverse down this track, but was shown a turning point hidden between two olive trees.

Outside, there is a large terrace laid with terracotta coloured stone giving a panoramic view of the Gulf of Solanto. East facing meant we would certainly have early mornings. All the windows were lined with mosquito nets. Hmmm. Even out here, the house had its own wrought iron lockable gate with a key with three different cross sections. Each window also had wrought iron grills in front, but these were very Italian in style so it didn't look or feel like a prison. Inside, there was a large bedroom with a vast matrimonial bed and a sofa bed that converted to two single beds. There was a small kitchen and a small shower room. It was plain, but definitely more upmarket than the Villaggio agli Androni.

We went off later in search off a beach, ice cream and some lunch.

We drove down to La Rotunda where we saw a job promotion scheme in operation. A gnarled man in his late sixties, white and wiry, was directing the car park with a whistle and collecting money off everyone.

It was worth the euro for our first Sicilian protection payment. The nearby bar had some simple but excellent food, toasted mozzarella cheese, spaghetti alle vongole etc. People were going into the gelateria and coming out with ice cream in a bun. Yes indeed, it was in a brioche. Very tasty, but as Eliza, George and Indigo witnessed very messy. Even in the springtime heat of a cool 23° C, it melted quickly enough to make it look as though I had cut my arm and that my blood had turned to chocolate.

Further round on the coast we found a port, where the locals were selling freshly caught fish. We needed to buy some food, but could not find any shops. We drove off to Bagheria where we found, at long last, a supermercato. Even this little town had numerous one-way systems. Round and round we went to try and find the entrance. Eventually we spotted the way in and a nifty u-turn enabled us to get there.

It was a straightforward supermarket, but it definitely felt poorer than those on the lakes in the north. There was a giant (so it seemed to Indigo) swordfish on the fish counter. Its nose was about half a metre long. Not to be sneered at.

Back to base camp we kept getting caught up in the Santa Flavia rush hour and by the level crossing: for the third time today. I'll not mention this again as I'm sure it will become very tedious. I'm just glad I don't live here, as this must be a real problem. The locals seemed relatively cool about it and despite the long queues only once or twice did anyone lean on horns.

As we approached the Villa, we learnt that you tell if the gates were open by the shadows they cast. With the sun setting the temperature dropped surprisingly fast and we had to resort to pullovers and even the electric fire before the evening was out. Indigo decided to throw a strop and her food was then randomly distributed about the table. Time for bed said Eliza. Short screams then silence from the other room as she drifted quickly off to sleep.

Casteldaccia
Day 5
Mileage 948
Sunday 28ᵗʰ April 2002
The Snake And Gecko

*Today I went to the villa and played football with three other children
and grazed both my KNEES! Within five minutes I had grazed both my
knees (my left first and then my right.) After that I went home and we
went for a walk and bought some prawns. (I didn't have any of this I
had some lovely Sicilian ham and melon.) on the way back to the house
(called Casetta Rosa) we saw a black serpent that slivered behind me
(he was just minding his own business if you don't mind me saying.)
This gave me a frightened shock that made me jump a foot in the air. I
asked a question. "Why do we have to be careful in the undergrowth?"
The serpent answered my question alright! When we had gone to the
Casetta Rosa we found a lizard (dad called him Art Grecko instead of
Art Decko.)*

*

We all slept soundly with one interruption overnight from Indigo
waking up and not really realising where she was. She's going to have
to learn to cope with this over the next few months else this will be hard
work.

It was blissful waking up without the worry of car thieves, car alarms
or just general mayhem. This morning was the first time when we were
together alone as a family. We decided that we would do no driving
today. Quite right too. We all went for a wander mid-morning but did
not find the local shops despite being told they were only 800m down
the road.

We found a man selling fish off the back of a barrow. It was obviously
fresh and local and we bought some enormous and some large size
prawns for our lunch. He had some very strange looking creatures on
his stall some of which were definitely still alive. "Eehh, yuck, they're
still breathing!" said George. We were warned not to touch as some of

the fish had poisonous spines. These certainly did not look appetising. The man quoted us a price in "eehhrose" and I'm dead certain it was more than the norm. He weighed out the prawns on old-fashioned scales held in one hand that probably would not have been out of place two thousand years ago. There was no way I could check his slight of hand. This guy looked well worn with the odd missing tooth and made all my jumpers look pristine and straight out of a modern fashion shoot. But he had a sidekick all dressed up in a suit and tie. If I didn't know better I would have thought that this guy was the stallkeeper's accountant whose sole job was to ensure that his customers got a fair deal and that the "eehroe" was used properly at the correct fixed exchange rate.

Having said all this, the prawns were actually extremely delicious. We'll be back for more if we ever see him again. I expect he was only arbitraging between the cost at the port and those poor suckers like us.

The old man was still whistling in the car park again, but this time we had no car and therefore he could whistle all he liked. He would not get anything from us today.

George met the three sons of Giovanni today and ended up terrorising them with her footballing skills. I must say I was impressed. Eliza and Giovanni talked about life, the universe and everything. Her Italian is definitely coming along, but how much of that is just reckless translation and how much of it is proper understanding and accuracy I haven't a clue. I tried mucking in a bit as Giovanni at least will helpfully try and correct you or slip into the odd bit of broken English (when it suits him, of course).

Franco, the concierge at the Brentano, our apartment on Lago di Como speaks some weird dialect. We only recently realised this when Vilia, a good Italian friend of ours from Chiavenna also had great difficulty understanding him. I always thought I was stupid and just couldn't speak Italian, so for most of the time I gave up trying. This I regret for everywhere else, but am entirely happy when I make heavy sign language with Franco.

We bought some olive oil and honey from Giovanni. The honey is made from orange blossom and is simply beautifully. He also showed us some nespole fruit growing in the garden. These were the colour and size of small apricots, but were more rounded like peaches. They had a smooth skin and contained two or three large pips. I'm not sure I liked the taste, it seemed like a cross between an apricot and a pear.

We ate some honey with fresh strawberries and mascapone. It was very tempting to eat the whole jar neat, there and then, but I did not think that George would understand or approve.

Walking back to the Casetta Rosa we saw lots of lizards and were telling George to be careful of the undergrowth. "Why?" she asked just as a three foot black snake shot out from under her feet. It made us all jump and some primitive instinct made the hairs on the back of my neck and spine all stand up. The snake moved a lot quicker than any of the lizards had. Some feat with no feet. Back in the house we had another visitor. High up on the inside wall of the house was a small lizard, different from the others with suckers on its feet. It was only about two or three inches long. He was quickly baptised as Art Gecko. He never moved when you watched him, but as if playing Grandmother's footsteps, had moved every time we looked up at him.

Day 6
Mileage 957
Monday 29th April 2002
Céfalu

I woke up first again before dad. When dad woke up and we had a game of cribbage. I won by 30pts. Then I got dressed and we went out to Céfalu. First we went to the museum and saw an excellent picture of an unknown man, the oil painting which dated back to 1465 (some paintings in the sixteenth century weren't as good as this!) After that we went to the beach. I dug a hole deep enough to find water. When we had dried off and got dressed again me, mum, dad and Indigo went for an ice cream before we went back to the Casetta Rosa

*

It was about time we did some sightseeing. So we made an early start, but by the time we had (sorry Eliza had) got everyone organised it was gone 10. We went to Céfalu on the north Tyrrhenian coast. We had the choice of driving on the motorway or taking the local state road SS113. We drove out on the local road.

This road took us through all the local towns. The biggest of which was Termini Imerese. The central parts of all these towns were full of old and stylish buildings and churches, but the newer parts appeared to be thrown together in simple cubic blocks. The outsides of all buildings tended to be very neglected with crumbling plaster and non-existent paintwork. This gave no real indication on the internal styles of the buildings. In the north, the Italians certainly didn't care about the outside of their houses, but were very keen that the insides were marble clad and furnished in elegant and mostly entirely impractical pieces of furniture. The more that your household looked like a museum, the better class of person you were. How families with children coped I just did not know. Maybe we mixed with the wrong sort.

Termini Imerese had a central square at the top of a hill and a large industrial area – mostly a Fiat factory – and port at the bottom. The square was pleasant enough and some of the buildings at the bottom of the hill were rather grand. There is supposedly a hot spring here where the waters are good for urological conditions. It would be nice to try and track this down if time permits.

On to Céfalu. The drive on the state road was straightforward, but we kept getting stuck behind paranoid Italian drivers who drove at 30kph in a Fiat cinquecento (so probably going as fast as he could without shaking the car to pieces) using the white line in the middle of the road as a steering guide. Got to keep it between the two front wheels and then you'll be safe. Some drivers used the white line at the edge of the road as their steering guide, but with walls and ditches close this never appeared to be safe for long.

Céfalu appeared to be like all the other towns with cubic architecture around the outside: shutters everywhere as protection against the heat. We found a parking spot down on the beach. Considering that this was late April, parking was quite difficult. The central part of the down dated back to the 1100s and nestled at the bottom of a large rock called La Rocca. The rock dominated the town and was fortified against various invaders in past centuries. The church in the main square underneath La Rocca also dominated the town. We took a stroll inside almost to immediately be expelled with cries of "Chiude, chiude". It was twelve o'clock and everything was shutting down for lunch. The interior was noticeably cooler even at this time of year and looked to my uneducated eye full of Norman style columns and arches. It was reputably built by King Roger II in thanks for his life being saved from a local shipwreck. Roger has a wonderfully Italian ring to it!

Away from the main square we visited a museum, which did not close for lunch. It was most famous for its "portrait of an unknown man" painted in 1465 by Antonello da Messina. He was handsome and had a knowing smirk as though the painter had regaled him with the equivalent of mediaeval double entendres or local gossip about a rival family. How he managed to keep that face still during the entire sitting, I've no idea. That is what makes the painting alive even today. There was quite of lot of other bits and pieces in the museum, but it obviously did not specialise in anything in particular. There were, of course, lots of religious paintings including Mary and her boy, boy on the cross, boy preaching, saints being martyred etc. All their faces were very much more formal and po faced. There was a collection of old coins that had been found in Sicily which contained not only Sicilian coins but coins from Germany, Belgium and Great Britain. There was a map showing where all the mints were in Sicily. Almost every town had one including Céfalu and Termini Imerese. There were about thirty mentioned. Now the same coins are equally legal throughout 12 countries.

There was also a shell collection, again featuring shells from around the world including Australia, South Africa, Canada, California and Taiwan; a stuffed animal collection, consisting of mostly birds, but including a crocodile, two porcupines, and a hedgehog; a collection of Greek urns (don't ask how much does a ….) and oil lamps; and a couple of wonderful tiled floors.

We bought a copy of their only postcard: the portrait of an unknown man, of course.

The temperature was definitely hotting up and after lunch it was 29°C. The beach looked very inviting. I could not tell if the sand was natural or not. It looked too good to be true. When we came by earlier they were grooming the beach making sure everything was smooth. The sea looked extremely inviting. George went to test the temperature with her toes and described it as "refreshing". Eliza would not go beyond her toes, but I went in fully. It was chilly, but definitely refreshing and became quickly more comfortable after submersion upto my neck.

Indigo became more adventurous over time, but never ventured in too far. George liked digging like a dog in the sand and found water when she dug down far enough. Both children wanted to be buried, but too many giggles meant that they were never still enough long enough for a posed photo.

Bought fruit, wine and ice cream and then drove back home on the motorway. This road was not only a lot quicker, but also had much more dramatic views of the landscape, both mountainous and coastal.

We came off at Casteldaccia to try and find a supermarket for some household bits and pieces. We found the town's central square, again with church and a few large pine trees. The square was enjoying a late spring early evening and the place was milling around with old men. Nobody was under fifty and there was only one woman who obviously was not a local. She was with two other men and they were all wearing shorts and carrying cameras.

Back at the house we all had outdoor showers to get rid of the sand. There is something liberating about "showing off yer bits" as George said to the great outdoors. No one could see us, but more importantly, I didn't care.

Day 7
Mileage 1023
Tuesday 30th April 2002
Villa Palagonia Monsters

Today we have gone to the Villa Palagonia where there are some stone statues, which looked more like monsters than people! The villa wasn't older than our house, but it looked much older! There was a hall of mirrors which would have been stunning if all the mirrors hadn't wasted away with the building. As we were leaving I noticed a big shabby dog, he looked so cute I could kiss him! Mum was determined to have a picnic so we had a picnic on the terrace. Afterwards all we did was mooch about.

*

We went off to Bagheria this morning to see Villa Palagonia. This was a villa built in the 18th century and is a most peculiar example. Throughout the gardens, around all the walls was a selection of statuary of weird and wonderful animals and people, but mostly phantasmagoria: serpents, dragons and groups of musicians.

There were statues of the original owners and friends and families all around. Inside there was a double staircase and upstairs there was only one room open to the public. It was called the hall of mirrors. The whole ceiling, which was a concave dome, and most of the walls were covered in mirrors except now most of the silver had perished.

The whole building was shaped like two sides only of a polygon. The angle was more obtuse than an octagon, but less so than a dodecagon. The front entrance was by the inside angle with a double staircase leading up to the first floor. A hallway went through the entire building and this was open to elements at both ends. In Sicily this meant it was cool and not cold.

The Italians thought that there was no point in letting this building stand unused and empty so the rest of the building had been rented out to at least one family, with private gardens and washing lines.

We wandered around Bagheria for another hour or so and stopped in a bar for refreshments. We tried an Arancia, a typical Sicilian delicacy. This looked a bit like a scotch egg but it was bigger. It turns out to be a mincemeat interior covered in rissole rice and then breadcrumbs. I quite liked it, but it was a bit too greasy for Eliza's taste.

At first Bagheria looked like it was shut. There may not have been many people on the streets, but once you got used to that fact and looked inside shops, it was obviously full of individuals and families who were going about their business. There were fish stalls and fruit shops and cafes and bars. There were fashion shops and photo shops.

Afterwards we drove down to Capo Zafferano, a headland that juts out into the sea. We hoped to be able to drive around the cape, but it was very rugged and there were no tracks or roads. We managed to find a parking place for the Galaxy and a rocky path that went towards the sea. The whole area had a fierce brutishness about it. The contrast in colours between the ochre sand, volcanic rocks, the turquoise sea and the deep polaroid blue sky was stark and immense. Between the sea and the sky the horizon was smudged with haze. In the far distance, the hills of nearby islands could be seen like the tips of icebergs. We followed the trail down to the sea. Here we could hear some people down by the water's edge, but could not see them. Eventually we gave up and had to go around a different way. This way too was very treacherous and at some points we had to pass Indigo along from arm to arm. I thought it was too dangerous to go right down to the sea and we stopped some ten feet short. George was very upset with me for stopping so close.

There were three or four young men on the rocks enjoying the spring sunshine. It was hot for us English, but mild for the Sicilian locals. Even they were wearing very hard shoes, as the rocks were very sharp. One managed to get in to swim and climbed out on the opposite rocks. We did not think he would be able to get back in. He was about ten feet up and the water only looked about four feet deep and was a mix of sand and rocks beneath. Eliza told George about a friend of hers, Jeremy. He had been very athletic as a young man and had gone to Greece on holiday one summer with some friends. They had all been larking about when he dove into some shallow water resulting in a broken neck. He was paralysed from the neck down and confined to a wheelchair from that day forth. Although we often saw him down the Nightingale in Balham, he remained bitter about his accident. His only remaining pleasures were Young's bitter and cigarettes. He died in his early thirties. Although this was an accident it was entirely avoidable with the proper care. We worried about the young man opposite and were quite anxious about what he was doing. With his friends watching him, but neither egging him on nor warning him off, the young man looked as though he would lose too much face if he asked for help. In the end he did a large belly flop and put his hands out flat in front of him to protect his face. The dive looked very sore, but he came out unscathed. His friends took no notice as if this was an everyday experience in the deadly heat of the midday Sicilian sun.

Back at the Casetta Rosa we started to make plans for the rest of the week. We wanted to spend a day in Palermo, but didn't want to drive and park there. So I decided to find out about the local train times. Also we needed some more fruit and vegetables for food. With a list in hand I went off to find the local Salumeria as recommended by Giovanni. It was 800 metres from the Villa Cefala. The railway station was also 800 metres from the Villa Cefala. As too was the nearest supermarket. This has become known as the Sicilian 800 metres. It means it is too far to advise walking in the heat of the day and yet hardly worth going by car, if at all possible use a moped.

The Salumeria was about a kilometre away and looked small and pokey. I ventured inside, much to the surprise of the people hanging around outside, who then promptly came in and switched the lights on. It was mostly just a cold meat and cheese counter with dried pasta, biscuits, tins and other non-perishable goods for tourists. For example, toothpaste and toiletries. The old man serving behind the meat counter looked as though parts of his fingers had seen the wrong side of the slicing machine in days long gone. He also had a touch of the shakes, which may have been nerves from being so close to a slicing machine. He laid out proscutto crudo and cotto neatly in the box with total care. Each slice was gently caught and laid down with tender affection alongside its brothers. The box was weighed and when complete was closed with the gentleness of a loved one saying his goodbyes to a friend.

I went over to the counter to pay for my purchases and the old man there asked me if I was staying in the Villa Cefala. I said yes and he immediately offered to drive me back (it was of course 800 metres away). I tried to say in broken English that I wanted to go to the railway station to find out about train times to Palermo for tomorrow. He shouted "Papa, Papa" to the old man behind the counter. So the old man at the till probably wasn't much older than me and had probably worked in this shop all his life. He found a local newspaper with the railway timetable inside and then promptly had big problems understanding it. He told me that tomorrow was festiva – a bank holiday – for the first of May. Everything would be closed. Except his shop of course. The railway timetable had trains marked as "Lav" and "Fes" meaning workdays and holidays. Some were marked with "Giorno" and some were left blank. It was obvious that there were more trains running on workdays than on the other days, but what did it all mean? It meant that we would go to Palermo on Thursday and not Wednesday after all. The son said he would take me to buy some train tickets. (You could not buy these at the railway station. It was too small.) I said okay and he drove me up to Casteldaccia. He pointed out were the station was (800 metres from Villa Cefala) and up to the main town square. We drove round the square and parked and he asked me to come with him. We went to the barber's shop where two customers were in the middle of a wet shave with cutthroat razors. I certainly didn't want to disturb them. I was asked how many tickets I wanted and I said two adults and two children. This completely flummoxed them as they did not know how to deal with child tickets. They knew they were not the same price as adult tickets, but how much? They did not have any. In the end they decided that I should have three adult tickets and the two children could share one as a concept. The exchange was done and we left. The son drove me the 800 metres to the Villa Cefala where I gratefully said thank you for his help.

I returned to the Casetta Rosa and explained that we were not going to Palermo tomorrow and that most of the shopping on the list I had failed to get. I could hardly ask the son to wait for me outside the supermarket while I did my other shopping. Nevertheless I went back up the 800 metres to the supermarket – this time in the car – to buy some supplies before the bank holiday.

When I got back to the flat again I discovered that we now had a second lizard. According to Indigo this was a squashed black one on the floor in the bathroom. When she showed me where it was it scuttled away. It was neither squashed nor dead but it was black. We decided to call this one Dec. So now we had Art and Dec. Art had reappeared in our bedroom on the wall and again remained motionless to the sight, but he had gone again by the morning.

Day 8
Mileage 1050
Wednesday 1ˢᵗ May 2002
Ruins, Ruins and Segesta

Today we went to ruins of Segesta which was an Ancient Greek Temple which was never finished because the ancient Greeks kept arguing and fighting. I took lots of pictures with my camera mum says that I do take after my dad. Before we went up the five minute walk both me and Indigo got hats – I've got a bright red one and Indigo got a straw one with a ribbon.

After this we went to a town called Trapani where we saw a fish market which was pretty amazing, there were eels, heads of swordfish, whole tuna and prawns. At lunchtime we met some Americans called Kay and Lou, they invited us to their island. Afterwards we mooched about on the beach. There was a shallow section where I broke lots of waves.

*

April was over and now we were in May. May 1st: it was another bank holiday in Italy. We decided to drive to Trapani on the east coast of Sicily. No traffic on the way to Palermo, but plenty coming out of Palermo. It looked like convoys were gathering by the side of the roads for large parties away from the city. After about three or four miles though the traffic had faded away, disappearing off the motorway to local seaside and mountainside places. The motorway became relatively deserted.

As we drove away from Palermo, the landscape became less craggy and turned into undulating low-level hills. These were much more fertile than the landscape around Palermo. The hills were covered with a patchwork of vines, orchards and olive groves.

On the way to Trapani we decided to stop at Segesta which was an ancient unfinished temple and city. When we arrived the whole place was heaving, but this was due to the large number of coaches that had done the tour and were soon to be leaving. We discovered that I had left our credit cards at home and that we only had 60 odd euros. We would have to be careful over lunch. We went to buy our tickets at the ticket office and were pleasantly surprised when we found out it was free entry today. However, the man in the ticket office insisted that we had our tickets and yes, later on, these were checked at the entrance to the temple to make sure we had paid. Yet another wonderful sign of Italian bureaucracy and job creation at work.

The temple was splendid. Unlike most ruins of this age that were falling down, these had not been completed. All the pillars were there together with the front and rear pediments plus a lot of the other bits with architectural names which I can't be bothered with. The exposed stone, lacking any marble protective cladding had been worn away over the centuries. There was no roof, but you could easily imagine how the place must have looked 2000 years ago. There was no other building in sight just the gentle sweep of the nearby Sicilian hills with craggy mountains and blue seas visible in the distance.

The birds had taken the temple over as their own. Swooping amongst the yellow-red pillars and nesting in the (virtual) eaves, their songs seemed to say "This is our nest, leave us alone. Leave us alone and go home". Small buddleia type plants had set root high up in the crevices at the top of the pillars. Eliza suggested to George that it would make a great football pitch.

We went on to Trapani via the motorway. Looking at the map this road was one of the only ways to get to the east coast. The state highway could be seen twisting up and down hills and through small villages, and this must have been very tiresome to drive along. Before the motorway, the easiest way to arrive at the east coast towns would have been by sea. Trapani had been laid out along a thin spit of land and had expanded westwards into an urban sprawl. All cubic houses and high rise flats. Most appeared to be locked up or shut against the impending summer weather.

The fish market was still going when we arrived with a good array of fish, prawns and other creatures such as octopus and squid. I was surprised not to see any shellfish such as vongole around, but maybe this was simply because we were too late.

As it was a festiva, everywhere was closed. Even most of the restaurants were closed, but we found one of the recommended restaurants open. We got there shortly after twelve. The doors were open to the Taverna La Porta, but it was deserted inside. We went in. It was a bit like intruding into the Marie Celeste. It was deserted, but tables were laid as if a large gathering was expected. Displays of fish and prawns were laid out for examination. After a short while we were noticed from the kitchen next door and shown to an unlaid table where we were sat with menus. Hmm this looked good. Later more people arrived and soon the place was bustling with people and yet others had to be turned away. I assume people had reserved and that we were early. We've not yet got into the Sicilian timetable, but never mind. The food here is certainly different from further north. The Moroccan influence can be seen as there is cous cous (spelt kus kus here) on the menu. Deliciously different from the way I cook it at home. All the fish looked fantastic and freshly caught in the Mediterranean. There was nothing frozen here. The fish with the cous cous was a real chunky white fish we asked its name it sounded like "cedi", but we've no real idea.

The restaurant had a knight in not-so-shining armour guarding the door and a brass model boat decorating the fish display.

Eliza, well Indigo really, got talking to a couple of Americans on the next door table. They lived in Milan and had a house on Favignana a nearby island. We told them about our adventure and they invited us to come and see them on the island.

We drove north along the coast to Pizzolungo where we spent a very pleasant couple of hours on the sand and in the sea. It was not as baking as a couple of days ago in Cefelu, but the water felt warmer. The nearby islands glistened enticingly in the distance. Like Sirens of old they beseeched us to come and visit.

The journey back to the Villa Cefala was uneventful except for being buzzed by police helicopters on both sides of Palermo. We are trying not to be paranoid about being here so we did not take this as a sign of police harassment. A bit further on with a police car leading the traffic another police car overtook at speed. Except this one had a Roma number plate and was unmarked except for the detachable siren on the roof. We wondered who he was after.

Day 9
Mileage 1221
Thursday 2nd May 2002
Palermo visited again

Today we went to Palermo by train which took about 20 minutes. When we first arrived, it wasn't just busy it was heaving. We found a market where mum spotted a nice pair of sandals in my size and they fitted like magic so mum bought them for me. Then we found a church. It was ok but for some reason we weren't allowed in for too long. Then we found the Chiesa San Giovanni degli Erementi which contains the Eunuchs bonnets and a pretty Cloister. The Eunuchs Bonnets are like little red domes. The pretty Cloister contains lots of different types of flowers. After that we went and had lunch mum said that this was a poor meal but my scallopina was the best. Next we had an icecream (which I threw at mum's back which explains her white mark on her back when she gets sunburnt – not). Then we went home.

*

Today we went to Palermo by train. The station was 800 metres from the Villa Cefala. Giovanni had promised Eliza that someone would give us a lift in the morning. It would have been fine for myself and Eliza and maybe George to have walked, but I would have ended up carrying Indigo or giving them all a lift, driving back and then walking back myself. There was no sign of Giovanni at 8:30 and we were aiming for the 8:58 train. As if by magic, one of his cohorts appeared out of nowhere. Our carriage awaited us. Or rather a small red fiat. The car certainly looked very dodgy and would not have been something I would have foistered on an enemy. We could have walked of course, but now we had been offered the lift and we were too late to walk we had no choice. Besides it would now have been very rude to turn down the lift. We all squeezed in and we were off. I made to put my seat belt on and was told that it was not worth it for the short distance we were going. There it was again, the Sicilian 800 metres.

We got to the station about ten minutes before the train was due and were the first waiting. When some other, more typical Sicilian commuters turned up, I asked George whether we looked like tourists. She said no why did I think so. Well we were pale, were wearing shorts had white t-shirts on, carried cameras, had two daughters with us who should have been at school. Whereas all the Italian around us looked downcast wore blue or grey, some wore coats to protect them from the cold, carried no cameras and generally looked like they had caught the same train hundreds of times before. Yes, we looked like tourists and we were playing the part. I didn't mind doing so, but I thought it was important for George to realise how everybody else saw us.

A man approached us on the bench and asked us if we were visiting Palermo (cunningly, he had spotted the fact that we were indeed tourists). We said we were and he then with the aid of our travel guides help us plot a route for the day. We were only planning on staying until early afternoon as neither George nor Indigo could take much more than this in any one hit. Whereas Eliza and I could have stayed on a lot longer before getting tired.

Once on the train neither of the girls was interested in looking at the passing scenery.

The train journey was quicker than I expected at about twenty minutes.

We walked down Vir Turkovy towards the Norman castle, but were quickly sidetracked into a fruit and veg market where right at the end we bought George a pair of sandals. We found our way back to the main drag, but by then all the girls were crying out for a loo stop. Its funny how in Italian cities and towns there are always hundreds of bars and cafes around until you actually would like to find one for a pressing emergency. Eventually we found one.

Next door was a pet shop where Indigo became fascinated by the tiny birds with red beaks.

We found our way to what we thought was the church and went inside. It was deserted. The lady putting out flowers was surprised to see us, but greeted us civilly.

When we left we realised that we were not in the "right" church and had just visited one of the hundred of "ordinary" churches in Palermo. Still ornate for all that. Almost straight next door was San Giovanni degli Eremit which is where we should have been visiting. This place was very much older and Moorish in style. The roof had five red domes known as the eunuchs bonnets. Inside it was very cool and quiet but also small and cellular. There were some very pretty cloisters with delicate arches and gardens. I could imagine this being a place of tranquillity and serenity to the religious order, but now everything around it was bearing down on the building.

Almost next door to this was the Norman palace (Palazzo dei Normanni), which Roger II had made into his principal residence. He did seem to get around a bit. The main feature here was the Palatine Chapel. Yet another chapel, but done up in glorious mosaics of African and Moorish designs interlaced with full blown portraits of all the famous characters in the new testament surrounded by gold mosaic tiles.

We wandered down the Corso Calatafimi through the Porta Nuova a giant Moorish gateway. There was a park here that was simply full of palm trees and cactus plants. A bit further along and we found the cathedral. Again this was very different from northern European cathedrals on the outside, but looked more conventional on the inside.

By this time the children were dying on their feet and we had to find somewhere to charge up their batteries. After a short stop for lunch we continued down to Quattro Canti where we wanted to see San Caterina, San Cataldo and the Piazza Pretoria. The first two were shut (for lunch) and the last was being restored. At this point we decided to call it a day and headed down Via Roma to the railway station. A quick ice cream, and then on to the train back to Casteldaccia.

A quiet afternoon was spent in the flat George doing her school and journal work and Indigo doing her scrapbook.

Day 10
Mileage 1221
Friday 3rd May 2002
Picnic On The Beach

Today mum finally got her picnic on the beach before lunch and afterwards we just mooched around on the beach making traps, contraptions and digging. The temperature soared at 30°C – 31°C. We left early afternoon so that dad could catch up with our journals and so mum could pack because we moving on tomorrow.

*

Today we thought the children needed a rest from sightseeing so we went back to the beach at Céfalu.

We drove up to Casteldaccia to the paneficio. Eliza went to buy some breakfast cakes and bread. This time the village square was full of middle aged women slowly exiting from church. There seemed to be no rush about their actions. The town definitely had a routine and a pace all of its own. Whatever speed we were doing or wanted to do the townspeople would carry on at their own pace. This spillage of women out of the church reminded me of when I first started living in Tooting Broadway. There the ornate 1930s' Odeon Cinema had been converted into a bingo hall. A real Mecca for the ladies in their fifties and above. At about nine o'clock in the evening you could be peacefully minding your own business walking home from the tube or the pub when suddenly, the doors of the Gala bingo palace would be flung wide and up to 900 women would come pouring out in less than five minutes. Not a place to be for the unwary. When it first happened to me I was just overcome by the rush, it was like trying to swim against the tide. In Casteldaccia, both the volume and the speed were only about 10% of the Tooting Broadway women's exodus.

The baker's shop was just a bit further up the hill. Eliza slipped out of the Galaxy while I waited. I noticed that four or five of the men, who were scuttling out of the way of the sprawling women, were limping and that three or four were with sticks and crutches. One of the limpers without a stick or a crutch came limping along past me in the Galaxy when suddenly a door opened up. My heart stopped as I thought the door would knock this man over, but no, a hand came out holding a crutch which the limper grabbed gratefully and proceeded to scuttle faster and with some dignity up the hill. I asked George if she knew the riddle about what has four legs in the morning, two at lunch time and three in the evening. She said she knew it and that the answer was a man, but that she didn't get it. I pointed at the men with three legs, but she still didn't get it. "Its not the evening" she cried, "Its still the morning." I explained once more and now, hopefully, she has got it.

As we now knew the way and where (-ish) to park it only took us an hour. There was plenty of time to see the cathedral before closing time at high noon. Unfortunately, Eliza had forgotten about the special piety which southern Europeans hold for their church and was improperly dressed and had not covered her shoulders or a sufficiency of leg. She was barred from admission and felt very silly. The children decided to show some much needed solidarity with their mother and declined to come round the cathedral with me.

Afterwards they all were desperate to go down to the beach. I was desperate to go for a walk and whilst the others wandered seaward, I wandered skyward. Up to the top of the Rocca and the Temple of Diana. The way up started with a well laid path and step. Half way up was a mediaeval wall and fortifications. Here, another job creation scheme, a young man with a book of tickets was selling entrances to the upper mount at 1 euro each. There was no notice of such a charge at the bottom of the hill and to come this far and turn around seemed rather daft. The view this far had been dramatic as the path huddled closely against the cliff, but once inside the fortifications where the cliff eased and there was more horizontal movement available to the walker, the view just opened up stunningly. The rock was alive with vegetation and flowers of all sorts of hues, red, blue and yellow. Insects crawled, buzzed and flittered everywhere. There were two specific types of butterflies that remain especially vibrant in the mind. The first was mostly white with large wing. Each wing was striped radially from the body in a deep golden yellow with a black striped outline. The second was more like a cross between a dragonfly and a moth. Very black except for speckled white dots on its wings.

Up here I could still hear the town clock strike. I heard ten and two quarters and ten and three quarters. But I did not hear eleven.

Up towards the top, the path split in two and I picked the contra path to everyone else, so I was always giving way to people descending. Not so bad really, as it meant I did have a breather every few minutes. The view just continued to open up as the town below shrank. Near the top four German ladies were setting out their picnic lunch. It all looked terribly just so. They were all in white and had a white table cloth. I did not look to closely as to whether they had tea and cucumber sandwiches. That would have been just too much like an English vicarage tea party.

The battlements at the top allowed you an uninterrupted view in all directions. Now, for the first time I could see west past Céfalu. Down on the front I could just make out our car, but could not pick out the George or the Indigo, much less the Eliza.

Just then there was a rumbling of thunder and the odd spot of rain. I though this was an excellent time to head downwards. The German ladies looked a bit peeved as they gathered up their belongings, put on some leg wear and generally made ready to dash for it. It did no more than spit though, even so, it still threatened to pour and thunder. This time I was still going counter to most of the traffic, but they gave way to me coming down and they were able to catch their breaths. One lady saw I was wearing sandals and said to her husband "See, some one else is not wearing proper walking boots." She asked me whether it got rough further up and I said not much worse, but that she would have to be careful. Well she was wearing high heels. At the other extreme, they were people wearing proper hiking boots with knee length socks and garters, people with sticks and at least one with a pair of sticks, not because she was unfit or anything, but it was part of the hiking apparel. A pity, because her tight bright blue flowery leggings just did not suit, but may well have been attractive on someone twenty or so years her junior who probably would not have needed the hiking sticks.

Down, down and down and then I heard the clock strike quarter to twelve. The upward flow of visitors was now busier than ever. Well, let me put that into context. There were probably half a dozen people a minute at most, so, busy was still very quiet compared with half past eight in the morning at Liverpool Street Station.

When I got down, I went off to find George and Indigo digging holes in the sand looking for water. They found it soon enough. When I pointed out the battlements around the Rocca and told her that that was where I had been George was most impressed.

The girls enjoyed getting sand everywhere, and George enjoyed both hitting and missing the tennis balls with her baseball bat.

We all enjoyed our picnic on the beach with the exception of the gritty sandy sandwiches.

We got back to the Casetta Rosa fairly early as we had to pack up shop in order to move on tomorrow.

Our friendly lizards were still about. The children started watching them and Art and Dec watched us back. Unfortunately Art had lost his tail. Eliza thought she had knock it off, but I'm not sure if he had ever had his tail since we were around.

We went out to dinner in Portocello at an expensive fish restaurant recommended and booked by Giovanni. When we had come down here to explore on Wednesday, the whole place had looked deserted. This evening, however, there was a mighty throng all along the front. It was as if the whole town and much more besides had come down to see us driving in Italian gridlock. Very surprisingly we managed to park just outside the restaurant. Giovanni sounded surprised when we wanted to book for seven thirty. Nobody opens until eight. But we had two children who would not last long so we settled for eight. We were definitely the first in the restaurant tonight, but still pleasantly welcomed. We had some most excellent fish, both as antipasti and as primo piatte. Excellent wine and followed by super sorbets.

Sciacca
Day 11
Mileage 1290
Saturday 4ᵗʰ May 2002
I Meet Lorenzo

We moved on today and there wasn't anything much that caught my eye today. Mum got lost again and again. When we finally arrived at Verdetecnica I met the two boys Lorenzo and Alessandro. Lorenzo spoke very good English compared to my broken Italian!

*

Moving day. Indigo had been up half the night with tummy ache. Poor child. Poor Eliza. I had swapped beds with Indigo to catch some sleep for today's driving.

Everything was packed up and loaded in about a couple of hours. Not bad for the first time, although some was done yesterday. The weather had changed since yesterday with some spotted showers and heavy looking rain clouds hanging expectantly in the air. The odd bar of sunlight still jutted through the clouds down onto the Gulf of Solunto.

We went off to say our goodbyes to Giovanni and to pay our bill. I tried to e-mail George's first school report back to England, but my e-mail address was not working, so had to use Giovanni's. I'm sure they won't mind.

Off, back up to the *paneficio*. This time, there were neither men nor women in the square and there were no three legged races up the hill. More breakfast cakes and off we went.

We were going to Sciacca on the south coast of Sicily, but we wanted to go to Monreale first to see the duomo. But getting there was a challenge to us poor navigators. Eliza managed to find the right turnoff from the Palermo by-pass with ease and we wound our way up towards Monreale in the drizzle and mist. Spotting where all the coaches were parked gave us the clue as to where the cathedral was sited.

We had to endure a *passagio turistichi* past stall keepers and a dozen or so ceramic shops selling their very nice but expensive hand made

Sicilian plates. I'm sure we can find some examples cheaper elsewhere. We were wary of the time and Eliza was today covered sufficiently. So we went straight into the Cathedral. There was a wedding going on, but this was fine. It was actually good to see a church in use.

There were lots of gold mosaic pictures around the walls showing bible stories. We saw the story of Adam and Eve and Noah's Ark amongst them. We tiptoed out of the church without wishing to disturb the wedding just as the couple were saying "Si" to each other. Eliza and I briefly looked at each other as we remembered our wedding with a quiet smile and a quick kiss.

Outside there was a fountain with a young man tying up some monstrous looking fish. There was a very tall pair of palm trees on either side of him. The tallest I have seen to date.

Back to the Galaxy and then on to Sciacca.

To get across to the state road that crossed the island we had to across a ravine. Down one side and back up the other. We thought this was preferable to going back down to Palermo. The road was fine, but the drizzle was still coming and the cloud base was getting lower. We could see the road we wanted sweeping into the distance. If only we could get there. We did and just at the slip road in the Sciacca direction were a pair of policemen waving their little red baton around refusing to let anyone onto the road. Okay. Let's follow the crowd. They would know where to go. Down, down, down. Down the tiny winding mountain roads to Palermo. Gradually we came closer to the road but on the wrong side and going in the wrong direction. We found ourselves nearly getting on the road, but decided against it and found our way over the top and then started to trail the road going south away from Palermo only to find ourselves reversing our footsteps so as to end up by the policemen again. I swallowed my pride and turned around again and went down the road towards Palermo. We joined the Palermo road and then saw what everyone else was doing: a u-turn in the middle of the carriageway. Oh for Italian free spirit. We did it too and then we were on our way. As we climbed, the cloud base stayed low and we were suddenly enclosed by mist. There were still two sorts of Italian drivers going up this hill: the hell-for-leather sort with no worry about speed and the pessimistically cautious sort going at half the pessimistic speed limit. Fairly quickly, the road climbed to its peak and descended below the cloud base. Shortly after that we were in glorious sunshine. The scenery had changed too as we left Palermo for the interior. All the ragged and jutting rocky escarpments around the coastline disappeared and we were left with a much more gentle landscape, more like a rumpled table cloth laid over the land.

The landscape continued to be remarkably refreshing and soothing after the harshness of the Palermo coast. It was not long before the Mediterranean snuck back into view and we dropped down into Sciacca. We had the address of where we were going and we had the instructions. Come off the motorway and follow the signs. Looking at the map there is a small mountain north of Sciacca and a road going all the way around it. The address was the name of this road. But could we find it? Eventually we found the other end of the road past Sciacca and drove up it all the way to the top and back down again. It was a magnificent drive and wonderful vistas, but by now I was getting tired and the kids were getting hungry and anxious about lunch. We were driving back down the mountain when we came across the sign for Verdetecnica (which is where we were staying).

And then we were there.

We were greeted by Pascale and Salvatore who showed us Angelica where we were staying. A bit more room than Casetta Rosa and better equipped although the view was not there.

George soon found the two boys Lorenzo and Alex. They had gameboys and a Nintendo 64 and played football. She was in heaven. They even thought she was a boy called George.

Then we realised that we only had one set of keys. Panic. Had we lost them or left them at the Villa Cefala. We thought we had left them at the Villa Cefala. Eliza rang up Giovanni, who had not been up to the Casetta Rosa. We thought he could put them in the post, but I decided that if they were there then I would fetch them tomorrow. Salvatore helped to speak to Giovanni and arranged for me to pick up the keys (which definitely were there) tomorrow.

After lunch both George and Indigo stayed with the boys and we went shopping.

Salvatore said that there was a restaurant 400 **yards** down the road and that there was a supermarket just beyond that. If we wanted to go into town then just carry on straight across at the traffic lights and there you'll be. All fine and dandy except that we did not find the supermarket. We did go into the town and went around a couple of times finding no supermarkets but signs that disappeared into thin air. I think we just do not have the Italian understanding of signs sorted out in our heads yet.

We found a supermarket in a residential area, but there really wasn't anything in there. No fresh meat and little fresh vegetables. We took the last litre of fresh milk.

We then drove around some more and found a *pollo* shop. Eliza bought all sorts of odd bits of chicken that we could cook on the barbeque in the house. Then we tried to find our way home.

We found where we had first come off the state road, which was right, but which we thought was wrong at the time. And then we did see some signs for the Verdetecnica. We followed them and crossed the state road but then they petered out. But now we saw a bigger supermarket and decided to try our luck here for food. Some success. Then we tried to find our way home.

We found where we had first come off the state road again. We followed some signs for the Verdetecnica again, but further this time, but then they petered out and we went around the town again. We recognised that we had been here before the first time we had been to the centre of Sciacca when we had taken the wrong turning off the state road and before we had driven around the mountain the wrong way. Eliza suggested that we do that route again, but I was determined not to. I needed to know how to get there for tomorrow when I had to return to Palermo. We went back on the state road and went back to the first exit. We calmly followed the signs to the Verdetecnica again this time took a left where we had gone straight ahead before. And lo and behold we were there.

This has confused me badly. Most of the time signposts on the right hand side of the road pointing left and signposts on the left hand side of the road pointing right mean straight on. Signposts on the right hand side pointing right mean right and signposts on the left hand side pointing left mean left. This one was a signpost on the right hand side pointing left so I felt justifiably aggrieved about this.

When we got home, Indigo had made a new friend, Bridgitta, and was being fed by her mother, Hannika. George was still playing with the boys and was not hungry.

We all were tired and even after trying to go to bed early it was half past ten before we settled down. And then Indigo woke up again with more of the same as last night, She was in quite a bit of pain and it was heart-wrenching watching her sob. Eliza sat with her for some time before she went to sleep.

Day 12
Mileage 1403
Sunday 5th May 2002
Casteldaccia and back again

Dad had to go back to the Casetta Rosa to get the keys (which were all his). After breakfast I went and played with the boys, we invited them round for lunch (we had a BBQ). After that me, Lorenzo, Indigo and her friend and mum and last, but not least, our mum went to the beach.

*

A second night's sleep was interrupted by Indigo. She was complaining about tummy ache and was very grisly. Eventually after much coaxing she fell asleep for a few hours.

Today I went off to drive back to Casetta Rosa to fetch the spare keys that we had left behind: car key, car crook lock key, safe lock key, computer lap top lock key and house keys. I had arranged to meet Giovanni at nine o'clock and so set off before eight, leaving everybody else still asleep in the Verdetecnica. It was bright and clear and there was virtually no traffic. The run across country was very therapeutic and calming. The Galaxy was purring along as I was listening to Dan Hicks, The Indigo Girls, Michelle Shocked and k d lang.

The countryside was very beautiful and unfolded in front of me as I drove along. Everything seemed neat and tidy and just so. Rank upon rank of vines and olive trees spread before me. Small and large handkerchief fields of corn and grass interleaved the vines and olives.

Small groups of olive trees crowned some hills and nestled alongside farmhouses in various states of repair. All along this stretch of road all side roads seemed to lead to Corleone, but no distances were ever marked. I later looked up Corleone on the map and the only way there was on narrow white roads.

The road, as it approached the northern side of the island, became more modern and there were longer and longer stretches of viaduct and bridges as the road builders compensated for the unevenness of the landscape. There was a long winding stretch rising slowly towards the craggy hills surrounding Palermo and then suddenly the long winding road downhill into the suburbs of Palermo. Out again to Casteldaccia and down to the Villa Cefela.

I had to wait for Giovanni and then turn around and go back again. Amazingly, I was back at the Verdetecnica by half past ten. After yesterday's drive through the mist and rain I began to realise how small Sicily actually was with only an hour or so separating the north and south coasts.

George and Indigo were playing with their new friends when I got back and we invited them all over for a barbeque. They had found a litter of kittens whose mother was feral and had made a nest under one of the windows in Salvatore's house.

The Sicilian sun played down strongly onto the garden, but we were semi shaded by the roof. The smell of wood smoke and cooking meat played enticingly over the garden. Garlic, tomatoes, cucumber and herbs added to the atmosphere. We had, as usual, over catered. Strong red Sicilian wine made me feel a little sleepy.

Later, they all went off to the beach with Lorenzo – the eldest boy – in charge of navigations and directions. I stayed behind and wrote and read.

Day 13
Mileage 1553
Monday 6th May 2002
Visiting The Valley Of The Temples

Today we went to a museum which had things from the bronze age hunting tools to ancient Greek moulds. There was even a giant statue which would have held up the roof of the temple of Zeus. Mum thought it was amazing that the ancient Greeks had their own tourist market! We arrived at the valley (of the Temples) carpark. Near the carpark there is a restaurant that has very poor food. Dad took a picture of me, mum and Indigo in a cave. We stayed there for a while while dad went for a walk. When it was raining me, Indigo and mum huddled up to keep warm.

*

Every one slept in trying to make up sleeping time.

Hannika and family went off to Agrigento to get a replacement hire car for theirs, which had broken down. We planned to go to the Valley of the Temples at Agrigento too and hoped we may meet up somewhere. The weather had cooled off and it was hazy and cloudy.

Agrigento was about an hour from Sciacca. This was another universal Sicilian measurement of length. From Sciacca, most places of interest were either an hour's drive away or on the way to somewhere else. The Valley of the Temples at Agrigento consists of a group of four or five Greek temples in various states of decay and unfinishedness. The phrase "the Valley of the temples" appears to have been made up by a tourist consultant who thought it would appeal to tourists and bring them in by the throng load. We went to the Archaeological Museum first as this was closing at lunchtime, but today was not opening again. The museum was well laid out and full of old things (as you would expect). One of the central exhibits was a giant 4 or 5 metre stone man standing upright but with head and neck bent in the prone position as if carrying a colossal weight on his shoulders. The temple of Zeus had about twenty of these statues supporting the buildings, but it was not clear where these giants had stood. The Temple itself was unfinished, as work had stopped after yet another invasion. The giants lay around the site in an undignified heap.

The museum had made great efforts to make itself wheelchair friendly with slopes in all the halls and a long curving ramp around an excavated amphitheatre as its entrance. Only to fail at the last. To get up from the entrance ramp to the museum itself were a dozen steps to negotiate. I just didn't see the point of all the effort they had obviously made yet not to actually get it right. What were the authorities afraid of? It could only be Daleks coming down to visit to understand some ancient Earth history.

We went further down the hill to the Valley of Temples itself. There were some terrific overall panoramas of the whole valley. In its glory, the site must have been amazingly awe-inspiring, an undoubted flaunting of prosperity and power for all to see. With its position uphill (despite its name), it would have been visible many miles out to sea.

We walked up to the temple at the top (The temple of Juno). Half way up we met Hannika and her family. She would have to wait until half past six that night for their replacement car. I felt very sorry for her to have to put up with this.

We went past the necropolis (cemetery) where a lot of the graves had been excavated and it then started spitting. George, Indigo and Eliza took shelter in one of a series of semi-circular stone excavations, while I carried on up to the Temple of Juno. George was upset that we couldn't go into the temples themselves unlike at Segesta where everyone could scramble everywhere. I told her that if she came back as an adult, it would be very surprising if the ruins at Segesta would still be so free.

The semi-circular excavation looked like tombs to me. They stretched a long way up the main drag towards the Temple of Juno. From the Temple of Juno you could see the town of Agrigento and the road up to from the coast. Like so many roads around Sicily and mainland Italy, there were long sections of viaduct, tall gracious structures sweeping over the ancient landscape. These were indeed the twentieth century equivalents of the ancient temples that we were marvelling at. These were dedicated to Fiat, Ferrari, Alfa Romeo, Lamborgini, Maserati, Pirelli and, I suppose, Ford.

On the way back from Agrigento to Sciacca we made a diversion to see Eraclea Minoa as recommended by Salvatore. We first went down to the beach. It was still spitting, but less so than before. The beach was a wonderful sweeping bay with real golden sand. And it was empty: partially because it was raining, but partially because of it remoteness. There were a large number of holiday homes around, but these would not have filled up the beach too much. South facing, the next landfall from here was Africa, and probably not too far either.

We drove up to the Eraclea Minoa, but now the rain was coming down steadily. The children and Eliza looked miserable at the prospect of looking at more ruins in the rain. So we didn't.

Day 14
Mileage 1644
Tuesday 7th May 2002
We Stay Put

Today we should have been moving on, but we haven't anywhere to stay so Salvatore said we could stay another two days. While I was having the best time on the holiday no trip (so far) mum and dad were searching in distress for a place for the next 8 days or so with no success what so ever!

*

Another day in the Verdetecnica. We needed to plan where we were going next. We had a ten day gap to fill and then three days in the Eolie Islands to fill. Partially because of the poor weather and partially because we liked it here and enjoyed Salvatore's and Pascale's company and the children enjoyed the boys' company, we decided to extend our stay here by another two days. That left eight to fill on the Sicilian mainland.

We needed to check out the Eolie Islands first, as we had no idea on ferry timetable or frequencies. From this information we could work our plans backwards. We already knew where we staying near Napoli and we were due to arrive there on Saturday 25th May. We originally planned to travel to the Eolie Islands and then to take the overnight ferry direct to Napoli. It was quite difficult finding times, but when we did, the trip to Napoli was just not right.

There are several islands in the group including Vulcano, Stromboli and Lipari. We decided to take the Galaxy across to Lipari and use that as a base, as we did not feel safe about the leaving the Galaxy on the Sicilian mainland for three nights even in a secured garage. We eventually found and booked a place on Lipari called Casa Gialla.

Then we had to find somewhere to stay on the Sicilian mainland for the remaining eight days. Although Salvatore was very helpful and supportive I could not work out whether he was guiding us or recommending places to us or trying to point us in different places. We quickly found somewhere for the last four days we needed but the previous four days was quite problematical. After a while we gave up.

We went down to Sciacca for a while and left Indigo with Hannika and Bridgitta to play in the park while we wandered around the town. Ceramics everywhere. It was interesting looking at all the plates and pots. There were a surprising number of different styles, but after a while they all began to look the same and swirled together in my mind. In the end we thought the best ones were in the very first couple of places we visited.

By now it was spitting and a threatening sky, well, threatened.

We also had visited the central square where there were numerous fish stalls. There were amongst other things anchovies, sardines, octopus, calamari, prawns, red snapper, large whelks like snails and some very very strange looking crustaceans. They looked to us like crayfish and were a light transparent sandy colour much larger than the prawns with two bright red false eyes on their tails. We had to try them. We bought a *mezzo chilo* of prawns and we asked for just four of these strange looking ones. The fishmonger gave us the prawns and then just kept piling the others in. We said, "Stop, Stop", but he shrugged his shoulders and gave us the whole bag for 4 euros. As the prawns were 3 we could not really argue.

By now, it was steadily drizzling, but not much to worry about.

We asked Salvatore what these were. He said that they had two names: *sparnocchie* and *cicale*. This second name was only used locally and meant the same as "those insects that go schick, schick in the trees in the summer." "Ahh, cicadas" I said. "Yes, yes, that's right. But why did you buy these? You will have to use your fingers to eat them." We said we didn't mind. We had never seen them before and they looked interesting.

By now, it was raining quite steadily.

And so it turned out. The *sparnocchie* were extremely difficult to eat. Their backs were particularly sharp and hard to break. The insides only had a small amount of meat, and, although very tasty were not worth all the hard work. Never mind, I had never eaten cicadas before and would probably never try them again.

While we were ploughing our way through the prawns and cicadas, George and Indigo were snuggled together watching a DVD and we were listening to the rain outside. They both went to sleep without much resistance and we settled down hoping for an undisturbed night.

Day 15
Mileage 1652
Wednesday 8ᵗʰ May 2002
Sciacca and Marsala
It Never Rains

Today we went to Marsala and went to an island and we found some half of mosaics and a house which is now a museum. On the way there we caught quite a big boat, however we caught quite a small boat on the way back. Before we went to Marsala I saved a kitten's life with the help of Lorenzo. We swapped houses with another house because the roof was leaking.

*

The rainstorm from yesterday evening continued unabated throughout the night. There were one or two thunderbolts only. Their loudness was emphasised by their unexpectedness. As I was lying in bed I thought I heard dripping. It was quite distinct and yet only a very small drip. I didn't want to wake Eliza, but I felt I had to investigate. I didn't so much mind dripping onto the floor, but I wanted to check whether our clothes were being dripped on or indeed whether the pc was being dripped on.

I went out into the other rooms and listened…

I looked at the phone. It was one thirty.

I could not hear dripping anywhere else. George and Indigo were sleeping oblivious to the storm. Only children seem to be able to sleep in such a thoroughly innocent manner through all this noise.

Just our luck it was in our bedroom only.

Our bed was on a raised wooden platform. Somehow, Salvatore had laid the floor with an inbuilt creak. Not your common or garden creak that you might find in the odd loose floorboard in our staircase, but a very substantial what-goes-creak-in-the-night fingernail-scrapping-down-black-board haunting sort of creak. So there I was, naked, in the pitch black, desperately, creeping around the bedroom trying to find this dripping noise, without stepping on the floor too much to avoid waking up Eliza. I felt a drip on my spine. And then another one. It was dripping on our bed. I then felt a drip on my head. And then on my arm. It was really dripping on our bed. And still I could here other dripping noises. So it was leaking in other places too.

"What on earth are you doing?" said Eliza. I had failed in not waking her up. "The roof is leaking," I said "and I'm trying to make sure that our things won't get wet." Eliza was suddenly wide awake. She switched on her bedside light and found her glasses.

Staring at the ceiling, we tried to fathom where the drips were coming from. Most were coming from one or two lateral beams where the water had run down from the apex, but there was no way we could see the cause of the leaks. We started putting down cups and saucepans to catch the leaks but this was no good.

Luckily for us, the apartment had a spare double bed. We just upended the mattress to avoid it getting any water damage and decamped to the other room. The rainstorm was still going on, but at least we were sure we would now be dry. Outside we could hear the kittens mewing as the mother cat moved them to a more sheltered site. Inside we could hear Salvatore and Pascale moving furniture around. They were obviously suffering from similar problems.

At last we fell asleep and too soon an uneasy dawn came and woke us up. The storm had abated.

"Never, in over ten years have we had such a storm", said Salvatore. "If it never rains, how can we tell if the roof leaks? It has been leaking in our house too and this has never happened before." We said that it we must have brought the English weather with us. Salvatore thought that if Eliza had made it rain then she would have a shrine erected in every town in Sicily as they were always short of water. During the night, Salvatore had been up as the electricity had been shorting out and he kept needing to reset the fuse box. We hadn't noticed.

Pascale and Salvatore were very helpful and said we should move into the newly vacated little cottage next door. We spent a couple of hours moving our stuff twenty metres.

The feral mother cat had moved only three out of four kittens in the night. The one that was left behind looked very bedraggled and lonesome. George managed to feed it some milk through a syringe. We didn't give this little one much hope without its mother. George would be very upset if it died.

Then we went back to Salvatore's office to try and once more fill in our accommodation gap. We tried a couple of places and we didn't get any answers. I said we needed to go out as I was going stir crazy.

Off we went in the Galaxy to Marsala. Eliza wanted to have some zabaglione made with local Marsala wine. The day was now hot and steaming, but it was still cloudy. We expected to arrive at Marsala at about noon and decided to go straight to lunch. The road into Marsala was long, narrow and dead straight. All the buildings on both sides were dull, square, concrete based and shuttered. The place was deserted except for the trail of slow moving vehicles of all shapes and sizes pottering up the road towards the town. We found a restaurant on Cape Lilybeo. Looking at the map, this seemed to me to be the westernmost point on the main island of Sicily. The buffet antipasto looked great and tasted just as good.

On the news on the television, it was apparent that the storm last night had been fairly unprecedented. There were floods mentioned in lots of places, but I think these were on the mainland rather than on the island. The very next item was concerned with the lack of water on Sicily and the current low level of water in their reservoirs. Hopefully, last night helped after all.

After lunch we headed up towards the salt flats. We visited the isle of Mothia where an English family, the Whittakers, had arrived with a load of port and learned to blend it with local Sicilian wine and invented Marsala wine. In those days, the local labour was cheap and their organisational abilities meant that they made a fortune. The island was originally inhabited by Phoenicians over 5 thousand years ago. Over the past century the place had been excavated to bits.

The trip over to the island was on a small boat across the salt flats. It was very shallow and the pilot had to take great care in avoiding grounding the boat. We thought that the place would not be busy as on our boat there was only one other person, but when we got to the island there was a large gaggle of grockles waiting to catch the boat back.

When we arrived the path up to the main house was entirely surrounded by Rosey Alloe cactus plants. They were dramatic in their own right and their sheer abundance and their banked up height made a wonderful sight. I wished we could see this path when they were in full bloom. We decided to go straight to the Whittaker museum dedicated to Englishman who had founded the island. It was shut. Again we had come across the Italian way of life.

Everywhere was full of cacti. The prickly pear style that grew into large clumps and bushes were now beginning to open up into gorgeous yellow blooms. The century plants, which I thought were named as they blossomed once every hundred years only to die afterward, were everywhere sending up shoots standing upright like sentries. At least a quarter of all these century plants were shooting up stalks this year alone. Row on row of them, everywhere you looked. And they were growing so fast you could almost hear them stretching upwards towards the sun.

The Aloe style again grew in clumps and were more like bushes than individual plants. There were cacti that rose up like trees and challenged the palm for size.

Wandering around the island we found some ancient mosaics that had been recently excavated and a long ancient street with sunken rooms.

Although it was hot and steaming I imagined the island in the full heat of the August Sicilian sun. Quite a challenge. It must also have been a challenge to the Whittaker family without today's luxuries like air conditioning and cold showers.

When we came back to the museum, it was now open and was well worth exploring. After a long lunch, there were hoards of school buses queuing to travel across to the islands. Leaving now looked like good timing to me.

We drove up further along the salt flats. It takes about six hot days to turn the seawater into salt. There were men sweeping the excess water off with squeezee mops, a bit like groundsmen clearing the outfields on English cricket pitches after a heavy downpour. It looked like very hard labour. Again, even harder under the full blaze of the August sun. I don't suppose that this sort of work would pay at all well either. Salt was definitely down the low end of the food chain even though it was an essential part of our diet. The salt was piled up and then tiled over with roof tiles to keep them dry. Those that were fully covered resembled huge turtles. Each one of these piles looked like several lifetimes supply, and there were dozens of these piles.

We drove into Marsala to try and find a place for Eliza to have her zabaglione, but failed miserable. Here was another Sicilian town that had sprawled and just had no discernable coherence about it. We could not even find the old centre, but I am sure it was there somewhere. We went on to Mazara del Vallo and tried the same. This time we found the centre and parked. We wandered the streets for a while, Indigo took her favourite riding position on my shoulders where she could see further than any of us. The place was decidedly in a pre-season mode. Places were closed and places were constructing outside shelters in preparation for the influx of holidaymakers over the next few months.

On the way back to Sciacca we saw olive trees: tree upon tree, row upon row, orchard upon orchard, solid from horizon to horizon. How many olives this produced and how much olive oil these made must be staggering.

Back home we found out that the mother cat had come back for her last kitten and they were successfully reunited. We were now in the new house. It was much more comfortable. Salvatore had built it in a month. We spent some more time with Salvatore finding the next place to stay. Eventually we found one up on Mount Etna. It looked and sounded great and, most importantly, it had spaces for us, so we booked it.

Day 16
Mileage 1765
Thursday 9th May 2002
Sciacca
Lorenzo's Foot

This morning mum went out and bought some plates. I played with Lorenzo all morning and most of the afternoon. Lorenzo was off school because he hurt his foot badly yesterday so he can't put his shoes on. After school had finished Lorenzo's friend came round and we had an awful amount of fun. Lorenzo may come and stay with us in the next summer holidays and Mark says he would like to come with Lorenzo to stay with us.

*

I woke up to calmness. The sunshine had come back.

Today was spent avoiding playing the tourist. All those household chores came back into play with washing and clearing up. Somehow these too seemed almost pleasant in the warm Sicilian sunshine.

Lorenzo had fallen at school and hurt his foot, so he and George played with their gameboys together. Laughter and raucous shouting told me that they were having fun. How much Italian George was using was debateable as I am sure they were relying on Lorenzo's schoolboy English, sign language and the universal language of Pokémon to get by.

In the apartments were some very simple yet effective plain white round porcelain handled platters. Eliza wanted to find out where they had been bought. Pascale told Eliza, but wisely – knowing our navigation record around Sciacca – offered to take her to the shop itself. When they came back Eliza had bought two of the round ones and two matching rectangular ones as well, plus a reproduction antique urn.

We had asked the family round for curry that night. Salvatore said he was vegetarian, but would eat fish and he would take Eliza to the fish stall later on to buy some. They went off later leaving me happily looking after the children.

We lit the barbecue and Salvatore said it was the first time that he had used the new one. They had only finished building it in February and, although it had been used already by some guests, he had not used it and not been able to prove that it worked. A bit like he had not been able to prove the roof in a storm.

We had some salmon steaks, some fresh sardines and some dogfish pieces. They were all excellent. It seemed very strange to us eating popadoms, vegetable curry, dhal and curried fish in Sicily on a barbecue. It seemed even stranger to the family. Salvatore had spent several years in England during his twenties and although he thought he had eaten curry before, he did not remember ever eating like this before. He said he spent most of his time with "posh" people and had typical English food. He was, as ever, generous in his appreciation. He said he used to eat Vespa curries and remembered that they had sultanas in them. I too certainly remember those sorts of dried pre-prepared curries from childhood, but I didn't think they were related to scooters.

They talked about their lives in Sciacca. Salvatore was born in Sciacca, but he felt that the townspeople were very introspective in their outlook on life. As an example, when the children went to school they had to state their religion. They were given two choices only: Catholic or Atheist. You were either with them or against them with no possibility for compromise. Pascale and he were content not to be part of that community. With their guests, they felt that they were more in touch with the outside world. People came from lots of different places to stay at the Verdetecnica. August was always very hot – up to 45°C. Even though he was born there, Salvatore liked to go away in August to escape the heat.

I went to bed realising that I had not been off the premises all day. This was the first time since leaving home where I had stayed in one place.

San Cataldo
Day 17
Mileage 1765
Friday 10ᵗʰ May 2002
Moving Again

Today we are moving again. But before we are moving I am going to do some quick trades of Pokémon. Afterwards we were on the move. Today we went to a villa with no walls or no roof but a wonderful mosaics. Then we were off to Mount Etna.

*

Today was moving on day. Eliza packed crates and I carried. Although this seemed easier today, it still took time. There was a lot of mess after last night's dinner and all the neighbourhood cats would be happy with the leftovers. Eventually we said our goodbyes and we were on our way.

We were going to Piazza Armerina to see a Roman villa and their mosaics. It turned out to be quite a drive and definitely not one hour from Sciacca.

The weather was glorious again. The snatches of the sea we saw through the rougher terrain were always stunningly beautiful and the beaches were enticing. We did not succumb to the pleasure. In this corner of Sicily, although there were lots of olives and vines, it was not these that caught the eye. Instead it was orchards of prickly pear cacti that took us by surprise. Large numbers of them but not horizons full.

The Roman villa was brilliant. We had seen some of the mosaics in pictures before, but this did not lead us to expect to see so much. The people and the faces in the mosaics were very vivid and full of life. They did not look staid and flat like most mosaics I had previously seen. There were hunting scenes and rooms full of intricate patterns, knots and interlinked loops. There was a room full of girls in bikinis (invented in the 20ᵗʰ Century, of course), a room with a semi-naked lady showing off her rear enticing a man in her arms, a room with a three-eyed man practicing something very odd, but I could not see what.

Eliza and I shared a sandwich for lunch.

After this we started our drive to Etna. I was excited by the prospect of seeing the mountain rise up over the horizon, but there was so much haze, it was very difficult to tell if we were actually seeing Etna or not. The autostrada around Catania was very busy as we caught the Italian rush hour. We found the road up to our *argitourismo* quite easily going through Gaggi, but then I failed to understand the Italian directions and took us up the wrong turning to Graniti. When Eliza eventually worked out from the Italian instructions that we should have gone **past** the turning to Graniti it was too late. Down the mountain we came and immediately after the junction we saw the signs to San Cataldo. These we followed and then turned off onto another road further north. This was much more fun although Eliza at the wheel did not seem to think so. It was narrow, windy, steep and *molto pericoloso*. It was treacherous and pitted and in some places un-tarmaced. There were however, occasional signs encouraging us forward towards the *agritourismo*. Each succeeding sign with a distance marked seemed to make the overall distance from the turnoff longer. And then, suddenly, we were there.

Eliza just wanted a vodka.

We unpacked some things, got changed and went to meet our hosts for dinner.

It had been cold but with a wood stove going it was fine. Food was rustic, thoroughly enjoyable and extremely filling. The room was clean simple and basic, but fine.

Day 18
Mileage 1982
Saturday 11th May 2002
Mooching

We mooched around our new apartment. And then we mooched around on the beach. We came back early because we were meant to go horse riding, but the was a communication problem and Fabrizzio had just fed the horses! But we went horse riding just before dinner. There was a lovely dog called Birillo (skittle).

*

I woke up early and was up writing the journal. It was misty and steamy. We were living up in the clouds. The lady of the house, Rita, gave me some homemade biscuits and coffee. After a while she said she was going up to feed the chickens and I decided to join her. We walked up the hill apiece so Rita could collect the chicken feed of yesterday's leftovers.

The chickens were in their own coop, but the gate was left open. There were at least thirty or forty chickens around and in their midst was a cat, quite nonchalantly, walking around as if he ruled the roost. The chickens showed no fear of the cat nor did the cat appear to want to attack them. It must be a chicken cat as opposed to a sheep dog.

After Rita had given the chickens their breakfast, we walked further up the hill to the goats. Her mother was inside a shack milking the goats. The goats had been corralled in an open pen and fed through to Rita's mother in single file so that she could milk them before being released back into their field. The goats were lined up patiently to be milked and once they were free they scampered up the hill. Some of the goats were nibbling grass and roots and some had even climbed some of the trees.

I asked how many goats they had. Over 150. These were milked daily and it took Rita's mother about an hour to do. She had filled two large buckets with the goats' milk. Rita told me that each bucket contained about 30 litres. The old lady had a yoke just fashioned out of a branch with notches at each end to hold the milk. She loaded this over her right shoulder balancing the yoke from front to back rather than from left to right as I expected. She the used another branch as her third leg. They took the milk off to make ricotta cheese.

I went back down to the main building and then went off to see the ostrich. They only had one and he looked rather sad and dishevelled. Lower down there was a large circular fishpond with – well – fish in it. This was set in a small orchard containing a variety of trees including walnuts, cherries, apricots or peaches, pears and olives. Further down still was the menagerie or horse riding school. No doubt George and Eliza will be down here later.

As the weather up here was still a bit cloudy, we decided that after breakfast we would venture down the mountain and try and find Hanneke. Up here in the mountain we had no signal for the telephone. We drove down the hill to the junction with the main road and still no signal so we decided to take a look at the Alcantara Gorge just up the road. This looked interesting, but being Saturday, it was busy and also it was now spitting so we thought we would come back after the weekend.

We drove down towards the sea at Gardini Naxos. Here, the houses come right down to the front promenade. The beach is sandy and has large rocks that interrupt the monotony of the sand. Even though it was placid there were enough waves to make it interesting to sit and watch. Everywhere has that pre-season feeling: places are open, but there is no real feeling to the resort. There are a few shorts walking around but they are a rarity at this time.

In the afternoon we arranged for Hanneke to come and meet us. It is their last day in Sicilia and Bridgitta and Indigo are happy to see each other again and play together. George just adores playing in the breaking waves. I'm the only one to actually go in and swim. Everyone thinks I am bonkers, but that's what fathers are for.

We say our farewells and say we'll keep in touch. Who knows whether we will or not. It rarely works. We drive back up the mountain to the San Cataldo. This time the road does begin to feel easier. I think we are just beginning to know its bends more intimately. We take a bit more notice of the scenery around us. Near San Cataldo there are various pieces of old cars lying around including two doors up separate trees. Could these be decorations to ward off evil spirits or were these used as nesting boxes for birds?

Eliza and George were expecting to go horse riding on our return, but apparently nobody had told Fabrizzio and the horses had all just been fed. There had been "a miscommunications". Later on an argument ensued – a short, very loud, shouting match with hand and arm gestures in the Italian fashion, it was all over in less than two minutes – between Fabrizzio and Filippo, his father, over the horses. An hour or so later the girls were all given a short ride around the school, including Indigo who thought it was so much fun and laughed and laughed. It was arranged to go out for a trek tomorrow morning at nine.

We have another splendid local dinner. Another English couple arrive to stay. Lots of chit chat, but I am tired and I am first to bed much to Indigo's delight.

Day 19
Mileage 2010
Sunday 12th May 2002
Pony Trekking

After breakfast we went on our long awaited pony trekking, I was easily one of the best riders there and I was the only kid! It was a lovely sunny morning for pony trekking. In the afternoon we went for a drive around Etna. We saw two craters: one was on a steep hill and I was scared to go up (I slipped and scared myself). The other we reached by car.

In the evening I was feeling ill so I went to bed and listened to Harry Potter.

*

It was Eliza's turn to get up early. I took her out to where the chickens and goats are, but she is too late to watch the goats being milked. Maria, Rita's mother, has already finished her milking and is loading up her yoke. Eliza goes off to watch the cheese making process itself. Eliza was very impressed that although the milk was turned into cheese out in the open, the women were extremely scrupulous over the hygiene conditions in the process. Cleanliness of all the equipment used and temperature control of the process itself was rigorously adhered to.

They poured the milk into a large wide wok-shaped bowl with a central hole filled with dried ferns to act as a filter. Then Maria added some rennet from a sheep's stomach and warmed the milk up to blood temperature by adding hot water. This mix was then stirred and when it began to solidify, she removed all the curds putting them into net baskets and added black pepper corns. These were put aside to drain and then put into the *crotto* to season and mature as pecorino. With the remnants of the liquor, Maria attempted to make some *ricotta frescha*, but for some reason this did not work today.

We are all up for breakfast. George has to be prodded several times to get up. "If you don't get up, you will miss your horse riding." The weather is bright and hot again, but storms are forecast for this afternoon. Nine o'clock turns into an Italian nine o'clock with no sign of horse riding preparations. Everyone is standing around talking in broken Italian and broken English.

The girls and the English couple go down to the menagerie and groom the horses. They tack up and get ready to go. Indigo is given a quick turn in the school and then the others are off for a short trek. Fabrizzio is riding bare back and the others are using American style saddles. Indigo is devastated. She desperately wanted to go, but she is far too small and totally inexperienced.

They were gone for about an hour. Indigo had a good cry and then calmed down.

We decided to drive to the top of the Etna Nord route. The weather had already closed in a piece and Etna itself was covered in cloud. It began to spot as we hit the main road and turned north towards Francavilla de Sicilia. Then up to Castiglione di Sicilia. The view as ever became dramatic as we climbed. All the small hilltops were crowned with villages. Houses, castles and churches were all shoehorned together. The roadside was full of wild fennel some of it was over six feet tall, with large yellow headed flowers. It looked like a wild version of cow parsley. The further we went up the mountain the more it rained. On to Linguaglossa where it became heavier and then relentless. We followed the road up to Mareneve, notable for the fact that as a town it no longer exists except on the map. We stopped near the top for a drink and then suddenly we were above the clouds and it was clear.

There was Etna in front of us. The top was covered in freshly fallen snow.

Further up, there was a sign pointing to a spent crater, so we followed it. It led up a very steep and blackened path with lots of loose lava. George became frightened of the steepness and the looseness of the stones and refused to climb all the way. Indigo was brave and reasonably sensible as we went up the last few metres slowly and very carefully. At the top we found ourselves at the lip of a crater where the middle was flat. Small plants were re-encroaching onto its surface, but the whole place had an eerie silence about it. The climb down was, if anything, even more treacherous than the ascent. Indigo was now very wary as we made our way back to George waiting patiently below.

We drove on, following the tourist route. We came across deep, wide and black solidified lava flows. These had crossed the roads, half-swallowed trees and partially covered houses. The flows looked very sharp and stark. You began to understand the irresistible nature of the lava flows slashing mercilessly down the mountainsides. At Zafferna Etnea we dropped down the mountain and drove quickly home along the autostrada. Hopefully we would take the southern route up later.

George was quite insistent on wanting to see the souvenir shops. Luckily only two out of about twelve were actually open. There were lots of lovely postcards, maps, rock and crystal samples and photographs of recent eruptions, but most of all there were religious icons made from lava and hand painted with glitter: gaudy green, ruby red and blissful blue. There were icons of the lovely Mary, her son, and a few other

Catholic dignitaries. I must say I was shocked at the sheer volume of Catholic imagery on sale in this, a Mount Etna, souvenir shop. I had forgotten how obsessed this country was with its religion.

They are getting used to us at San Cataldo and the people are much more talkative. Rita is trying to learn English and is having a hard time with her pronunciation. "Sweater, shirt, skirt and shoes", "Cooking the chicken in the kitchen" are two exercises she is trying. We learn the Italian for tongue twister. What's funny is that our Italian pronunciation is bound to be just as bad to their ears. Several years ago we had a Czech au pair called Simone. Her English was very good and improved dramatically after a few weeks. One Christmas her parents came to stay and they had no English at all. We played "guess the word". They would pick an English word from the dictionary and try to say it. Then we would try to guess what it was. Afterwards we would pick a Czech word from the dictionary and they would try to guess what it was. Simone acted as referee. This was surprisingly highly amusing. So I could well understand the mutual amusement that all the broken language was causing. Everyone was helping each other understand what we all were trying to say. It was great fun.

It was Sunday. At lunchtime, the farm had been very busy and despite the rain and the 5km drive up a narrow and windy single track road, they had had over a hundred places for lunch. The Italians love to come out into the country on a Sunday. Fillippo told us that most of these weren't local, but, like us were tourists or had come some distant to celebrate something in particular.

More food as dinnertime came around again. This time, George was not feeling so good, but had some *stellini* pasta in broth. This must be the Italian equivalent of chicken noodle soup. She went to bed soon after.

I must give a description of a typical meal here, so tonight's is as good as any.

We had antipasti as normal. All made from their own produce: *salami piccant*, *pecorino* with embedded olives and peppercorns, sliced grilled melanzine (aubergines) in a tangy dressing, large green and very strong olives, funghi, omelettes – two varieties: potato and pecorino, slices of sweet and salty ricotta, *pane fritta* – bread fried in batter, potato salad with thin sliced onion.

We had pasta. Macaroni with home made pesto – beaten anchovies, salt, garlic, olive oil, pine nuts and wild fennel **and** lasagne with béchamel sauce made with homemade cheese and milk.

We had *carni*. Chicken roasted and falling off the bone with potatoes from the oven. A green lettuce salad in a vinaigrette as a consolation prize for any vegetarians present.

We were well and truly full, but it was not over yet. Fillippo profusely and loudly apologised that the next course was not his produce, but was brought by a friend. We all said that this was quite acceptable and encouraged him to bring it out: *cozze* (muscles) followed and were quickly snapped up by Indigo – one of her favourites. Shortly these were followed by *lumanche* (very small snails). At this point I had given up eating altogether even though this was very impolite.

We had fruit of nespole and caffe and a cinnamon based liquor.

Definitely time for bed.

The day had been very full of contrasts and activities. A truly delightful experience.

Day 20
Mileage 2038
Monday 13ᵗʰ May 2002
San Cataldo
Ill

Today we just mooched about because I was feeling under the weather and I caught up with my school work and things like that.

But the view of the mountain was just lovely just like the weather.

It was a little girl's birthday and I ended up a piece of cake which cheered me up. (I was still feeling bad.)

*

Early on, it was blustery and cloudy. You could see most of Etna and its fresh covering in snow showed strongly. After a while the sun had come out from behind us and there was this tremendously strong rainbow arcing solidly across a smoking Etna and its cloud cover. I took a couple of pictures, but my experiences with photographing rainbows have not been encouraging. Still we would see. I had to wake up Eliza specially to see. She was not pleased, but pleased at the same time. Her ruffled feathers were smoothed by the offer of freshly made tea in bed.

George was still not feeling well so we decided on just chilling out up on this mountain – with the wonderful name of Montangna Grande or Big Mountain. I'm sure it was original once. As the morning progressed the wind blew all the cloud cover away. By mid-afternoon we were left with a spectacular panoramic view of the whole area. Etna, still snow covered and smoking, dominated the horizon. You could very easily see what had attracted peoples throughout history to live on its sides. Today, the San Cataldo was a touch of paradise, but what we had seen of the people living here showed us that they all worked hard each and every day to make it so for them. There was definitely no such thing as a free lunch this high up and remote in the hills. They had earned every euro-cent and deserved to reap their rich rewards.

Indigo and I went for a walk up the mountain in search of chickens and goats. We found the chickens, but we did not find the goats. She enjoyed picking flowers for mummy and I was very surprised at how far she walked with no encouragement or complaint or asking to be carried.

Earlier, Eliza and Indigo had volunteered to work in the kitchens. Indigo was busy shelling peas and Eliza was stuffing pasta in the shape of conch shells. More food came our way in the form of lunch. Wine and Italian food together with warmth, wind and glorious sunshine and views made for another perfectly structured afternoon. George improved and spent much of her time – after doing some journal work and spelling – making friends with the horses. Indigo dressed up and wandered around. A large Italian family had come up for lunch and celebrated their daughter, Serena's, sixth birthday with cake and *prosecco* for everyone. It was rude not to join in.

Eliza stayed in the kitchen talking Italian with the ladies and making English scones for tea.

Scillichenti
Day 21
Mileage 2085
Tuesday 14ᵗʰ May 2002
We Get Lost

We are moving on yet again but this has a different "tale". Me and Indigo went on a shetland pony I found easier than riding Nita (the pony I was riding on the trek). Afterwards we all jumped into the car and we were off. We spent two hours going up and down the same stupid bit of road looking for the place were going to stay. Finally we stopped at a place which we hoped to point us in the right direction. But the woman kept saying there was a family room up the road. Dad phoned up Salvatore to give us the address, and it was the one down the road after all! We broke out laughing. This evening we saw the moon setting behind Etna. But (the) thing that was so amazing was we saw earthlight that meant we could see the whole disk of the moon.

*

All quiet this morning, everybody was sleeping like babies.

Started packing up and brought the Galaxy down to help load up.

Indigo wanted to have another go on the horses. Fabrizzio was only too willing. This time, he tacked up the very small Shetland pony. He had to make up a bridle for him from odd bits of leather. For me the time taken from the decision to go horse riding to being ready was too long. I got hot and sweaty standing around and I did not like all the flies buzzing around all the horse muck. Eliza was very impressed with his skills. Indigo went first and simply grinned at being on horseback. George went next and scampered around the school. Then George and Indigo went together.

After all this it was time to go.

We drove the mountain for the last time and headed for the Alcantara Gorge. This was now nearly empty compared with the weekend, and today the temperature was much warmer. We climbed down to the water level. It was very dramatic and very still and quiet. The stratifications in the rock formations were remarkable. Some people had come here for the day with picnics and all, but we only stayed for half an hour or so. Without any speedy water flow, it was a slight disappointment.

We drove down the mountain towards Gardini Naxos. Stopped at a supermarket on the way down to buy some lunch.

We decided to take the coast road rather than the motorway to Acireale as we had plenty of time. The road varied from the state road to smaller white roads as we wove our way down towards the coastal strip. Unfortunately there wasn't a single road or track that followed the sea front and we had to keep doubling back along various paths and dead ends. There was one point where all the signs led to Riposto no matter what direction we were going in. We were aiming for a small village called Scillichenti which wasn't on our map, but we knew it was just north of Acireale on the minor roads. From Acireale we dropped down to the coastal plain called the Ciclopi Riviera. The view and the richness of the sea colour was stunning. We travelled the road to Scillichenti and beyond and back again with no signs of Il Limoneto where we were staying. Up down round and round we went. The whole area was a like network of capillaries, everywhere were very small roads indeed and still no signs. We decided to go to Acireale and find the tourist office and ask there. I had written down neither the address, nor the phone number, nor the Italian instructions, so this was going to be fun.

Round and round we went through Aceriale. It had a very baroque centre, but no tourist office that we could find. We drove down a very narrow road only slightly wider than our car and with no possibility of reversing or turning around. We went back up to the motorway to see if we had came off the motorway there would be signs, but no, nothing.

We went back to Scillichenti and had another look. The view as we dropped down to the coastal plain was still stunning and the sea still deep blue and turquoise and still we had no luck. Eventually we decided to stop and ask! We stopped at the Villa Palomba, a restaurant in the middle of Scillichenti. I was very impressed with Eliza's ability to communicate. We explained that we were lost and needed some assistance. They were very kind and asked us in, offered us a drink and, once I had fetched George and Indigo, offered us ice cream too.

We asked about Il Limoneto an agritourismo place in Scillichenti. No such place. The old lady said there was one agritourism place called La Cocchenigli. Yes we had seen lots of signs to this and had found it, but it was closed and was not where we were looking. But no Il Limoneto.

She thought there was such a place years ago, but it had closed. But we had made a reservation five days ago and no we didn't have a telephone number. There was a Limoneto in Syracuse (about 50 kms away), had we booked there instead. We rang this place up and once they realised we were not trying to book, but trying to see if we had booked, it was obvious that we had not booked there.

I rang Salvatore who had helped us book it in the first place, but he was out and about in the town, I would need to ring him back when he back home.

The old lady said there was a place in a nearby street which had family rooms and that we should try there. I thought she was inviting us to stay at her house, but apparently not, just my misunderstanding of Italian and hand gestures.

I rang Salvatore back and he had the address and telephone number ready for us. I thanked him very much. The address was indeed just around the corner and was in the same street as the family rooms. They telephoned the number and discovered where it was. We decided that we would come down here for dinner and discussed the menu. Then they escorted us up to Il Limoneto.

We would never have found it without the address and vowed to look at the website when we got home to check on what instructions there were. Never mind, we knew a lot more about Scillichenti that we would have done otherwise. The setting in Il Limonetto was really beautiful within lemon groves and delicious views both towards the sea and up to ever-smoking Etna. The area outside the apartment was rustic with a well and stone benches. Eliza thinks that the apartments are converted cowsheds.

After unpacking the Galaxy, Indigo and I went for a walk around the grounds. There was a solarium signposted so we went off in search of it. It turned out to be a small suntrap with sun loungers and chairs. Of course the Sicilian weather was reliable enough not to require artificial tanning machines.

There were acres and acres of lemons groves. This was one of the problems with the Sicilian economy. Lemons are no longer a viable crop. They were so low in value that it was just not worth picking.

Back down in the village, there was a stunning new crescent moon with Venus above it. The whole of the moon was visible not just the thin sliver of a crescent illuminated by the sun. The earth itself was reflecting light and this earthlight was illuminating the dark side of the moon.

The Grateful Dead started playing Terrapin Station in my head about counting stars and brand new cresent moons.

Supper was good. George and Indigo were glued to the cartoons on the television in the background. We had some good wine made from Nero d'Avola grapes blended with Sauvignion and Merlot. When we left they also gave us another bottle made only from Nero d'Avola. I look forward to trying it.

We came out in the car park just in time to see the new moon set behind Etna. It was very surprising how fast the crescent limbs sunk below the edge of the mountain. Even after the crescent has set, the earth lit portion of the moon was still visible for a couple of short minutes.

Day 22
Mileage 2151
Wednesday 15th May 2002
A House Of Shells

Today we went to a stony beach we found a house full of shells. Indigo filled her bucket with water so we could find hermit crabs so they could have a hermit crab party. The beach had sea on BOTH sides! There were stones large and small. The view was beautiful and I could see the mainland of Italy's toe. We went for lunch and next we went to the old town of Castelmola. We were going to go to Taormina, but mum left her keys and phone in Letojanni so we had to there and get 'em.

*

In the early morning, Indigo and I went off to find a shop for things for breakfast. We drove again around and around through the capillaries trying to spot one. After a while we found one. Inside was a little old woman who looked more surprised at us than we were at finding her. We bought some bread, zola (as Indigo calls gorgonzola) Calabrese salami, pears, apples, bananas, cherry tomatoes and milk and pear juice.

Breakfast was outside on the stone table in the early sunshine.

After yesterday's shenanigans trying to find Scillichenti, we decided that we needed some time chilling out and went off to find a beach near Taormina. The town of Taormina is up in the hills and there is a cable car between the town and the sea. We could not find it. We found the beach, which was a very narrow strip of shingle out to a tiny island *belle isola*. The shingle was no more than four metres wide. It was odd to be on a beach with water on both sides. There were rocks in both sides. One side seem to have water currents swirling around, while the other side was tranquil.

George and Indigo started looking for shells in the sand. The ones we found were all very small, and some were really tiny. Later we went in the water and Indigo found a hermit crab. George and Indigo went off collecting lots of them and put them in Indigo's bucket with some water and shingle. After a while, all the hermits came out of their shells, just slightly, trying to find out where they were. When they found out just how crowded it was in the bucket, a real hermit crab dance ensued. Everyone who was anyone was out and about strutting their stuff (like the Italians with their evening *passegiata*) and embracing each other in a complex set of manoeuvres. This was made more complicated still when I added a sea urchin into the melee. Shortly after, we let them all go back into the sea.

We drove along the coast to Letojani for some lunch and then drove up the mountain. Taormina is especially beautiful and everyone recommends a visit. We went straight through and up to Castelmola as the view north up towards Catania and Etna. At the top it was the clearest that we have seen. Up to the North, Etna was smoking. Across to the East we could see the mainland limb of Italy for the first time sneaking up closely to Sicily. George and Indigo discovered a playground and proceeded to play on the highest slide and swing of the tour so far. Eliza then discovered that we had left her telephone and keys at lunch. Do we go and find them or go for an ice cream in Taormina? We had to go and find the keys, it was the only sensible thing to do. We drove down from

Castelmola through Taormina. Here we were, in the middle of May, late on a Wednesday afternoon and it was heaving. Even now there was nowhere to park and busloads (not just one or two but ten or twenty) were busily unloading tourists. Undoubtedly, it was a wonderful place to visit, but it did not look like our cup of tea and certainly not at the moment.

We drove back to Letojani. There are two entrances into Letojani: one across the railway tracks and one under the railway tracks. In the morning we had been on the entrance under the tracks. It was narrow and low. Indeed it was only when we saw other cars going back and forth did we really believe that it was not a pedestrian entrance, but there again this is Sicily. The road was about a foot wider and two foot taller than the Galaxy. Enough to make me nervous. The level crossing was also quite nerve wrecking. The railway runs alongside the main state road and you simply slip across the tracks. There is no corner and no signs, but the barrier was down when we wanted to cross and we managed to cause a tail back just by waiting for the train. I suffered from a touch of English guilt, but not for long. Back on the front, we found the restaurant and Eliza went off in search of her belongings. She returned empty-handed. Not because they did not have her keys and phone, but because the whole place was deserted. The restaurant was locked, there was no bell and nobody seemed to be around. I went around the back to try and find another entrance. But again everything was locked up.

We went for a Letojani ice cream and a long walk on the beach in order to wait for the restaurant to re-open. An hour later I went back for the keys and the telephone and they took one look and me and even before I had opened my mouth they knew what I was after.

So it was one all on forgetting keys.

We drove back to Acireale and then to Scillichenti. And then to bed.

Day 23
Mileage 2229
Thursday 16th May 2002
Legolas' Dad

Today we really went up Mount Etna. We caught a small bus no bigger than a small school bus which took us round some heart thumping turns and some awesome jumps. When the bus finally stopped, me, Indigo, mum and dad got to our feet and went out. A guide took us round a crater which was the one that erupted last year. We stopped at a piece of rock which looked like any piece of rock, but then a man put a scroll of white newspaper which caught up in flames in seconds, it was 400^0C which is four times hotter than boiling water! On the way down we stopped at a sight which was the platform of the cablecar that was blownup by the eruption last year. Back down the mountain we met Legolas' dad and I bought a green crystal and Indigo got a pink one.

*

The morning was crystal clear, a perfectly blue sky and no haze.

After a lazy start we set off to go up Mount Etna. We grabbed some savoury and sweet pastries for breakfast at the local bar and drove off to Acireale to buy some money from an ATM. Again, we had trouble finding our way around a Sicilian city even though we had been around the centre several times a couple of days ago. This time I decided to park Italian style and just aimed the Galaxy at a row of parked cars and stopped double-parked, but not quite blocking the road. I left Eliza in charge and dashed to the bank. Mission accomplished, I jumped back in the Galaxy and surprised Eliza by asking her to drive. "Well, yes, as long as you don't take me down any narrow roads". Mission impossible, I thought. Still we would try our best. Off we went and followed the occasional Etna Sud signs in yellow on a brown background. Eliza drove well, but somehow was no longer seeing her surroundings and was concentrating so hard on immediate and mundane matters such as free wandering pedestrians, other cars – moving and stationery, mopeds – driven with 4 year olds in control, walls, occasional dogs and other animals. When the signs disappeared, which was the standard Sicilian practise and I spotted one pointing the way we had just come, we decided that I had better drive. She later told me that she was not feeling well and that her brain wasn't entirely with it. I know from past experience that when Eliza felt like that she needed help and that this wasn't a reflection on her normal driving skills.

We drove up to Zafferano Etneo, the starting point of the drive from the foothills. I was surprised at how little traffic was going this way. Soon, the landscape changed. More and more lava floes showed their trails with black uncompromising scars across the landscape. They disregarded forests, orchards, houses, railway tracks and roads. The Sicilians still believe in divine intervention and this was only reinforced recently when the lava floe split in two passing around a church and leaving it completely unscathed. This church is now a shrine.

As we neared the top of the road, it was obvious that this was a tourist spot. There were hundreds of cars and coaches milling around. People were wandering up black paths and up to the top of some of the lower craters. We wanted to get up to the top. I had always harboured an ambition to get to the top of Etna. There used to be a cable car that went up further, but this had been severely damaged in the eruption of July 2001, only 10 months ago. Instead there were four-wheel drive small buses that we could catch. Up to this point we were not sure if we would all go because Indigo was frightened about going up a volcano. Now that she saw it was currently quiet she became keen to go. So we all went. It was quite an expensive trip at 33 euros each (George half price and Indigo free) plus a euro each to hire a coat.

The drive up was slow and painful and the road was just a flattened lava trail: steep and windy and with innumerable potholes. Cloud, mist and smoke swirled all around together. There was no telling which was which. After about twenty minutes we stopped and disembarked into a black and eerily quiet inhospitable landscape. You could see where the lava had swirled and curled just before it had set solid. A local guide met us and walked us up a few minutes further. He pointed up to a crater which he told us was the source of last year's eruption. The rock underfoot was still warm to the touch. Further up still you could feel the heat of the rock on your face and you could no longer touch it with hands. The guide brought out some paper and inserted it into a hole in the rock. After a few seconds the paper had ignited itself. Fahrenheit 451 came to mind. This was the temperature where paper spontaneously combusted. The heat from the rocks and the cold from the air made for a volatile sensation.

Further up still we came to a sign telling us that it was dangerous above this level from unpredictable explosive activity. This did not stop people wandering up, some well wrapped in appropriate clothing, but some in short sleeves, shorts and sandals. I did not understand what these people had to prove, but I suspect they did it because they could and with only a notice to stop them carried on regardless.

We took the risk of standing around the sign to pose.

Indigo opened her hand and showed us two ladybirds that she had found. Two bright red black-spotted bugs in this ocean of black lava. A bit further on she found a third. Quite extraordinary.

Back on the way down, we stopped at the top of the cable car and looked at the destruction. It was fairly impressive, with mangled girders and dislodged pylons poking out through the black lava. Some people thought it was a good idea to walk through the building, testing the strength of its remains by leaning on walls and jumping up and down on the floors. The Italians felt they were as indestructible as when they drive, and, if they weren't protected, then, what the hell, the lady Madonna and son would protect them and see them through to a better place where there were neither taxes nor bureaucrats. Hurrah!

We got talking to the two Englishmen sat next to us on the bus. George was astonished that Charles was Legolas's dad. Yes, you got it, the very same Legolas as the one in Lord of the Rings. Charles's claim to fame made George's day! She would be able say she met Legolas's dad on Mount Etna. Not many people can say that.

The bus drivers were selling crystal samples from the mountain. George bought a green one and Indigo a pink one. Don't ask me what they were, I don't know.

We went back down to Il Limonetto and after cooling off a bit we all went to sit in the Solarium except for George who had the grumps about something. She eventually joined us later. This was a most beautiful spot, a few sun-loungers and chairs surrounded by a lemon grove. There were also a couple of nespole and banana trees growing near by. A strange metal pole grew out of the earth too. It was an electricity pole, but was now in splendid isolation. It was completely disconnected, but still stood there proud with just its insulators hiding its nakedness. It would be many years before rust would fell this tree.

Indigo and George found a hammock and enjoyed wrestling and then just resting in it being hand-fed nespole picked and peeled by their father. A scene of domestic bliss which I'm sure they'll forget about soon enough.

As we sat and the evening drew on, the air became full of swallows. A first just a few came darting around and coming close over our heads and then more and more. Just watching them was exhilarating. They dove, twisted and turned, narrowly avoiding each other as they went for the same flying insect. They came so close you could hear the gentle "whoosh" as they swept past. Mid air collisions were avoided by the birds turning their breasts towards each other at the last possible moment.

After the sun settled down over Etna we went off in search of pizza. Fabrizzo had recommended a restaurant just down the road as a pizzeria so we decided to give it a try. We drove down there, surprised we knew where to find it only to find it was an expensive looking restaurant and with no pizzas. Interesting, but not what we were after tonight. We followed the coast road up toward Aceriale where we had seen some signs before and then down a road to Santa Maria (another original name) and found a pizzeria near a campsite that was open.

Here the menu was in Sicilian which made life a bit tricky. There were some great sounding names here such as *Muscalora, Friscanzana, Cicchiciacchi* and so on. I settled for a *Zzappagghiuna* with *pomodoro fresco, mozzarella nuvoletta Sole, zucchine frite, ricotta salata*, pancetta, *origano e olio.* Much more interesting than *Margherita* or *Quatro Frommaggi.* These were truly great pizzas produced with enthusiasm and flair at a very ordinary sleepy campsite only half awake awaiting for the summer season to kick in.

Day 24
Mileage 2305
Friday 17ᵗʰ May 2002
Syracusa

Today we went to Syracusa. We went to a market with lots of fresh fruit and fish. There were some funny spotty fish. We bought some peaches, apricots and cherries.

We then went to see an aquarium with all types of fish you could think of. In one tank there were three giant eels like the one we saw in the market, in another tank there was a blue fish with a white spiral on its belly. We saw as well the natural spring. The spring has natural water and it has its own legend. Legend of the Nymph Arethusa. Three ducks were running around the edge of the spring!

After lunch we went to see Diyoncas' ear (which is a cave where a king would shut his enemies in and listen to their conversations.)

Next we visited the greek theatre, and later that night we watched a greek play. (I had no idea what was going on or what the show was about, but I just sat there and watched and I enjoyed it anyway.) The bits I enjoyed the most were a man that looked like he was flying (he used a crane, we think he was playing Zeus.) When he was flying the movement looked mythical. At the very end through a hand of the statue a burst of flame erupted out, it looked extremely hot that would badly burn you.

*

This morning we got up early to go to Syracusa on the southeast corner of Sicilia. It was a straight run down the motorway around Catania, but somehow we managed to come off the *tangenziale* and dove into the Catanian traffic. What was really sad, was that it was some while until we realised what we had done and we just sat in traffic wondering whether all Italian motorways were this busy in rush hour and full of pedestrians and buses and school children and traffic lights. We suddenly started seeing signs for Messina, which is on the northeast corner of Sicily, and this gave us the clue that we were driving around

Catania. We found our way back to the autostrada and went around Catania again. We realised that our mistake was made near the Palermo motorway turnoff. We knew we didn't want to go to Palermo and so we had simply followed the other route.

Other than that, the drive down to Syracusa was uneventful. We did not originally have any intention of going into Catania but we did agree with all the guide books that Catania was not the sort of place for tourists to go to unless you were really interested in something specific.

The historic centre of Syracusa is in two parts, one an island connected to the mainland by a bridge and the second part the archaeological zone a mile or so inland from the bridge. We drove onto the island and found a spot to park near the busy local market. Everything was flourishing there with lots of fruit, vegetable and fish stalls all together and intermingled with each other. It was very colourful with local produce. The ubiquitous nespole, oranges – normal and sanguine – and lemons were on all fruit stalls, but there were also strawberries, melons, bananas and early cherries. We were starting to see peaches – both *bianca* and *romana* – and apricots for the first time. Amongst the vegetables were yard long twisty *zucchine*, broad beans, red-spotted beans, *raddichio*, artichokes, tomatoes of many varieties and sizes, white onions, red onions, small onions, large onions, *rucola*, *frizzante* lettuce, iceberg lettuce, two sorts of *melanzane* – one the sort you get in England and another more spherical and much lighter in colour. On the *pescetore* stalls were shrimp and prawns – both large and giant – half a dozen varieties of *vongole*, octopus, *calamari*, cuttlefish, snapper, tuna, sword fish, silver fish, enormous eels, sardines, more tuna, lobsters and crabs. There were more stone fish and other spiny fish and more I could not identify. These fish were definitely fresh as some were still slowly dying in the air, slithering and twitching on the stalls or, for the shellfish, gently moving around in their own buckets. There were jars and jars of *porcini*, olives, anchovies, artichoke hearts, *pepperoni*, I. There were fresh and dried herbs: basil, rosemary, thyme, parsley and of course garlic.

We went up to the main tourist drag along to the cathedral. Very pretty walkway lined with tourist shops, but we kept to the straight and narrow. We were heading for the Fonte Aretusa. This was the centre of many legends. It was a freshwater spring right on the edge of the sea named after the nymph Aretusa. She had swam here all the way from the Peleponnese in Greece after Artemis had changed her into a spring. Aretusa was trying to avoid the amorous pursuits of Apheus the river god. But alas, Alpheus pursued Aretusa to this spot where they embraced together in their watery form.

The only way down to the spring was to go through the aquarium. We decided to go in as the children are always interested in moving creatures and this would be a good distraction. And so it was. Most of the fish market was also on display here, except that it was much more alive than down on the market.

The spring was a very quiet spot although we were looked down at but a throng of fellow tourists (who were all wondering how we got down here). Indigo had fun trying to catch the almost tame geese and trying to tickle the fish with her fingers. A large clump of papyrus grew in the middle of the spring.

After lunch on a hot terrace overlooking the sea – it was very bright – we drove out to the archaeological site to look at the bits and pieces there. In one area the Latomie del Paradiso is a quarry from which stone was excavated for monuments.

Inside here is the *Orecchio di Dionisio* (Dionysius' Ear) which is a cave where all sounds are amplified. This was supposedly used to eavesdrop on the conversations of prisoners and conspirators held here. Then there is the Greek theatre which is the largest in Sicily. It is well preserved and has a large number of rows of seats.

As luck would have it, today was the first day of a six week season of performances here. I was dubious as to whether the children would be able to cope with this but they were both keen, so we bought some tickets and stayed for the evening performance. They use the theatre every other year on even numbered years, so this was a good year to be here.

We had unnumbered seats and so we were in the melee with loads of Italians. The doors were supposed to open at five, but this was a Sicilian five and it was nearer six by the time the gates were unlocked. They had to ensure that all the archaeological visitors from the afternoon had left before they could let us in and then they waited, but I've no idea what for. We just knew they wouldn't let us in until they were good and ready. The crowd was good natured but were queuing in Italian style: there was no discernible sequence to it. People would amble (later squeeze) to the front and give off the impression that they had been there for hours.

There was plenty of room to spread out amongst the unnumbered seats, but the numbered seats were closely packed together. Overall, it must have been about half full. The audience was mostly Italian youngsters, tourists and local dignitaries. The police were there in some numbers all in their best dress uniform. We even saw a couple of ceremonial swords.

We had the Sicilian wave where different groups of students screamed at each other across the auditorium in turns. And we had the Italian "sshh" as the production started pronounced "sskkk, sskkk".

We saw the Incantation of Prometheus an ancient Greek tragedy. I thought it would be spoken in Greek, but it was spoken in Italian – which actually didn't help at all. Prometheus was up there chained to a rock for his punishment for giving man fire. There was lots of wailing and gnashing of teeth from him, the Greek chorus, and two other women, one of whom took the form of a cow. I think Prometheus was chained to the rock by the producer to stop his enthusiastic Italian arm movements. There was a cameo role for Zeus who came flying across the stage twice suspended by a crane. (There was also an earth-bound Zeus who did a lot of talking).

Afterwards, everyone wanted to hang around and talk. Idea, the theatre restaurant looked as if it was just opening for business. We had to go as it would be late by the time we got back to Il Limonetto. The drive back was quite stressful along twisting unlit Italian roads where the oncoming traffic came in long waves all bunched up behind the slow Italian drivers. We managed to drive around Catania successfully tonight unlike this morning.

Colamarco
Day 25
Mileage 2435
Saturday 18ᵗʰ May 2002
A Cable Car Ride

Today we went to Taormina, this time to the old town, we went up by the cablecar which goes every 15 minutes. The ride was first slow then quite fast and when we went over the pylons it was quite bumpy. The total ride was no more than five minutes.

After the cable car ride we trudged up to another Greek theatre, but this one is the second largest theatre in Sicily after the one in Syracusa. You cannot see the wonderful view, because when the Romans came to power they made the theatre into a gladiator's ring. They dug trenches around the outline of the ring and build a huge stone wall right in front of the view.

We drove over the mountains and through the highest town in Sicily, Floresta, and to Colamarco, an Azienda Agrituristica, without getting lost once. We first had an apartment downstairs but mum found some beetles down behind the bunk beds, upstairs was much nicer so we moved upstairs. (Heaven in mum's eyes is upstairs, downstairs however is HELL for mum.).

*

Moving day. Despite yesterday's late night, we managed to pack up in a couple of hours. Fabrizzio and father were amazed at just how much stuff we managed to get into the Galaxy. I told Fabrizzio that if there were just Eliza and I we could travel in a Fiat Uno, but the children…. He laughed. I asked if he had children and he said "No, I am unmarried." I asked him if he had a girl friend. "Yes", he said, and then with a cheeky twinkle in his eye and a smirk on his face, he added "Two".

We took the autostrada to Taormina and this time managed to find the *funivia* from the coast up to the old town. It was a far superior idea than driving up the mountain and parking. The ride up was quick and spectacular. At the top we went to see the Greek theatre. The centre of town was a lot quieter than it had been on our last visit, when we didn't stop, and very picture postcardy with flowers overhanging from every possible corner and every balcony. Lots of shops selling tourist souvenirs, expensive designer clothes, ties and shoes, ceramic shops, restaurants and the odd sprinkling of *ottofruta, macelleria, samuleria, alimentari* shops to make sure no one starved to death.

The Greek theatre was high up on the hill and had the most magnificent backdrop view of the Ciclopi coastline and a smoking Etna. This view had been obscured by the Roman portion of the theatre. The Romans had built a wall totally obscuring the view with columns and arches (this wall had since mostly fallen down to reveal the view again). This theatre was more compact than that at Syracusa, but it was still the second largest in Sicily. The Romans had used this exclusively for gladiatorial contests. The views were stunning, but for me, the best view was not south towards Etna but north. To see this view you had to go round the back of the toilet block (lovely).

Maybe it was the time of the day and the angle of the sun. I have never seen such an immense intensity of blues. Its purity was just awesome. But it wasn't a simple single shade. The sky and the sea smudged together in a hazy whitish-blue line. I could stare at this view for a long time. And there, hazily in the distance stretching northward was the enticing leg of Italy.

We took the cable car down and then we were on our way to Castelli'Umbertti for our next stop.

We took the road up from the autostrada to Linguaglossa and onto the road going anticlockwise around Etna. The road kept rubbing up against the railway line that also ran around the mountain and we crossed and re-crossed it several times at all levels. We came across the occasional black lava floe constantly reminding us of Etna's power.

When we came to Randazzo, we came off this road and headed off to Capo d'Orlando. Here, the road suddenly rose out of the valley around Etna into a different direction. As we drove off, the town shrank rapidly and soon its three church domes stood out proudly together in classic pose. Then we were over the hill and out of sight, but not before seeing one lava floe that had spilled over the land and had spread out into a circular shape. It had been stopped by the rise of the hills on the far side of the valley.

The area we were driving through was climbing up to a pass near Floresta. This was the highest town in Sicily. The atmosphere of the area had changed from volcanic to almost alpine, but without the neatness of the Swiss where every building looked pristine and well cared for and every field looked as if it had been trimmed with nail clippers and even the cows and horses seemed to go around with chaperones.

The road followed the contours of the hillside and was very twisty and gave onto the most amazing valley views. Eventually we arrived at Castelli'Umberti and looked out for the signs to Colamarco. Amazingly we found one and followed it. The sign took us out of the village and down, down, down into the valley below. The road became steep and narrow, but it looked even more like Heidi country with its small yellow and pink flowers everywhere and with the grass sprouting out in tall clumps into the roadside.

Yes, there was another sign for Colamarco and then another. 200m. A mile later there was another sign and then we found it. We turned up into the drive and were greeted by Fabio. "Dave Horth from Essex, Welcome!" Not quiet the embrace for a long lost prodigal son, but certainly the greeting of a man amazed that we had arrived when we said we would, yet alone at all.

He sat us down and offered us drinks. Orange juice freshly squeezed from his own oranges, beer and *fragoline – frizzante* wine flavoured with small wild strawberries. He then showed us his olive press. Not exactly what we had in mind at this time, but nevertheless important. The Sicilians all seemed to be obsessed with olive oil. Everyone we had met implied that the olive oil that they grew was simply the best.

The process of turning olives into olive oil was not too complicated but had to be done just so. Everything had to be weighed, washed, milled, pressed and finally centrifuged. For the pressing, the milled paste had to be spread onto two foot wide mats. These were then stacked and put into the press. The press at Fabio's exerted 30 atmosphere pressures onto this paste to exude the juices from the paste. This liquid was then put through a centrifuge which separated out the oil and any excess water.

I wanted to know how much olive oil a typical tree could produce. Fabio was not very forthcoming about this, but said that in a good year a large tree might produce 70 kilos of olives which would produce about 20 litres of oil.

The press machinery was quite expensive and not only did Fabio press his own olives, but also the olives of neighbours. Everyone's olives had to be pressed separately. Nobody wanted to blend their oils; they considered this to be a sacrilege. Everyone considered their own oil to be the best.

Fabio then took us to the house where we were staying. This was about half a kilometre away on the other side of the road. The track off the road was so steep that you felt as if you were driving off the edge of a cliff on a leap of faith. Luckily the track was right there, bit it was a bit scary the first time. The house itself was set in the middle of some olive trees. We were shown into the ground floor. Fabio left us to get organised.

Outside the house there was a tree with fruit on that I did not recognise. It looked like mulberries, but they were white as if not yet ripe. They were indeed mulberries – *gesli* – and were a different variety than those seen in England. The white mulberry trees are used to cultivate silkworms.

Although there was plenty of room, it was badly laid out and somehow was not all satisfactory. All the beds were in the same room and we immediately had arguments about who was sleeping on the top bunk. The bed linen felt damp, the place smelt of moth balls, the fridge was falling apart, there were bugs and insects all over the floor – some dead and some very much alive scurrying everywhere just to be out of sight, there was a dead wasp in the sugar. We were not happy, the whole place was a disgrace.

The children were desperate for food, so we tried and failed to light the gas. Although Fabio had turned on the hot water, it remained decidedly *freddo*. It was getting late and the sun was going down. Eliza wanted to move on and her face looked as if she had been sucking sour lemons.

I had to go and find Fabio.

As I was walking up to the house he came to me on his motor bike. I told him we had no gas, no hot water and he needed to sort this out pronto. He got to the house before I got back and tried to work out why no gas was in the house. After a while we had success. We told him we were not happy about the state of the apartment. He said we could have a look upstairs if we liked, but the apartments were both the same. We went upstairs where the apartment was of a completely different standard although it was about the same size. Everywhere was better furnished and better finished, clean and dry, but still very basic. We could not understand how he could possibly think the apartments were the same! We moved upstairs.

We had dinner with the family. Fabio's partner Nuncadine and his son Ugo.

We had orange salad which was a savoury salad with cut oranges, olive oil and herbs. It was very Sicilian and regional, we had not seen it in any restaurant. The pasta was served with grated breadcrumbs instead of cheese. Digestives of homemade *limoncello* and a cream version were very nice.

Altogether a very tiring day.

Day 26
Mileage 2523
Sunday 19th May 2002
Oranges for Breakfast

Today we had breakfast at Fabio's house, we walked from our apartment, and I forget to mention the rabbits and the chicken that we saw yesterday. I went in and picked up an egg which I didn't have for breakfast because I had filled myself with lovely freshly made orange juice.

Then we went out in car. We went past Tindari and didn't stop there because there were too many tourists.

We tried to find somewhere to have lunch, but we ended up in a funny place up the mountain and then we went home. On our way back home we came back along a piece of road which had collapsed on a land slide. It was scary crossing it.

*

We had breakfast in the house with Fabio and family. George simply adored the freshly squeezed oranges from Fabio's trees. The olive trees here were also in full bloom and I started suffering from hay fever and/or a head cold. Later that day Eliza would develop the same symptoms.

The day was not very bright, but we decided to go and drive around and see some of the sights. Fabio recommended that we go to Tindari so off we went. We drove down into the valley and along the river road, but the river Zappulla was dry and obviously just used as a storm drain. This route was certainly quicker and easier than attempting the climb back up to Castelli'Umberti and driving on top of the ridge.

The drive was along the autostrada a bit and then along the state road and then some white roads. Eventually as we approached Tindari we became aware of the crowd that was gathering. We then remembered that it was Sunday and that one of the Sicilians favourite pastimes was to take the mother-in-law off to see a religious icon as a special Sunday treat after church and before lunch. Tindari was both a religious site and an ancient Greek site. We had hoped to see the Greek part, but we would have had to endure the religious site first. We turned around and drove off leaving the Sicilians and their families alone.

We then went to Patti a nearby resort which also had a roman villa. This one was empty, but didn't look worth dragging the children round. Eliza spotted a shop that was open. It was a cheap factory outlet for designer clothes and shoes. We spent some time here buying shoes and discovered that the Sicilians that hadn't gone up to Tindari that morning were indulging in another favourite pastime – shopping.

We drove up and down and there was nowhere of much interest. We were looking for an open *supermacato* to buy some food, but they were all *chiuso*. We then started looking for somewhere to eat. The resorts on the front were definitely still in pre-season mode. Those that were open were full. We followed a knife and fork sign up the hill and found a restaurant in the middle of a sea of new houses and roundabouts. It was faintly reminiscent of a cross between Milton Keynes and the Marie Celeste

In Castoreale Terme we also found the thermal baths which in the guide books were noted for being good for liver and urological complaints. Well what the hell, anything would be more interesting that driving around on a dull Sunday. The Terme Hotel was deserted. I peeked inside and a lady receptionist appeared after a few minutes to inform me that everything was closed. I asked when they were open to be told tomorrow from 7 to 10 in the morning. We didn't need to make appointments but could turn up. This was better than the thermal baths in Sciacca where you need to have a doctor's prescription before you could make an appointment for a couple of week's time.

I politely said "*A domani*" and left.

We went back to Colamarco driving along the coast road. Capo d'Orlando was the main town on this route. This was also completely deserted. The sea was relatively rough, but the beaches looked fine. If the sun shone we would be back.

Over dinner we spoke to them about our drive and the fact that we hadn't been up to Tindari. Fabio and his girlfriend, Ugo and their two guests Renato (who introduced himself as "King born") and his wife Rosa were aghast that we were not full of remorse for not seeing the shrine and could not understand that being surrounded by bus loads of Sicilian worshippers was not our idea of fun. We blamed the tiredness of the children.

We told them that we were not impressed by Patti and Ugo, struggling for words, described Patti as *squalido*. Nuff said.

Day 27
Mileage 2632
Monday 20th May 2002
No Roast Dinner

Fabio came to wake us up this morning because we had a late night at Fabio's house for dinner and had slept late.

After breakfast we went to the supermarket and got some weird vampire teeth, burgers and lots of bready things. After that we went back home and I had an early night.

*

It was another day of cloud and wind. We got up too late to go to the baths. No one was upset. Not a lot going on. We went off in search of a *supermacato* so I could cook a Sunday roast for us. We found a *supermacato*, and some lamb. The lady behind the counter was most surprised when I didn't want it chopped up (bone and all).

We spent more time wandering around Patti and Cap d'Orlando again. We were still not impressed.

We went back to Colamarco and I wandered up to the house to try and find some *rosemarino* and *cipolle* from Fabio for our dinner with success. I told him in broken Italian that I was going to cook lamb in the oven in the English style. He nodded knowingly.

After I had peeled the potatoes and prepared the lamb, I tried to turn the oven on. At this point I noticed that the oven was electric (the rings were gas) and that the wire from the back of the oven was not wired in. In very small letters on a notice behind the cooker, it said that the oven was *non funzione*. Now I realised why Fabio had nodded so sagely at me when I told him what I was going to cook. I ended up having to improvise a lamb stew. Very tasty, but not what the taste buds had yearned for.

Day 28
Mileage 2699
Tuesday 21st May 2002
In The Waves

We went to the beach. It looked like a very cobbly one and dad said, "I'll go and see if it's sandy up there of if there is just fine pebbles." It was sandy so we dragged our bags over the soft sand and finally KERPLUNK! Dad, mum and I had dropped our bags or boxes at the same time.

After we got changed into our swimming stuff mum ACTUALLY went into the sea! Mum and dad threatened to throw me into the sea if I didn't come quietly. Mum said I had to go past where the waves broke. I said I would come quietly, but they dragged me in and there were two giant waves, the first one hit this wasn't too bad but anyhow I was scared and I shouted, "let go, let go of me!" But as dad was holding on tight there was no way he was going to let go. I could see this giant wave rising and leaning over me, I froze, I was rooted to the spot and WHAM! It had crashed down on me and mum. I went off sobbing over the beach to our things.

Mum finally tempted me with 15 Euros to spend on whatever I liked except sweets. I did it. It was fantastic to be bobbing up and down over the waves. After this I was sopping, so we decided to go home.

But mum said go away to me so I took this so seriously I went over to a bunch of rocks working out where I was going to sleep, what I was going to eat and so on, but mum stopped me and we went home as a family.

*

Today the sun came out again. We went off to Capo d'Orlando for a few hours on the beach. It was quiet and the beach was almost deserted. The sand was a fine grey colour. Quite unusual for English eyes. I had an internment in the sand and tried to frighten George and Indigo with my impersonation of the Mummy (failed miserably, but raised a few giggles and a facial expression from George which said "Dad, you are sooo embarrassing" – a foretaste of things to come during the teenage years).

The slope of the beach was shallow until you got about two feet out and then went steeply down. Before this point the waves broke with some force and George enjoyed breaking them with her feet. Beyond this points the waves did not break and you could bob up and down with them. No matter how much we tried to persuade George we could not get her to go past this point. Indigo was quite happy to do so in my arms.

We returned back to the Colamarco to pack and pay. Fabio was off to Messina this evening as he was in court tomorrow. He is a practicing lawyer, not a defendant.

I paid Fabio and he told me how unhappy he was with the euros. He hated all those pesky coins and wished that there were a fifty-euro cent note. This would be equivalent to the 1000 lire note. Everybody used to leave coins as tips, but now the smallest note was almost 10,000 lire and that would mean leaving too much! Beside, how can you carry coins in trousers? The whole idea was ridiculous. Fabio gave me two Colamarco t-shirts: one for Eliza and one for me. I thanked him and thought that they would useful for wearing while decorating.

It was dark before we had finished packing up the Galaxy.

Lipari
Day 29
Mileage 2721
Wednesday 22nd May 2002
To The Islands

Mum woke us up really early again (about 6:30).
We got to the car ferry at 7:30 but the boat didn't start to load until 8:30. A long wait dragged on, finally the boat started loading.
The boat went to Vulcano then to Lipari. We went to Casa Gialla. We went to lunch. It was very hot at 34°C. We had a mini siesta (about 2 hours) then we went for a passeggiata and a gelato.
We went to bed

*

We got up early so we could be sure of catching the ferry to the Eolie islands. It was still grey and dull. Suddenly, the heavens opened, but it was not rain but hail. It was all over in a matter of minutes.

We finished packing, woke the children and then we were off. The drive to Milazzo was straight down the motorway, past all those places we had been haunting for the past three days. We were not sorry to leave, although the people had been friendly, the accommodation had been miserable, the weather had been against us and there was nothing worthwhile nearby that we had seen.

There were three different boat companies that operated ferry services to the islands so we just tried one after the other. The first one offered us a day trip to Vulcano and Lipari. The second didn't take cars and the third was not open. We hung about until the office opened, bought our ticket (we could not buy a return) and went to where the only empty boat was docked. After ten minutes we were still the only car in the queue, so I went to ask a sailor, who just happened to be sauntering past what time this boat left. He said half past ten. We were booked on the nine o'clock.

We quickly dove back in the Galaxy and drove back to the other end of the dock and back to the ticket office where we were informed that the boat had not yet arrived. We went away sheepishly and formed a queue where we thought appropriate. We have found this a lot in Sicily, that unless you have local or inside information, it is quite difficult to tell what we have to do, where and when.

At last the boat arrived, probably the six am ferry from Lipari. About a dozen cars came off the ferry and then there was a scrum to get onto the ferry. Cars materialised from all directions. Everyone had to reverse on to the ferry. Salvatore had told us these were roll-on, roll-off ferries. Reverse-on, roll-off more like. They were also first on last off (FOLO) or last on first off (LOFO) ferries, so why there was a rush to be first on by the Sicilians rather than a polite stand off to be last on (after you please, I want to be first off) I don't know.

Despite the late arrival of the ferry, it left on time. I think this was helped by the relative emptiness of the boat. Apart from a few cars, there were a couple of sets of school children on day trips. All the other day-trippers were on another ferry scheduled to leave and arrive at the same time as us but without carrying cars.

The first stop was on Vulcano. We had been warned that Vulcano would smell of bad eggs. There was a slight whiff in the air, but unless you were on the look out (smell out?) you would never have noticed. Lipari was another twenty minutes or so away. It reminded me very much of approaching some Cycladean island in the seventies and eighties. We drove off the ferry and there we were met by Emmanuella knocking on our Galaxy door. "Follow my grey opal". Eliza said "That's funny, I was expecting to follow a blue polo." Well we were in a silver Galaxy. These were all sweets, so somehow this made some sort of universal truth.

We followed Emmanuella up the mountain road to Pianoconte and to the Casa Gialla where we were staying. Everything here was beautiful and I breathed a great sigh of relief after the disaster of Colamarco. The weather was crystal clear and hot, the view was absolutely stunning over the sea, and the house was covered in lots of colourful flowers. We had two terraces on either side of the house and we immediately felt at home.

We unpacked just a couple of the crates that we needed and then drove on down to Lipari town to find some lunch. It was hot. The temperature soared to 34°C.

Indigo and George talked us into buying some bandanas for them to keep off the sun. The family in the shop were very friendly and once they realised that we spoke English and a bit of Italian they got very agitated. The old lady persuaded us to stay for a while while her husband disappeared into the back room. He came out with a broad smile on his face, the drooping moustache covering up the gaps in his teeth and his beard sharp and stubbly almost threatening by the way it all stood on end and handed Eliza a letter. These were from some Australians who had befriended the family a couple of years ago. Eliza ended up acting as a translator. It was not a professional job, but it was interesting with arm and hand signals filling in the gaps left by verbs, conjunctions, tenses and a whole lot else. The family were very pleased and at least understood the gist of the letter. Most important was that the Australians had had a baby and had moved. Their new address was enclosed.

After Eliza's good deed of the day, we went back to the Galaxy. We were glad to get back to the top of the hill where the temperature dropped to a mere 27°C.

Day 30
Mileage 2790
Thursday 23rd May 2002
A Long Boat Ride

At half past two pm we went on a boat ride. The boat had a flatish bottom and so it would exaggerate the large waves and tip the boat from side to side. It took about 2 hours to get to Stromboli. The people on the boat gave us three hours to give us enough time to explore the island and recover from the boat ride.

The island had black sand which I thought was rather weird. Stromboli is a large island and is a very strange shape. This may be due to the terrific landslides or some huge monster eruptions.

On the actual island everything seemed to be geared up to be used by tourists. Me, Indigo, mum and dad, all got t-shirts (except mum and dad – they shared one). I got a t-shirt with two cats hugging. Indigo got one with the island of Stromboli and mum got one saying "On Stromboli, even the cats are on holiday" in Italian.

At 7:30 we got back on the rocky little boat (not as in real rocks!) We sailed over smaller waves, than when we sailed into port, round the island until about 8:30. Then, out of the pitch black we saw it. Stromboli, spitting out flames randomly for 5 minutes or so, first on the left then on the right and finally flames were spurting, shooting and spitting in every direction up the middle.

*

We went down to the town to organise a boat trip that afternoon and evening to Stromboli. Although the day was clear it was not nearly as hot as yesterday.

While we were wandering around the town in the morning, there was a wedding going on. The church was overflowing with people hanging around outside. We had lunch in a restaurant and as the wedding party went by, one on the waiters said, "There goes another mistake."

Once on the boat the motion created a breeze strong enough to refresh us. Stromboli was about an hour and half away. We all enjoyed the ride and could see the pumice stone mines. Some of the scars scoured out by the miners were supposedly used, by those more adventurous than us, as a 30m slide into the sea. My backside felt raw just at the thought. We motored past Panarea and some other small islands en route. Even though there was very little wind, there was still an underlying swell on the sea which made the ride more interesting. George was surprised at how big the waves were for the Mediterranean. As was typical with the Mediterranean boats, they were very flat bottomed and so they exaggerated the effect of the waves.

We tried to land at the harbour on Stromboli, but the waves here were too strong. The boat had to sail around the corner to get into the lee where we disembarked onto the beach.

The sand was deepest black. It was volcanic ash and was mixed with stones of various sizes. I tried to get into the sea but the stones at the waters edge were just too painful to walk on. We walked along the road and up to the town. It was just one street of small buildings strung along like a necklace. A few shops were there for the day tripper market all a bit arty-farty and trendy. We bought some Stomboli t-shirts. George had wanted some t-shirts from Lipari, but they were all manufactured elsewhere and the designs were anonymous: you could have bought them anywhere including London. There was a *supermacato* and a *farmacia*, a couple of bars and restaurants. From here you could also get guided tours up to the crater. These tours ran from mid afternoon and came back down again in the late evening. In the main square by the church, life buzzed with a mix of day-trippers and locals. The standard means of transport for the locals was either moped or one of the three wheeler trucks. These are called *ape* in Italian which means bee. The local community appeared to be a mix of indigenous locals and outsiders staying for a period or a season or two. There was a pair of men who had great manes of bushy long grey hair and beards wearing open toed sandals and dishevelled shirts and trousers. They both looked like "its" who had escaped Monty Python.

We were not the only boat here today; there were at least two other, both were bigger than us. In the height of the season this place must be crawling with them, but after 7:30 everything must get quiet as the day trippers leave.

Stromboli is famous for its active volcano. This volcano has been active continuously for over two thousand years with eruptions about every 20 minutes or so. This is what we had come to see.

We went back down to the boat where we then motored across to the Lanterna Strombolicchio– the lighthouse set on a small island off Stromboli and on to the other side of the island to the Sciara del Fuoco. This was an incredibly steep and smooth lava flow running straight down from the volcano crater. You could see climbers going up the sides and along the ridge positioning themselves for the spectacle.

We stopped and floated in an eerie calm with half a dozen other small boats, bobbing around in the calm sea. The moon was now gibbous and shone down brightly on the scene. We did not have to wait long, but it seemed an age at the time. First there was more smoke and then you could see the rocks rise in the air, both black and bright red. A couple more spurts and it was over. Ten minutes later there was a bigger eruption round the corner from the first. This lasted a little longer. And then a third.

After this we started to motor back to Lipari. It seemed a long ride in the gathering night. As darkness set in and the temperature dropped we all huddled together inside. The ride out had been exhilarating, but this was just tedious.

Got back and drove up to the Casa Gialla exhausted but very satisfied.

Day 31
Mileage 2800
Friday 24ᵗʰ May 2002
A Rainy Day

Today when I woke up it was windy, and it was raining quite hard by the time I had got out of bed and got dressed.
After I had caught up with a bit of my journal, Indigo woke up, I had to keep her amused for a while so I played: Sammy's Science House, Trudy's Time and Place House and at long last my and Indigo's favourite Millie's Maths House, this has funny houses to make and shoes to give and cookies to bake.
In the afternoon we spent what seemed a very boring 9 hours in a crockery shop (a slight exaggeration there my dear) trying to buy eight big plates.

*

We woke up to the rain. The cloud base was less than 100 metres above us. We could not see the sea either.

I decided that it was a good day to visit the Internet point and do various stuff.

I left the children in their pyjamas playing on the computer.

On the way to the Galaxy I met Bartolomio who was most apologetic and shocked. It never rains in Lipari in May he told me. I told him that it would do his garden good. He agreed and then waved for me to come over to his store and gave me a jar of salted capers. These he had grown himself on and around Casa Gialle. He told me what to do with them. I needed to soak them in cold water for two days regularly changing the water. He emphasised "*freddo, freddo*" several times. After two days

101

they needed to be spread on a cloth and dried for a couple of hours. Then you could put them in a jar, cover them in olive oil and add other seasoning such as garlic, *pepperoncino*, fennel etc. I thanked him and went off down to the town.

I also had to find out what time the ferries went back to Millazzo tomorrow for our long drive to Sorrento. The ferry ticket office was shut but the timetable outside said 6:30 and 11:45 am. The 11:45 would make it far to late, so the 6:30 it would have to be and yet another dawn-crackingly early start.

Got back to the house and found the children happily still playing computer games. We had to go down to the town again to buy our ferry ticket. This time we all went after lunch. The whole day stayed grey and rainy. We tried not to get wet, but it was inevitable. Eliza and I spent a fair bit of time trawling around the ceramic shops, much to the chagrin of George and Indigo, looking for plates to take home. Between shops we explored more of Lipari town. We bribed George and Indigo with ice cream and tit-bits. We found the second harbour and the citadel amongst the maze of tiny streets. The afternoon actually went very quickly. We bought tickets for the 10:15 ferry which I had not recognised on the timetable because I was reading Friday's timetable (i.e. Today's) rather than Saturday's.

We had dinner out near Pianoconte. The children were very good despite being tired and grumpy. We had some roasted rabbit in a sweet sauce, *coniglio in agrodolce*. It was most delicious and delicate. The children enjoyed their pizzas and were nodding off before we left.

Day 32
Mileage 2820
Saturday 25th May 2002
Yet Again Four Move On

Mum woke me up at 8:30 because we were aiming to leave the house by 9:00 in order to catch a 10:30 boat from Lipari first to Vulcano and then back to the main land Sicilia.
It was obviously an Italian 10:30 we didn't get on the boat until 11:15. When after a long hour we arrived at Vulcano it stank like rotten eggs.

*

Overnight the weather worsened and there were heavy storms and wind overnight. This time we were dry and warm snuggled up in our beds. The morning arrived quietly, although there was still some low level cloud around.

We were up and packed quite promptly this morning thanks to Eliza being well prepared. Today we were leaving Sicily and driving up to near Sorrento – our next stop – where we would be in one place for two weeks. A real luxury we hoped.

We left the Casa Gialla at about nine, having said goodbye to everyone and to the cats. The sun was back again, but everything was still damp from the rain. We drove down to the town and passed the panoramic viewpoint for the last time. This gave a brilliant view towards Vulcano and the intermediate rocky outcrops. Whenever it had been clear and sunny I had been driving and had not stopped to take the inevitable photo. Still these would be better in a guide book anyway.

We got some nibbles from the baker's shop to keep us going on the boat. 10:15 turned out to be a Sicilian 10:15. The boat was delayed. It arrived about quarter to 11. Some cars and trucks disembarked and some very ashen faced people also got off. This must have been the overnight ferry from Napoli which must have been caught up in the storm.

The ferry was much bigger than the one we had caught out, but still had very little space to sit indoors. There were people sitting around who had had no cabin all looking rather grim.

We boarded and were off.

We took the reverse route from the way out with a first stop at Vulcano. This time the rotten eggs smell was unmissable. George and Indigo went round with their noses held shut pulling faces. The people disembarking looked upset but still willing to play the tourist game in high spirits.

The trip to Millazzo was otherwise uneventful and I managed to catch twenty winks.

After Lipari, Millazzo seemed a very busy place. Throbbing with cars and buses as we docked. We had to drive to Messina for the next boat and followed the signs to the motorway. It was easier just following everyone else as I think they were all off to the autostrada as well. This was an excellent strategy as the road to the autostrada was blocked and there were diversions and roadworks all around. Following locals in the know worked very well. The autostrada went around the northeast tip of Sicily; the final piece in our tour. Sicily looked extra green today, probably because of the extra rain that it had had in our visit.

At Messina we followed the signs down to the docks where we discovered there were two routes across the straights both available from two different ports. We just picked one and decided to take the route to the northern most point, Villa San Giovanni. In typical Sicilian style the road layout was incorrectly marked, all the locals knew where to go so our suspicions were aroused when everyone drove in a different direction from the signs. Still, like the good English people that we were, we followed the signs. They took us to the other port and then around the docks and back up to the first dock. They were busy running a new tramway all along the roadside. The road itself was all cut up and potholed. We realised that all the signposts were still pointing in their original directions as if none of the road works had started. Hmm, that explained a lot.

We were finally approaching the ferry point and as yet we did not have any tickets. I thought maybe they were set up like the autostrada tollbooths where we just rolled through. There were large numbers of lanes which were all empty gradually converging on the ferry. Suddenly, there was the ticket office in the middle of the road. Everyone was just parked in a higgardly-piggardly fashion. The drivers were all queuing at the ticket office. Lanes were blocked by cars waiting for tickets. It was a wonderful shambles and scrum.

Once we were past the ticket office we rolled straight onto a ferry.

The rear door lifted and closed behind us with an ominous clang. We could not see anything around us, but we knew that our time in Sicily was now over.

Part 2: The Central Tour

Le Tore
Day 32
Mileage 2849
Saturday 25th May 2002
Yet Again Four Move On

After we arrived back at mainland of Sicilia it was about an hour to get the boat to the mainland of Italy. Next a five hour drive followed. We saw lots of beautiful scenery. When we arrived we saw lots of fireflies.

*

Once over the straights of Messina, the doors of our ferry opened onto the Italian mainland. Now we would be heading north for the next part of our tour. The autostrada was only a couple of kilometres up from the ferry port. We hit the autostrada and immediately started to climb. As we drove north, Sicily was there very close on our left hand side. The very tip of Sicily looked close enough to touch and yet was a good few kilometres away. There, further away to our left in the soft distant blue haze, we could also make out the Eolie islands of Stromboli, Lipari and Vulcano smudged on the horizon.

Soon, however, as we continued to climb around the mountainous ankle of Italy, Sicily slipped out of view. There were over four hundred kilometres of autostrada to travel to get to Salerno and we wanted to press ahead with top speed.

There were road works very regularly along the route. Sometimes, parts of the carriageway looked as if it had been disturbed over the winter, sometimes, it looked as if it had fallen away completely. Sometimes we went to two-way traffic on the other carriageway. Sometimes the other carriageway no longer appeared to exist. This was not just road maintenance going on here, but wholesale rebuilding and widening. We suspect that during the height of summer this autostrada carries a great deal of traffic.

The motorway wended it way across mountains, through valleys and plains. It went through the Parco Nationale della Calabria and cut a swathe through the forest. All the way it was simple and stunning scenery. The trees and fields looked more lush than Sicily. The olive trees seemed to stretch ever upward compared to the dwarf and stunted varieties on Sicily. Only the Indian fig cactus plants looked small compared with their Sicilian cousins.

The road works slowed our average speed down considerably and we arrived at Salerno a lot later than we had hoped. After Salerno we turned off the motorway and followed the yellow roads through Castellmare towards Sorrento. We hoped that the road would be quiet, but it was the wrong time of day. Early Saturday evening in Italy was *passagiata* time or, rather, everyone was trying desperately to get to wherever they wanted to get to to have their *passagiata*. Everyone appeared to be on the move. Except that as everyone is on the move, nobody moves fast. The quickest way forward were the mopedists with one, two, three and even four people on board, weaving their way through the cars like a hot knife cutting through butter. They overtook and undertook. They mounted the pavement and, if there was an opportunity, I'm sure they would go up and down steps. They even went round roundabouts the wrong way. It was like an example of a cross between Brownian motion and Heisenberg's uncertainty principal applied to the macro world. Mopeds were too numerous to count and flitted in a seemingly random manner. If you knew where a moped was, then you couldn't tell how fast it was going. If you knew how fast it was going then you didn't know where it was.

Suddenly, we were through the Gordian knot of cars and mopeds and out on to the coastal road down to Sorrento. But the traffic was not yet finished. Now the cars and coaches were queued up patiently waiting in the traffic jam to get to their destination. This road was very reminiscent of the lakeside road around Como, where on Friday and Saturday evenings the Comoese and Milanese drove out to the lake to their second homes and flats or to visit friends and relations. It was just our bad luck and misfortune to time our arrival with everyone else's. We were just in with the in crowd.

Before getting to Sorrento we had to turn off at Meta and then find the road to Sant'Agata. At Sant'Agata we would find the road to Le Tore where we were staying. Because time was running late Eliza rung on ahead to let Vittoria know we were on our way. We were recognised.

We found the turning off to Sant'Agata and then Eliza saw a sign to Le Tore earlier than we expected so we took it. This went up the mountain and the road turned into a dust track. No worse than we had already been on on this tour, but still narrow. The signs to Le Tore did not reappear. The moon was now virtually full and glistened amazingly on the waters below; we had risen up the Sorrento side and now were on the top looking down on the Amalfi side. There, two small islands pock marked the moon's reflection in the sea. Then we were at the Le Tore Refuge. This was not what we expected and we needed to get down the mountain. But how? I did not relish reversing all the way by moonlight, nor could we find a place to turn around. On my right there was a fence with a steep drop beyond and on my left was the forest. I finally found a corner where I made an x point turn (where x is greater than 5) and drove down the mountain.

Back onto the main road we continued into Sant'Agata and quickly found the road we should have gone up. This too went up into the mountains, but the landmarks matched the directions! The entrance to Le Tore was signposted at the junction of three roads. We took the middle one which was a mud track through fruit trees. We got to a corner which was blocked by a car. It was very dark and I could not see anything. I reversed out and followed the entrance on the right which was tarmaced. This suddenly shot up further into the mountain so I thought this was wrong too. We went back down. The path on the left looked even less promising than the middle way. Eliza told me that she saw a house when we went down the middle track. So we tried again. Round the corner there was a house but with no lights. Suddenly we were surrounded by lights; the whole place was alive with the dim green light of fireflies. We stopped the Galaxy switched off the lights and looked around in wonder. I got out and walked down to check out this house. Round the back there were lights and people eating. Vittoria came out to greet me. She told us to come back on the left hand track, as this would bring the Galaxy nearest to our apartment. She said she would bring us food and drink after we arrived.

So back up to the entrance and we took the left hand path. The fireflies were quite astounding. When we turned the corner all the diners had come out to meet us. They had finished their dinner. Germans, Italians and Dutch finding it strange to meet some Brits coming out of the gloom illuminated by fire flies and the full moon.

We were just glad to be here.

Vittoria's food was rustic and hearty: pasta and meatloaf. The wine would have been undrinkable if we were not thirsty. It was good to sit down at our own table, but the apartment downstairs was gloomy and shabby.

Day 33
Mileage 3151
Sunday 26th May 2002
A Recovery Day

This morning I woke up early and so I tried to get back to sleep. About an hour later I was suddenly woken up by a loud engine roaring and a rooster crowing, "Cockadoola do". Checking my watch I stretched and got out of be and reached for some clothes and got dressed.

At about 2 o'clock a party arrived to celebrate Frederick's first communion. Frederick is a boy I made friends with and I also made friends with another boy called Stefano. We played football, basket ball and running races. It was fun to have some people to play with especially when we did running races because the wind was flicking my hair wildly around. I had a light breeze on my face. For the first time in a while I was enjoying having company.

While Frederick's family were having lunch, me Frederick and Stefano found a little dog who had killed a grass snake and had ripped its head off and had eaten it but just left the rest of the body!

*

The apartment was on two floors. The upper floor was spacious and airy. There were three bedrooms and a bathroom with a proper bathtub. Downstairs was the kitchen /dining/ living area which was definitely worse for wear and needed an overhaul. The fridge was mouldy inside, the flush to the downstairs toilet did not appear to be working, there were tell-tale signs of damp plaster and mould around the bottoms of the walls – luckily it was now dry and did not smell. Two sofa beds downstairs were blown making them very uncomfortable to sit in. This was not a bad as Colamarco, but if we had been more fussy we would have moved on.

As this was Sunday we would not try and wander around like last week, but instead just chill out here. Yesterday's journey had been more tiring than we expected and last night's traffic was definitely a warning of things to come at the weekends.

Around the farm, we discovered fruit trees, vines, vegetables and four calves. There was a constant supply of dogs which I found distasteful. We started talking to an old woman whose relationship with the farm was unclear. She lived next door to us, but had her own small holding as well. She showed us around her part. She grew oranges, lemons and nespole (there's a surprise), artichokes, raspberries, kiwi fruit, and cherries. She had chickens and ducks and ten piglets belonging to one sow. The poor sow was in a cage where she could not move, she could only lie down and offer her teats to her young. The piglets were very inquisitive and pleased to see us. The sow just looked miserable. The animals stank worse than most farms I have been on.

For lunch, Le Tore was expecting between 20 and 30 people. Tables were set in the gardens around the house. The place was decorated with flowers and tree branches. Fires were lit and barbecues were laid. People came and went. George and Indigo made friends with children and had fun playing football and running around. One group was celebrating a boy's first communion emphasising again the strength of religious fervour in this country.

Baptisms, birthdays, weddings, first communions, saints' days, crucifixions, Christmas, New Year, and funerals seemed to be what the Italians celebrated. Oh, and, of course, a multitude of sporting events especially football. Not much difference from the English then except the number of publicly recognised saints' days.

In the evening we ate with the other guests, but the food was dull, flavourless and uninspiring and the wine was unpalatable.

Day 34
Mileage 3151
Monday 27th May 2002
We Discover A Beach

First thing I did today was trying to get back to sleep. But in the end I forced myself to get up. This is a boring bit so I will not tell you it but I will just tell you the next bit.

When I finally got up we jumped into the car and headed straight for a tourist office to see if there were any maps to show us where a beach is. Dad came strolling back to the car with a map grasped in his hand, he looked as if he had some bad news to tell. When he finally reached the car he said, "Here's a map that shows where B-E-A-C-H-E-S are, but there's only one on it!" After hearing this we decided to find this beach.

After driving for about an hour or more, we found a cove/bay sort of beach, which was good enough for me.

As soon as I could I got changed into my swimming stuff and ran. I ran straight for the sea jumping on to a rock which looked like a number eight. I gave a final leap and splash, I had jumped into the sea.

It was colder than I expected and so I jumped straight out again. This time I went further out and started to tread water.

*

We wanted to go to Napoli and Capri and we needed to find out how to get there, so we decided to drive to Sorrento and find out about boats and trains. The road down to Sorrento was twisty and steep with magnificent views all the way. Sorrento itself was a busy and bustling holiday resort and looked as if the very walls oozed wealth. Coming after Sicily this was a complete contrast. Its affluence was on display and it wasn't in pre-season mode. Everywhere was busy already. I hate to think how packed this place would be in August.

We drove down to the port and parked.

The view across the bay of Naples was terrific. Vesuvius loomed over

Naples. Although it was a volcano, it was not nearly as large and did not look as menacing as Etna. There was no visible smoke coming out of the crater.

There were queues for the hydrofoils going to Capri snaking up the gangplank and along the front. All nice orderly tourists in shorts and (mostly) white shirts, hats and skin. Coming this way, it was obvious we would have to make an earlier start to avoid the rush. We decided to drive around the coastline in search of less busy places. On the way out of the town we found the Circumvesuvius railway for trains to Pompeii and Napoli.

As we wove our way around the coast roads, we could see occasional bays and coves between the rocky shoreline, but access looked frightenly difficult to us. Eventually we ended on the Amalfi side where the road was known as the road with a thousand bends. It is narrow and bendy so there is no overtaking, but there are signs in four different languages saying, "give way to overtaking traffic". This is a concession to the fact that Italians will overtake at every possible and often, to our eyes, impossible opportunity. How they overtake buses which can hardly go round the bends you need to see to believe. I can understand why they do it, as the buses are very slow.

We stopped above Positano for refreshments and to look at the view. It was again stunning. In this part of the world you run out of different superlatives to use.

The elusive beach remained that way until eventually we stumbled upon one. It took two or three attempts to get the Galaxy around the corner. The road down was full of empty parking spaces and we could park right near the bottom. The beach was at Marina di Praia, it was shingle and sloped down to a small entrance into the sea. There were some small waves and George and I spent time floating in the sea enjoying its refreshing feel.

On the way back we came across a whole model village carved into the rock face. There must have been about fifty small houses and churches in this little group.

Then we searched for an open supermarket, but failed miserably to find one. So dinner, not with Vittoria, was relatively modest.

113

Day 35
Mileage 3205
Tuesday 28th May 2002
Visiting Pompeii

When we had got to Pompeii (yes the actual one which was blown up by Vesuvius in 79 AD) Dad had only bought two tickets because it said that children are free, but when we came to the ticket gate the man said that children needed a ticket as well even though we were free! Dad got very angry and then said "Can I have the purse please just in case." When at last dad came back he was only holding one ticket and said, "It's for them to share"

When we finally got in I was listening to what happened on the fateful day in August.

As we walked through the main entrance gate to Pompeii, the audio guide explained to me that that was the only entrance into Pompeii because Pompeii has a high wall around it.

As we walked around I discovered that urine (pee-pee) contains ammonia so it was used to clean walls and to clean clothes!!! (YUCK!!!!)

Just before we went to go home we found a gladiator ring (one where they practice). And the shrine to Hercules who according to the legend founded Pompeii.

*

Back to being tourists. We drove back along the coast to find Pompeii. This time we stuck to the motorway and followed the signs. This by-passed Castellmare completely and dropped us right on the doorstep of Pompeii.

It was already hot by the time we arrived and Indigo and George were desperate for ice cream. We parked under trees in the campsite and went off to the ruins.

The whole place was full of tourists (of course, it is the most popular tourist site in the whole of Italy – what did we expect). Up into the ruins

we went and of course there was no way we could see it all. If we were lucky we would be able to stay here for two hours before overwhelming weariness set in to George and Indigo. We first saw the Temple of Apollo again with Vesuvius looming benignly in the background, just like in times gone by except on 24th August 79AD when it was not benign but both menacing and deadly.

I hadn't realised, but there had been a serious earthquake just seventeen years prior to the eruption in, 62 AD, which had seriously damaged Pompeii. I suspect there will need to be another earthquake before the Napolese take talks of an eruption seriously and even then I doubt it. The whole bay area is so beautiful, it would be hard to give it up under any circumstances especially if it is your home.

Next came the Basilica, a large roofed rectangular public building (55m x 24m) that was used as a meeting place and to conduct business. At one end was a raised podium used by magistrates as a tribunal. Then there is the Forum. This had much more open space and was flanked by rows of public buildings and shops. Off the Forum there was the Eumachia Building dedicated to the priestess Eumachia who was the patron of wool makers. This had the most beautiful preserved marble architrave surrounding its entrance. George particularly liked this as there was an area in the entrance hall which was used to publicly collect urine.

Wandering down one of the main streets, it was not hard to imagine this as a genuine live and working city. There were so many houses in various states of repair. In the laundry, there were many deep vats. Apparently they hadn't invented the plug as each vat had to be emptied by hand. Urine was used in the washing process for the ammonia it contained and clay was also used as a fabric conditioner. Both of these items seem strange to us. I wonder how often clothes were sent to the laundry?

Further along there was another house, where the walls were much better preserved. You could see paintings and decorations still in place throughout. This one had a "garden room" and much like many urban houses in England it didn't really have a garden at all. All the houses were very much back to back squeezed into a compact area, instead the room had a large mural depicting rural scenes of animal fighting

and chasing each other. Drains were disguised with pictures of nymphs pouring water.

As we walked down towards the theatres we noticed that the roads had very large stepping stones in them. These were there because the main roads were used as open sewers. These were then washed clean by the rainfall. (I hope that they got more rain here than in Sicily where there is never any rain in May.)

There were two theatres, large and small, both showed signs of roofing or shading. The large one had a capacity of about five thousand. This was about one quarter of Pompeii's population at the time. Next to the large theatre was a smaller theatre with a capacity of about 1300. Behind the theatres was a large open space where the crowds could mingle between or after performances, much like the crowd in Syracuse were doing after our attendance at the Greek play. Some things in society obviously do not change very much. I still would not like to have lived in Roman times. For the great majority of the population life would have been very simple and to us mind bogglingly hard graft from dawn to dusk day in day out. The very rich and those in charge may have done well for themselves, but most people were the grafters and the slaves. Even compared with the very richest of Pompeii society, most of us have a very high quality of life.

Day 36
Mileage 3250
Wednesday 29th May 2002
A Quiet Beach

Today we went to another beach which we didn't see on the way down to the little cove we found on Monday.

We parked under the olive groves at the top of the slope which is a steep walk down and up. (Another great parking spot mum, very good.)

When we had at last trooped down the very steep winding road (that lead down the slope) At last, at long last, I saw the sea, the sand and the waves.

When we actually got on to the beach mum saw other people had sun

beds and she wanted to see how much they were. Mum bought two sun beds.

For lunch we had a picnic on the beach. We had jam sandwiches, Pringles and fruit. After we had relished on a filling lunch the dreadful thought of climbing the slope again made me lose my spirit.

Before we left we saw three people get on a moped!

When we left we stopped at a port to see a time table to see what time boats leave to Capri (a small island off the coast).

*

We wanted to find somewhere nearer to Le Tore to relax. So we headed off to Massa Lubrense on the way to Sorrento. There I found the tourist office and was given a more detailed map of the local area. I asked if there were any nearby beaches and was told this one is sandy, this one is rocky and this one has shingle. We decided to try the sandy beach at Poulu only a few minutes away. There were two roads down to this beach so we took the first. We had not gone more than ten yards down this road when we realised it was a mistake. It was too steep and too narrow. A three wheeler ape truck was struggling up the track and we had to reverse back to the main road. We drove to the second way down and this was much more successful. We parked in an olive grove. There was room for hundreds of cars here, but we must have been one of the first. It looked as if the olive grove had been deliberately planted with enough space for cars to manoeuvre between them. If only the designers of multi-storey and underground car parks in the UK were as generous with their proportions as this place, then my world would be a far, far happier space.

We were pointed down to the direction of the beach. It was still a considerable amble down, but quite acceptable. Further down there was another car park in the open. This was, of course, much closer. Never mind.

The beach itself was small and un-crowded and did feel pre-season. This suited us entirely. George again enjoyed playing in the sea and the waves. Indigo was busy in the sand and paddling. I very much enjoyed being here with Eliza just watching our children relax in this way. It was very pleasant to see them enjoying just being children. We went off to explore the rocks that formed the sea break. They were both becoming confident on climbing these rocks, but with a sensible amount of caution thrown in. They could see gaps between rocks and said that they had to be careful to avoid falling between them. We ate sandwiches and fruit for lunch and let the hours slip away peacefully.

There was an Italian couple and small girl next to us. Indigo made friends with the little girl, who could not have been more than three. They all played together quite nicely with Indigo asking Dad for "Aqua" on several occasions smiling one of her more beguiling smiles and Daddy trotting off ever so obediently to fill up her bucket or watering can for her.

Soon they prepared to leave. They got out their moped. Papa sat at the front with his bright blue helmet, Mama sat at the back with a carrier bag in each hand to keep her balanced, and the little girl sat squeezed between her parents. Once the moped was started, they slowly wobbled along the seafront and then up the hill. It all looked very precarious, but, as I keep reminding ourselves, this is Italy after all.

Later we took all our belongings and wandered up the hill to our Galaxy. There were another two or three cars parked there when we arrived. The shaded olive grove parking meant that the Galaxy was cool. We drove back to Massa Lubrensa and went down to find the small port there. We wanted to find if there were trips to Capri from here as this would be far easier for us than going to Sorrento. Eliza talked to a man by the side of the harbour and he told us that the trips to Capri ran every morning at nine o'clock. We also found that the parking here was free during the week – a veritable bargain compared with 1.5 €/hour in Sorrento.

Day 37
Mileage 3265
Thursday 30th May 2002
A Boat Ride To Capri

After another early start to catch a small boat to Capri. Just as we were leaving another small boat stopped by us and another load crammed on to the fully laden boat. By the time we had got past the harbour the waves started and they gradually got larger and larger until it was really rough for the med.

Eventually we reached the island of Capri. It was ten o'clock and we had until quarter past four to explore the island of Capri. We caught a taxi up to the town Capri (it is very usual that a small island will call its main town/city the same name as the island itself).

I asked mum what's typical of Capri? (the island), she said that there was nothing typical of Capri, but it is a tourist trap! But at the end of travelling around Capri (the town) I saw a blue grotto tee-shirt for a low price compared with to the rest of the town!!!!!

At long last we were going down to Marina Piccola. At last we were going down to the beach and go swimming. Marina Piccola is a beautiful place with lots of rocks and holes in them. Me and Dad swam round the rocks in and out of the wide holes. We stopped at a rock and a sharp one at that. Dad got on the rock first then I followed. Steadily climbing up the rock and I sat on the top of it next to dad.

On the way back me and Indigo sat up front where we got splashed. With one wave the boat broke everyone in the front got splashed. By now we had reached the blue grotto. You could see that each time the swell came, the grotto almost closed up (that was our chance gone of seeing the blue grotto!)

We came to another landing place, but it was to rough to land so we went to the port where we had landed and we went home.

*

We were up early in order to make sure we caught the nine o'clock boat from Massa Lubrense for Capri. We were the first passengers there, so early enough for breakfast at a local bar with coffee, juice and croissants.

As the time approached nine, a boat and a couple of smaller boats approached the harbour. We were not going alone as the harbour acted as a collection point from other nearby pick up points.

We all sat on the side at the back and enjoyed the sunshine and the sea. We were definitely beginning to look like old hands as everybody else (except the crew) looked unbelievably pale and pasty. The trip to Capri was only about half an hour – a lot less than from Lipari to Stromboli.

We thought that the boat was just taking us to and from Capri and expected to land in the main harbour. Instead, the boat took us clockwise around the island. We saw Tiberius's leap where the Tiberius is supposed to have "invited" people to jump from 300 ft to their deaths on the cliffs below. I wondered what fate lay in store for anyone who refused this invitation. We went round the island where there were very tall cliffs with incredibly sharp promontories and rocks. There were some tiny islands where there were natural arches in the rocks. One was big enough for our boat to pass through. Here there was almost a queue of traffic in both directions. We landed in Marina Piccolo – the little port of Capri town where we would be picked up again in about four and a half hours.

We walked up past the beach and to the bus stop. There was a small bus service up to Capri Town but we just missed it. A smart open topped taxi arrived and we let the people who had been on our boat with luggage take the taxi. Except the taxi didn't want to take them! He had plenty of room for them all, but no room for luggage…and he didn't want to spoil his nice white leather upholstery. What a great introduction to the island. So, as it was there and free, we took the cab up into the town. It was a real touch of luxury that the children simply adored. It was unimaginable travelling in an open-topped car in England except for one or two days a year.

Capri Town was on the top of the ridge looking down to the main harbour – Marina Grande. Here there was a funicular railway, taking people up and down to the port. The town was the place to come for expensive designer clothes, expensive hotels, restaurants and bars and tourist tatt. There were lots of nice things set in beautiful scenery. There were lots of beautiful people set in nice scenery. And then there were the tourists and the wannabies just loitering and littering the streets. We saw our first wisteria of the season open here. It was quiet and peaceful with only a few taxis and buses to spoil the pedestrianisation of the island. We would have liked to have gone to see Tiberius's Villa Jovis, but we would have to walk and Indigo would not have been able to manage. We settled for a walk admiring things, an expensive coffee and beer followed by a leisurely lunch in an expensive restaurant. Elton John, Kirk Douglas, Bianca Jagger had left their autographs which adorned the menu. I'm sure there were lots of other famous names, but their signatures were too obscure.

Afterwards, we wandered around the town some more, found ourselves in the middle of wedding photographs on the steps of the church, caught the bus back down to Marina Piccolo and we waited for our boat on the beach playing on the stones and in the sea. George managed to swim out to some rocks and climbed out of the sea with me. Indigo allowed me to take her around the sea in her rubber ring. She was very brave and happy.

The boat picked us up and we continued around the island. George and Indigo sat at the front where they enjoyed the spray and getting wet from the occasional wave. As we went around the island we saw more steep rock faces and lighthouses. There were occasional bays with long steep paths leading down from the higher hills occupied by sun-seekers and bathers. We came to the entrance of the famous blue grotto, but the swell in the sea was too rough to allow us in. The entrance was semi-circular and barely a metre in diameter. It needed to be very calm for anyone to enter without being decapitated. There was a notice saying that swimming in the blue grotto was absolutely forbidden. So that was that. In true Neapolitan style a boat with a man and a woman drew up, the man dove off and swam into the blue grotto. The swell did its best to knock him out, his head missed the rocks on an uplift by less than a foot. We never did see him come out, but we didn't stay for long.

Further around we came to the Marina Grande and looked up to Capri Town on the top of the ridge. It was lit up with the late afternoon sun. At the end of the island was a statue of a siren, whose legendary powers lured men onto her rocks below.

We motored across the gap back to the Italian mainland watching the other boats coming and going, the swell of the afternoon sea picking up again. Seagulls were travelling at high speed leaving the mainland for Capri. Their wingtips slung low and playing chicken with the waves below them. As we approached the mainland, the spray from the waves reached up high onto the rocky coastline. Although the boat was rolling and pitching the movement was enjoyable in the sunshine. Our harbour soon came into view and we landed safely.

Day 38
Mileage 3276
Friday 31st May 2002
The Road of 1000 Bends

Today we had a plan to go to Positano without success, so we decided to go to see the Smeraldo Grotto.

When we got there we went in a lift down 72m according to the man at the lift. After we had dropped down the drop (in a lift of course) we entered a little cave called the Smeraldo Grotto.

The Smeraldo Grotto is a little cave with stalactites hanging on the ceiling and there was water not just any water and at one end there was some lovely turquoise coloured water. There were two boats with guides. We went round on one who wasn't very good at English but he tried his best and it was good enough for us to understand. Anyway, he took us round and explained how the turquoise water was natural, there was an underwater tunnel and it made the water turquoise. Also when he slashed the water with his oar, the ripple was turquoise.

We went to the cove beach and we had lunch there. We spent a pleasant afternoon on the beach playing with the waves.

*

This morning we drove out to take a closer look at Positano along the road with a thousand bends. It was a hot and crystal clear day. The sea looked a lot calmer from the cliff top mountain road, but we were sure that there was some underlying swell that was difficult to see. We were wondering about whether we would have been able to enter the blue grotto today.

To get down to the front at Positano, we could walk down the long windy road, but I would end up having to carry Indigo most of the way down and all of the way up, so we drove down the road slowly and found an expensive car park. Just by the car park there was a second model village. I wondered whether this was a common feature around here. It certainly made a change from the ubiquitous shrine. I looked for but didn't notice if there was a miniature church in this model village. This was another town full of delightfully expensive shops and restaurants. The beach front was flat and wide and full of rows and rows of sunbeds and umbrellas. It was very hot. We decided that this really was not our cup of tea and that we should move on. Indigo by this time was refusing to walk as predicted and needed to be carried. I took her up to the point where the road came down and left the others while I went off to fetch the Galaxy. We poked our heads into some very expensive looking restaurants just to look. In one, the outdoor surroundings were very plush, but the place was empty – it was closed at lunch time.

I came back with the Galaxy and parked like all good Italians, blocking everybody else's way while everyone got on board. Then we drove back up to the cliff top road and further along to the Grotta della Smerlado – a smaller version of the blue grotto accessible from land.

To gain access, there was a lift down to the water's edge. A drop of 72 metres we were told. There we could enter the grotto through a narrow and low doorway carved out of the rock. Inside, it took some time to get used to the dark. There were two boats being slowly rowed around the water each with a guide. It was soon our turn. The boat took about 20 and the guide decided to speak English.

There were stalactites hanging from the ceiling which we were invited to "lookee here" and use our "imagination, fantasieeeer" to visualise the leaning tower of Pisa. There was an underwater tunnel connecting the cave to the outside. It was the natural light from this that gave the grotto its light and its name. It was a very glorious green and when the guide splashed water around the whole surface shimmered and sparkled in the light.

Further around there was another stalagmite who we were invited to "lookee here". According to the guide this was supposed to look like the silhouette of Garibaldi, but he went on, according to other Italians this was also Mussolini. Americans thought this was Abraham Lincoln or Bill Clinton or George Bush. English people thought it was Tony Blair. It was all down to "imagination, fantasieeeer". Very tongue in cheek and quite amusing.

Further around still, the Italians had imagined the Madonna and child on the ceiling. Well the Italians would. And yet further there was a nativity scene below the waterline except this one was not natural. It was ceramic and had been deliberately put there by a television company that had been allowed to film in the grotto as a measure of thanks to the boatmen. The guide seemed especially pleased by this. I was very bemused that anyone would have thought of doing this yet alone find it pleasurable, but this is Italy and they certainly love their religious icons and shrines and put them in every conceivable place and niche. So, yet another victory for the Catholic Church.

We decided that we would go back to Marina di Praia, the beach we had been to on Monday and spend the rest of the afternoon down there. Approaching the turn off down to the sea front from this side was a lot easier. Even since Monday the beach looked more switched on for the season. There were sunbeds available and all the pedalos were being given a fresh lick of paint. George no longer had any fear about the sea here, but it was a lot calmer than on Monday.

After a while Indigo got bored and I took her for a walk along a path that had been cut into the cliff. We followed this round as it went up and up. Near the top there was the entrance to a tower called Torre a Mare. There was a sign saying that the entrance was free so we wandered along the path to the tower. Indigo discovered three little baby kid goats lying in the shade next to the path. They could only have been a couple of weeks old. She tried to touch and pet them, but they were rather nervous. At the tower there was a man inside who invited us in. He was working on a sculpture that he called "the girl and cock". This showed a naked girl astride a rooster embraced in a strange whirling dance. Both the girl and the rooster were the same size. It was neither erotic nor rude, but reminiscent of Beryl Reid. I must say I liked it, the features were well balanced and there were good expressions in the bodies and on the faces and life in the motion. He showed me some of his other sculptures and seemed particularly pleased with his swimmers. These sculptures were part above and part below a flat translucent surface which when put into a large glass bowl gave the illusion of swimmers in water. He said he taught local children sculpting and showed a series of small heads that were made by his class last year as self-portraits. They were rather good, but did they resemble the class?

We went off back down to the beach. Later Indigo took Eliza to see Torre a Mare and the artist. He did not live there, but simply used it as his studio. I imagine that this must have been a touch of paradise for an artist. Here surrounded by some of the most picturesque landscapes in the world.

We drove back to Le Tore where tonight we would be eating in the house. We took the precaution of buying some Nero d'Avola wine from Sicilia this time, as the wine last week was unpalatable. Today, we were two among seven and, although we had booked with Vittoria, the kitchen staff were unaware that we were eating, but coped without any problem. The food tonight was more interesting and tasty than on Sunday. It was all rustic and peasant food. There was definitely nothing here you could buy in a restaurant with freshly made cheese, pasta with legumes, stuffed cabbage leaves, roasted chicken and, to finish, fresh raspberries.

Day 39
Mileage 3310
Saturday 1ˢᵗ June 2002
Amalfi Coast

Today we went to see Jo, Stephen and of course baby Mathew. When we arrived they were round by the pool. As soon as I was changed I headed straight for the pool. It was warm, lovely and warm, even mum went in.

Before lunch, I received presseys from my friends. I got a Harry Potter t-shirts and DVD, Kitten pictures, White Horse book, Secrets book and two cards. Thank you everybody. It was great to get some presents. They were very nice.

There was the most spectacular view imaginable.

*

This was the first day of June. May had been a very full and rich month for us, but June we would definitely see more and more crowds as the summer tourist season started to kick in.

Today we had arranged to meet Jo and Stephen who were out from Saffron Walden for halfterm with their youngest Mathew. They were staying at the Palazzo Sasso in Ravello. We set off on our usual route towards Positano. I was definitely becoming familiar with all the bends and adopted some Italian overtaking practices to get past the newly arrived Dutch and Germans and even the occasional bus.

We drove past Positano, Praiano, Grotta della Smerlado – the furthest we had been, Amalfi, Atrani and up to Ravello. The drive was quite tiring and the bends slowed our average speed down to a mere 17 mph. – surprisingly slower than in London. Ravello itself was high up on the mountainside. I dropped Eliza, George and Indigo near the top and then went to park the Galaxy a bit further down. The hotel itself had a discrete entrance. It was so discrete that there were no signs and no name on the door. It just looked rich inside. I walked past it twice before daring to go in. The entrance was spacious and well marbled and furnished with elegant chairs and tables. I walked in as if I owned the place, but was politely stopped by the receptionist who asked my business. I told them who I was meeting and was directed down to the pool.

The pool-side terrace was green and lush. This was a very different world from the Agritourismo world we were inhabiting. Steve, Jo and Mathew were all there looking calm and relaxed and we were all under-dressed. They had arrived yesterday as could be seen by their skin colour. It was good to see them all and we spent a very pleasant few hours in their company. George and Indigo loved the pool, the first we had used since being away. All the other pools we had seen were still inoperative. It was shallow and fountains gushed water around and into the pool.

Indigo very much enjoyed all the other waterfalls and fountains set around the gardens. The gardens were immaculately kept with Swiss efficiency and not a leaf out of place. The view down to the sea was very very spectacular. Today there was no wind at all. The sea was a long way down and looked very flat indeed, with only the pale blue and white trails of the slow-moving boats disturbing its smoothness.

George was given a parcel of presents from her school friends as an early birthday present. She had great fun unwrapping them. For her, the best was a CD full of photographs of Fleku's kittens aged about 5 weeks.

After lunch, young Mathew, who had been given royal attention by all the waiters and was revelling in every minute of it, started becoming fractious. He had not slept much the day before and needed a good sleep. We said our goodbyes and wished them a good holiday – they were moving further south on Tuesday for the rest of their week. It took some while to drag George and Indigo out of the swimming pool and off to the Galaxy.

Back down at Amalfi, we needed to buy some money and to find a *macellaria* for some food for George and so spent an hour or so here casually wandering around. Amalfi was more of a genuine town than Positano. It was busy, but there were Italians as well as foreigners wandering around. Amalfi had one main street perpendicular to the coast containing all the shops. The further away from the sea you got the less the shops were aimed at the tourist, with butchers and greengrocers and grocer shops. In one shop window long strings of scarlet chilli were being sold as natural Viagra. Still, it was very evident that this town's main income was the tourist trade.

At this time of day the view along the coast was very different. You could see a number of different headlands stacked up one behind the other. Their colours were washed out and each successive headland was fainter than the previous. The sun caught the peaks and cast shadows across the sea. Despite the clarity of the air, there was enough dust to see the edges of these shadows hanging in the air.

Day 40
Mileage 3360
Sunday 2nd June 2002
A Busy Beach

Today we stayed on the beach for five hours non-stop. In-out of the water in-out-in-out-in-and-out again running backwards and forwards. After say four hours Indigo and dad found a sea snail. Dad said if you left it upside down it would right itself.

Instead of walking up the steep hill me and Indigo jogged.

*

We didn't want to go too far this Sunday. The children wanted a beach so it was back to Poulu. Today it was crowded. We knew this before we even got down to the beach as the car park was heaving. Down on the shore there was room, but you had to fit in between others.

The girls were now familiar with the layout and lost no time going down to the sea and continually splashing and fooling about. Indigo and I spent what seemed forever watching small fish and crabs hiding from us in the rock pools. This was the day we should have brought nets, but we hadn't.

Sand intruded into our homemade on the beach *mozzerella, proscutio* and *pomodoro panini*. Here the mass of people were Italians, either local or from Napoli enjoying a day on the beach. Unlike Capri, the beautiful people stayed away leaving only the red and white skins, the balding, the plump, the bawling babies, scrawny teenagers and the big fat *nonnas*. Everyone seemed content with the way they were and were obviously very happy just to be spending a day here on the beach. A million miles away from their work lives tomorrow.

Day 41
Mileage 3372
Monday 3rd June 2002
Napoli (not)

Today we are going to Naples. The drive to the station was one of the worst. I kept thinking I was going to be sick. When we stopped at the train station I walked a few steps then threw up (this was not a pretty picture.) So we went home again.

I didn't do anything much today because I threw up three more times later.

*

We wanted desperately to do a day in Napoli. All the guidebooks stressed that driving in Napoli was anarchic and that cars, especially foreign cars, disappeared here with amazing regularity – don't take your car into Napoli. We decided to drive to Sorrento and get the

Circumvesuviana railway. We were up and out early. George started complaining about headache and tummy ache, but we put this down to not enough sleep. We drove the seven kilometres to Sorrento and surprised ourselves by finding somewhere to park right by the station. In order to stay for the day we had to buy a pack of cards - parking cards for the Galaxy. However, immediately after parking George got out and promptly threw up on the pavement.

This changed everything. We hoped that the act of vomiting would make George feel better. So we went for a walk towards the central square to find a café and maybe let George unwind. This didn't work very well and George continued to look ashen faced like one of Vesuvius's victims.

We aborted the day and went back to Sant'Agata. George sat in the Galaxy with a plastic bag in her hand just in case. She went back to bed. We suspected it was the amount of sea water she swallowed yesterday that was causing the problem.

Indigo and I went for a walk following the vines and came out near the front entrance to the Farm. The footpaths led down to a nearby village. I wanted to get some fresh bottled water for George. There was a small bar open where there was world cup football on the television, but even with such an attraction we were still the only customers. Indigo does seem to like these little walks and coped very well with them.

We bought some water and climbed back up the hill. Indigo managed very well without grumbling except for one long flight of stairs where I carried her on my shoulders. Indigo found some peach trees and then further up picked some cherries to give to Eliza.

George was still in bed when we got back, but was pleased to see us and delighted to have some cold water to drink. Even so this was enough to make her throw up again. George spent the rest of the entire day listening to Harry Potter. She continued to throw up during the day and felt very sorry for herself (quite right too). The rest of us just pottered around.

By the evening George appeared much better and was able to eat some plain pasta without throwing up further.

Day 42
Mileage 3390
Tuesday 4th June 2002
A Day In Herculaneum

Today we catch a train, but we didn't go to Naples we went to Herculaneum. Herculaneum is another site which was destroyed in 79 AD by Vesuvius but Herculaneum was not covered like Pompeii but hot mud came down the mountain and killed any people in its path.

What I found amazing was that most of the mosaics weren't just like the old ones which you find half or something like that but you can see the whole thing. It's amazing. What mum found amazing was that the style of the houses then are much like the style used today. This style of houses is 2100 years old, where as our house is only 400 years old, but no one would build it today though would they?

*

George was much better today. We did not want to push it today, but we wanted to send a couple of crates home rather than cart them around with us for another three months. Tina from Le Tore found us some boxes, string, bubble wrap and packing tape. It was quite amazing how much we managed to pack away. We went down to the local post office. Unwittingly one of the boxes was too heavy as there was a 20kg limit. So we had to unwrap a box and remove some items.

After wandering around the local area we discovered there were bus timetables posted in the local tourist office. We decided to get the bus to Sorrento and if George survived that then we would get the train to Eroclano. George was quite keen to go and see these ruins.

The bus was fine, but we were quite astonished at how fast the driver took all the bends. Mind you, he had had enough practice doing this drive and the bus itself was one of the few vehicles that we had seen with no scratches or dents. It also gave me a chance to take a proper look at the scenery. At some points you could see the coast on both sides of the peninsular simultaneously. At others, the mountains blocked your view of the sea completely. The whole way was lined with orange, lemon and olive groves. Everywhere nets were up to help catch the fruit at harvest time. The lemons here were enormous compared with those in Sicilia. Some of them were the size of small melons, but were contorted into gnarled gargoyle deformed faces.

In order to test George we went for a snack lunch in the middle of Sorrento. Everything was well. George was happy and felt much better. So off to the train, catching it with barely a minute to spare (they were every half hour). We hadn't realised just how far Eroclano was and it took over an hour on the train. At Eroclano it was hot and sticky, and, unlike at Pompeii, it was a long hot stroll down the hill to the ruins. We tried to buy ice creams but all the bars sold Aglida factory made ice cream. It seemed daft to go all the way to Italy and eat Wall's, but that's all there was here.

Eroclano was much more compact a site than Pompeii and was not anywhere near as busy. It had been destroyed by the same earthquake that had affected Pompeii. Some of the ruins were much better preserved than those we saw in Pompeii. In particular there were the baths. These were split into male and female baths and the female baths were the better preserved. They each had three rooms: a changing room, a tepid room and a hot room. Each room had black and white mosaics on the floor. I particularly liked the ones in the ladies baths. In the changing room there was a picture of Poseidon surrounded by dolphins and an octopus and squid.

In the tepid room, the floor was covered in regular black and white pattern with small objects inserted into the pattern such as jars, tridents, fish etc. The male bath additionally had a *fridgidarium* or cold bath. Here the roof had been decorated with fish to give the illusion of fish swimming in the water. Both neat and clever. Changing rooms could learn a thing or two from here.

There were four or five other buildings with well preserved mosaics in quite astounding bright colours considering their age. The best was in the Casa di Nettuno and Anfitrite. Here there were pictures of the gods on one wall in gold surrounded by reds and blues. On the wall next to this were hunting scenes where the main background colour was deep rich blue.

There was a two storey villa where some of the staircases were still preserved. The floors were still laid with marble. You could walk around it like I always imagined a Roman villa with a central square courtyard garden.

There were at least three shops which looked like the equivalent of city sandwich bars with half a dozen urns sunk into a marble surface worktop for selling hot and cold food to the public.

Eventually we decided to go home. The train journey seemed longer than on the way out, but was fine. There even was a bus connection at the station and we only had to wait ten minutes or so.

Day 43
Mileage 3392
Wednesday 5ᵗʰ June 2002
   Visiting Naples at last

Today we are finally going to Naples. We are going by train from Pompeii.

The first thing we went and saw was the Duomo, the cathedral with vials of blood which according to the legends the blood of the saint is to have liquefied three times. There is also a skull somewhere. However, apart from how gross this seems there are pictures you could die for.

Next we found somewhere to eat, this wasn't what we expected, but it was fine all the same except when a man came in and started to sing an Italian song.

Dad spotted it first, there it was looming in front of us. Mum kicked herself for being so blind. Staring in front of us was the Catacombs (underground tunnels under Naples). The catacombs were used in the second world war for the bombs couldn't get past the top of them. Most of the way was lit but at the last bit we had a candle each even me but not Indigo.

Finally, we went to the train station (the nearest one) we had to catch the train so we can catch another train so we could catch another train. We caught the wrong train everything went horribly wrong and we didn't get back until at least 10:45!!!!!!!!!

*

Today we tried again to go to Napoli. After yesterday with the bus and the train we decided to drive to Pompeii and catch the train from there. This may not be any quicker, but it would be more convenient for us all. It was still a long time to get to Pompeii and even longer to get to Napoli. We had decided to go as light as possible to Napoli so as not to attract thieves and pickpockets. When we were leaving the farm it was shrouded in cloud, and there looked as if there was every chance of rain. So into the backpack went a fleecy each making it more bulky than I had wished. We had decided that there was no way we could do much so had picked on only a couple of things that we wanted to see. We were especially intrigued to find Da Michele, which was recommended in two guide books as selling the best pizzas in Naples (and hence, some would say, the best pizzas in the world). When we emerged from the central station at Piazza Garibaldi everywhere was chaos. The whole square seemed to be one big hole. Spiderman was advertised along the front on an entire office block. I'm sure that they were building a new underground line.

We walked to where our maps had placed Da Michele. I was surprised at how small all the streets were in this quarter. Some of the main thoroughfares you could hardly pass two mopeds yet alone two cars. Hence, most of these streets were necessarily one way. We could not find Da Michele nor even the street that it was on, but if the map we had was right we could not have been more than 20 metres from where it should have been. We walked up to where the Doll's Hospital was and I was relieved to say it was there, so my navigation was not askew. Unfortunately, there was a notice on the door saying back in half an hour. It was more of a shop than a hospital, with lots of old fashioned dolls in the window, but they also fixed life-sized mannequins and there were a few of these with odd limbs and broken heads lying around. Looking around us I was surprised to see that just in this little street there were three or four shops specialising in selling shrines and all sorts of other Catholic idolatry. We went up to the Duomo. Unlike St Paul's in London, you could not see this building until you were virtually in front of it. All this emphasised the clutter and claustrophobic nature of the little streets in this area. The Duomo was a place of peace in a sea of chaos, no wonder the Italians turned to religion. Inside, it was a fairly typical cathedral with marble-clad floor, statues and murals on the walls and ceilings. There was also a side chapel to San Gennaro. One of the busts is supposed to contain his skull and there are some vials in the church that contained some of his blood. It is one of the miracles of this church that San Gennaro's blood has liquefied three times in the past.

Walking down Via Tribuli, we passed several pizza joints with their *pizza vero vecchia* signs – a symbol of the real Neapolitan pizza made to special rules – but there was nowhere to sit at any of these and the children needed to sit to eat. The pizzas all looked very good, if simple and doughy. We found a small family run trattoria and had a simple, but very rewarding lunch. A wiry old man came into the restaurant and suddenly the air was filled with music from a cassette as we were given a taste of opera karaoke. He did have a better voice than most. After about ten minutes here, with a lady collecting money, they left and hopped onto a moped and were off to the next trattoria. By going from trattoria to trattoria he probably made a better living than a lot of other down-and-out opera singers. We had some delicious fried anchovies and lamb and potato stew. The wine was rough to say the least, but after the first glass, unlike at Le Tore, it became much more palatable.

As we sat there I noticed that across the street there was the entrance to Napoli Sottoterranean. We had intended to visit the catacombs under the Royal Palace, and knew that this was an alternative, but had not realised that it was here. The next tour was at two, so we took it.

The tour started by the guide putting on her leather coat and her woollen bobble hat. I got the impression that it was going to be colder than the normal Neapolitan temperature for the beginning of June. There was a group of about a dozen of us who descended into Naopli's underground passageways. Originally, these passageways were dug by the Greeks. The Greeks had found that the tufa stone that was here in the ground made for good building material. It was strong and robust and, because it was volcanic in origin, it was very light. This stone was quarried out by the Greeks for use in their buildings both locally and also for Pompeii and Herculaneum. After a while the Greeks also discovered that these underground quarries were useful as wells for water storage. Some wells were communal and had more than one well-hole drilled down to it, others must have been private as there was only one well-hole into it. The water was shipped in via Roman built aqueducts. Even after the fall of the Roman Empire during the fifth century AD, the system of aqueducts and underwater wells worked very well. In fact they were still operational up to the eighteenth century when the water started to become contaminated from the volume of sewage emanating from the city. Multiple and regular cholera epidemics ensured that the Greek and Roman system of water transport and storage finally broke down. Nevertheless, these underground spaces continued to have their uses. Before the Second World War the wells were often used as rubbish dumps. During the war, the wells were capped so as to stop bombs from dropping into the subterranean area and the underground tunnels were used as air-raid shelters. During 1944, when the Napoli resistance rose up against the Germans in four days, the underground tunnels played an important role in communications.

There are stories of underground ghost dwellers who were used to explain mysterious disappearances or appearances of items such as money. A bit like the Borrowers in England. Sometimes mysterious visitors to women were explained away in this fashion and sometimes the unexplained arrival of little children was also blamed on these phantoms.

In one part of the tunnels we had to walk along a very narrow pathway where we had only candles to see our way. These parts of the tunnels, although narrow, were also very tall. Apparently, they were designed so that water would sluice quickly down from the water source to the wells. These parts could be a bit claustrophobic if one was that way inclined, but George and Indigo both revelled in it.

There were areas where some toys had been left behind after the Second World War and another area where German military remnants had been gathered for a display.

There was an area under a nunnery which had been used to brew and store wines. These were legendarily miraculous in the medicinal properties. Then it was discovered that it was not the nuns that were producing the miracles, but the very stones where the wine was stored. The fellow citizens were not amused. The storehouse under the nunnery also led up to an entrance to a nearby monastery. The nun's wine when mixed with visitors from the monastery apparently led to some great times until they were discovered. This is certainly not the first time we have come across secret passageways between nunneries and monasteries in Italy.

When we re-emerged into the Napoli daylight, it was hot, sunny and steamy. Our guide then took us to see the remains of a Greek and Roman theatre. This was very surprising as to enter the ruins we had to go into an ordinary house in a back street. Until two years ago, the previous owner, who had now died, refused to let anyone see what was hidden in his basement. We had to open a trapdoor in the ground floor and climb down a couple of flights of stairs. There we could see just a small fraction of the ancient theatre. Any further excavations had to be extremely careful in case the buildings on top collapsed. In ancient Napoli (the name itself derives from Neo Polis or new city) there were regulations preventing building outside the city limits. Over time, space was very much at a premium and new buildings were simply erected on top of existing ones. This was how the Greek theatre had come to be buried in situ. There were other buildings in the area where one could see part of a row of seats or a bit of doorway.

As we walked away from here, we saw some firemen struggling with a ladder. Along with a wealth of other people we stopped to watch. They appeared to be trying to get onto a balcony two floors up, but there was no evidence of smoke or flames. They had a ladder in three parts and were struggling to put it together. This looked like something out of Laurel and Hardy. There were now five of them struggling with this ladder. Eventually, they managed. Then they had to erect it. The only problem was that the pavement was full of street cafes and there was nowhere to stand it up. They got it up: straight up against the wall. Now, all they had to do was move it to the balcony. This meant twisting it through 90°. As they slid the ladder across and twisted it, it slid over and nearly came down on the people nonchalantly sipping their coffees and reading their newspapers. Suddenly a fireman appeared on the balcony on the second floor. He caught the top section of the ladder and disaster was averted. The top section of the ladder came away and he took inside the building. The bottom two sections were lowered and separated. The firemen then all went away happy. So had someone found their key? Who knows? Just a small incident in a big city.

After all this we decided that we needed to have some gelato. A few minutes walk away there was a gelateria called La Scimmia – as far as we could tell this meant cheeky monkey. The ice cream was home made and excellent with a wide variety of flavours. I was surprised at how little "real" ice cream there was in Napoli and how much was branded by Aglida and Néstle.

Up on the funicular railway we hoped to get a good view of the city, but when we had got to the top, it became obvious that the children were past caring and that it was time to go home. We found our way to the Metro entrance and followed the map and the signs. We would have to change once before getting to Piazza Garibaldi where we would get our connection to the Circumvesviana railway. Little did we realise that this metro line was only partially finished. There was a half an hour wait for a train – hardly suitable for a mass transit system. Then at the change point the stations were not next to each other, but a ten minute walk away. By this time we were all desperate for a drink. We went into an empty looking bar at the entrance to the station to buy a bottle of water and found ourselves suddenly surrounded by locals. I did not worry about this until I saw a wallet drop on the floor (not ours) and felt a hand (not mine or anyone else's in my family) in my trouser pocket. We got out and checked our belongings. Two or three of the zips on the backpack were open, but they had not been able to rummage below the bulky fleecies that we were carrying. They had also missed George's purse which was behind the dictionary. We were lucky, but we knew that we had deliberately not taken much into the city with us. We vowed that, in future if we needed a bottle of water in a bar in this kind of area, only one of us would go in.

We caught the next metro train quickly and without incident and then we saw that the next train to Pompeii left in three minutes. We dashed for it, caught it, and felt very smug with ourselves. The train went fine and we recognised the stations until the stop before Pompeii. Just as we were getting ready to get off we realised we were not at Pompeii at all but somewhere else. We got off anyway. The station master told us that there were two Pompeiis – one was the town, where this train was going and one was the old city Pompeii Scavi (Pompeii excavations). To get back to Pompeii Scavi we had to go back one stop and change. I felt such an idiot. This delay cost us an hour in all as the trains only ran twice an hour.

On the way back to Sant'Agata everyone was hungry and we stopped off at a restaurant overlooking the bay of Sorrento. Again the view was wonderful. As dusk fell and the evening lights came on, the whole horizon shimmered with silver and gold. Distant churches began to light up and their bells sounded out across the valley to us. Pizza and pasta recharged both George and Indigo. Now it was my turn to be tired.

A very long, but highly rewarding day.

Day 44
Mileage 3437
Thursday 6th June 2002
Sant'Agata

Today we just lounged about, I caught up with my journal and did a bit of Italian and a bit of English this is very hard work, this made me very tired indeed. We were very tired from the trip to Naples yesterday so we stayed at home. Later me and Indigo went to the farm and looked at all the animals, we went to see the piglets, the cows (which were both in bad condition in their own poo), the chickens, the turkeys and the rabbits. One of the rabbits had babies one of which had got stuck in the bars of the cage and the chickens had eaten its legs and insides!! (gross!!!).

*

The sunshine this morning was all in vain, everyone was sleeping in after yesterday's exhausting activities. The children played near the apartment and spent time at the farmyard looking at the piglets and their mother. Half the chickens had been replaced by turkeys. Where had they disappeared?

Indigo and I went down for a walk to Sant'Agata where we went to see if we could find Don Alfonso – a very expensive restaurant. We bought some fruit and vegetables and some large prawns and fresh anchovies for supper. The prawns had a bright blue tinge around their middles. On closer inspection these were eggs. I had never seen them like this before.

Later, we all drove down to Sant'Agata in order to buy some food for dinner. We went to Don Alfonso to book a meal, but they said we would have to come back next week for an evening meal. We booked for tomorrow lunchtime as then the children could enjoy it too.

The prawns were very tasty, but the anchovies would have been better filleted first.

Day 45
Mileage 3440
Friday 7ᵗʰ June 2002
Don Alfonso's

This morning we had soothing baths and mum did a lot of packing, but we helped by packing our own things because tomorrow we are moving on.

We got into some lovely clothes because "we are going to one of the best restaurants in south Italy" according to mum. The restaurant was made up of tiles, two glass lights which glimmered with the light, some quiet Tom Jones music and quite a few mirrors. The food was served in such a way that it could well have been a piece of art work. When the food arrived it had a little silver dome on top. I had scallopini and chips.

*

This was a day where we indulged ourselves at Sant'Agata. Eliza had done most of the packing by mid-morning so we could quickly load up the Galaxy for our escape tomorrow.

Indigo wanted to dress up for our lunch at Don Alfonso. She looked very beautiful in her red sequinned top. Her hair was done up in a bun and she had had glitter sprayed on her hair and arms. George and I looked quite smart for us and Eliza was simply stunning.

It was quite late when we got to Don Alfonso's. We spent ages looking at the menu and trying to decide what we would have. George and

Indigo would just have some pasta and *scallopini*, it was their parents who were having difficulty choosing.

Everything was carried out with a calm precision, almost a military air, but without the forced pace of the military music played at Waterloo station accompanying the morning rush hour. As usual in a restaurant this expensive, everybody had their own specific rôle. The headwaiter was tall and looked officious in his black suit, he was definitely in charge, but he was very friendly and even Indigo did not mind him, his broad smile stretching his grey square and squat moustache. The wine waiter had very short hair and looked as if he had escaped recently from the North Bank at West Ham, he wore a long black apron and passed out the wine list. This extravagant list was a thick book, far far larger than the menu, with wines ranging in price up to €1,500. When asked for help, however, he quickly honed on to a bottle of local red wine which was not extravagantly priced – at least in comparison with the rest of the list. The water waiter ensured that our water glasses were topped up throughout the meal without us having to. The bread waiter hurried from table to table handing out individual slices of bread including a bright orange tomato bread and a bright green spinach bread formed into the shape of a clenched fist. The table waiters carried plates covered in silver domes to the tables and ceremoniously removed them to reveal their contents. The crumb waitress went round sweeping up breadcrumbs and other debris with a special silver tool: simple, elegant and clearly effective.

The chef and his wife came out to talk to their customers and check if they too were having a wonderful time. I had thought that the head waiter was Don Alfonso. He certainly looked like him in the pictures I had seen, but it was evident he was just a doppelganger and that the chef was the real Don Alfonso. The food was truly excellent, delicate and well presented. It was a lovely occasion and one that will be remembered for some time.

Afterwards we went to the shop and showroom next door and spent some time and money in there. They ran a large local farm where they grew a lot of their own produce. This produce formed the very backbone of their traditional local cuisine.

Later I took Indigo out for a walk up towards the woods and mountains.

We followed a path that took us towards the coast. I wished we had found this path earlier. It was very easy, but the views changed quickly and radically. The whole of the Amalfi coast started to stretch away in front of us. We could see for miles. There were a few small islands scattered along the coast, all looking inviting in their own right. I could not imagine a car driving down this path, but there was the odd house that we past. Finally the track came to an end and we had to return the way we came. Then as we climbed up the road a car came racing down towards us, both sides over the edge of the path, but still it came. We were able to get out of its way easily, but I was just dumbstruck seeing it at all.

Where the path was even narrower, tall grasses grew. By now Indigo was having a comfy ride on my shoulders, but even with this extra height, some of the grass grew over her head.

Back at Le Tore, we loaded the rest of the luggage and sat down for some peace and quiet. Nobody wanted to eat after today's lunch.

The air was clear and still, the sunset was very golden. Streaks of light lit the clouds from underneath giving a rich set of colours this evening. The fireflies were still glowing hot on the trail of a mate. I thought that their season was less than two weeks.

San Gimignano
Day 46
Mileage 3442
Saturday 8ᵗʰ June 2002
To San Gimignano

We packed up the car because we are moving on today. We drove for ages and stopped for lunch. I was happy for this I got bored in the car. Italy were on the telly we saw Italy score two goals that weren't allowed, then Italy lost the final score being 2-1 to the other side.

When we finally arrived at San Gimignano the place we were staying at we found out that we could not park our car there but in a pay car park!

We found a place that looked like Hogwarts, take that Oliver!!!!!

*

We were up bright and early as we were on our travels again. We were pleased to be going: two weeks here was definitely too long, we were too far away from the places we wanted to visit and this place had never felt like home to us which was a great shame. The accommodation was fine upstairs, but downstairs was simple shabby and worn out.

The drive was straightforward: we knew where we were going! We stopped on the motorway near Rome where everyone was glued to the television watching Italy play Croatia. As we were queuing for some food there were sounds of great cheers followed by moans as two Italian goals were disallowed. There were half strangled cheers as goals were missed. In the end the final whistle blew and the crowd spontaneously dissipated in stunned silence. Italy had lost 2-1.

The motorway made its way cross country to San Gimignano. It was heaving. Saturday afternoon and the place was crawling with coaches, cars, bicycles and people: all swilling around the place. As usual, we did not have a detailed map of where we were going, but we knew that it was accessible from the outside of the town walls. We drove around looking at signs until we recognised the name and nimbly nipped into a courtyard behind some gates. We had found it. We had also seen some signs for the Museum of Torture. "Wicked" said George gleefully. "We must see that!"

After settling down in our apartment we went for a stroll around the town. It would be a delight to be able to eat out and not have to drive home. The towers were as magnificent as they had always been. Some had been standing for six or seven hundred years. We just wandered absorbing the atmosphere, after about six, the day-trippers were no longer around and the town settled down to a quiet evening. It may have been a Saturday night and it was quite busy, but it was far nicer at this time of day.

George thought that the whole place looked like a set out of Hogwarts. It was very old and there were primary coloured flags on the main streets. In the courtyard of the commune palazzo there were shields and various murals on the wall.

Day 47
Mileage 3457
Sunday 9ᵗʰ June 2002
The Torture Museum

We finally went to the torture museum. It was absolutely disgusting what people used to do to each other! For example, they used to cut people in half and the saw had to reach your middle before you became unconscious – gross. There was a chair which had spikes on it and there was also a note saying "Don't sit down please!"

*

I got up early to try and find some shops for breakfast. Overnight rain had damp dusted the streets. A bar was open and locals were watching more world cup football.

I asked a couple of people if there was a *paneficio* or an *alimentary*. I was given disparate advice and even though I followed them all up I could not find anything. I found signs to the Antico Forno (marked in English as a baker's shop). I went up and down the road trying to find it as the signs pointed both back and forth. I then saw bread being handed out of a doorway. I went and asked where the baker's shop was. It's here, I was told, but it didn't open for another hour. I went back to the apartment empty-handed and everyone decided to get up and go to get croissants and a drink at the bar. Just as we walked through the gate into the town I looked to my left and there was an *alimentary*. Our bedroom window was almost directly above it. Unfortunately, it was closed.

At the bar, the football was still going on much to George's delight.

The newspapers were full of speculation over Italy's chances after yesterday's defeat. All the different results of the Mexico vs Ecuador match were shown giving the different possible routes for Italy to qualify for the second stage.

As we walked towards the Piazza di Duomo, some of the artefact shops were beginning to open. I was still trying to find this baker shop. We followed the signs again and this time it was perfectly clear. The sign on the door was up and it was open. Inside the front of the shop had been taken over by wine. This happened too at a lot of the other shops. The true local shop was at the back, but the front of the shop was used for tourist goods. But at last we had some fresh bread, milk, salami and, oh yes, a bottle of Chianti Classico.

We walked down to the far end of the town looking at the various shops. There was a steady influx of tourists and yet it was only nine o'clock. We managed to get out of the gate and here was a grocer's shop. Fresh fruit, and salad.

After lunch and a nap, we just had to go to the torture museum. The girls seemed really enthusiastic about going, but it was quite an horrific experience. Although the exhibits themselves were not nasty, the descriptions in English were very explicit and quite gruesome. It was absolutely frightening what rulers, the church and ordinary people could do to other people in the name of justice, religion, interrogation, revenge or simple humiliation or a combination of all of these. More worrying some of these methods and instruments were still in use throughout the world.

One chair had wooden spikes all over it, back, sides and seat. There was a notice on it saying "Please do not sit down". Obviously, some people took their tourist experiences of reality too far.

Day 48
Mileage 3763
Monday 10th June 2002
Tony's Ice Cream

We hit the road again, not to move on, but to find somewhere to stay after my birthday for three weeks. We did find somewhere to stay in the end.

When we got back we went up the great tower and to a museum which was just paintings "boring." Up the tower we could see for about ten miles.

We had a wonderful dinner somewhere granddad recommended to celebrate mum and dad's 9th wedding anniversary (it's actually tomorrow, but this restaurant was closed tomorrow.) On our way back we saw a satellite circling over our heads.

*

We needed to find somewhere to stay later in the month. We always had intended to stay in Tuscany for some of this later period as we wanted to spend time in Frienze, Pisa, Lucca etc. We also wanted to have a pool. Yes we could have gone to the municipal pool, but that would have meant planning and smothered our impulsive natures.

The Tourist Office offered us some advice and found us a place with availability for the whole of the three weeks. We decided to go for a look see. It was only a few kilometres away and we would have more space than we were used to.

We had seen a couple of places on the way in to San Gimignano on Saturday and decided to visit these as a quality and price sensibility check. We found one by the roadside with a pool and went to have a look. It was right by the local prison. Also there were so many apartments that the poolside would be heaving when it was busy. Each apartment looked small from the outside. There was nobody around so we moved on.

There were two more signs for apartments with pools along the same road. The first one we stopped had some impressive iron gates and a phone number. Again there was no one around. At the second there were some people milling around and the lady who ran the establishment was around. The gardens had a pool with a stunning backdrop of San Gimignano and its towers. They had one apartment and it was free during the period we wanted. It was nicely finished, but it would have meant that George and Indigo would have had to sleep in the living room. They quoted us a reasonable price for the three weeks. We took her card and said we would ring her back later in the day.

An Agritourismo place was signposted so we decided to follow it. This time the road quickly became a dirt track and then there was another sign which implied that they also did food. 7kms later we arrived, without even looking at the place we knew that this was too far off the main road to be of use. Our experience at Le Tore in particular told us this. The place looked run down and miserable. We still went in and talked to the lady of the house and had lunch. There were a dozen builders having lunch too. They told us they were from Napoli and had been working on a building project on the farm for eight months. Lunch was alright, but nothing I would want on a regular basis. We gave the lady a friendly farewell and left.

We had an appointment to keep and were running late. The signal on our phone kept coming and going as we rang up the lady we were meeting. We think they understood that we were going to be late after half a dozen broken conversations. We found the place and had a good look round. We were under the impression that we would be in the same apartment for three weeks, but we were told that we could have one apartment for two weeks and change for the third. Again, the apartments were well furnished – this was their first season – and there was an extra room so that the children had their own bedroom without having to sleep in the kitchen space. There were only four apartments so the swimming pool would never get too crowded. We left as we had one more apartment we were going to try and see again with the promise of going to the tourist office in San Gimignano or ringing back later in the day.

After another failed attempt to contact the third woman, on the phone more than once, we decided that the last apartments would be fine. We just had to decide if we really wanted to be in the same place for three weeks. In the end that's what we did.

After we got back to San Gimignano, we took the children up the great tower and into the civic museum. Despite complaining about her legs all the time and asking to be carried, Indigo climbed up the tower with relish. 199 steps according to George. The views from the top were simple glorious. Today the sky was clear and blue so everywhere emphasised the soft blanket look of the Tuscan landscape: all vines, olive groves, villas and tall long avenues of tall thin straight cypress trees. Three main colours dominated: the sky was blue and where there was not green then there was terracotta.

Eliza's father, Mike, had recommended La Cisterna Hotel for dinner. We originally planned to come tomorrow for our wedding anniversary, but it was closed on Tuesdays. We happily settled for a window table with a gorgeous view of the surrounding countryside. As the sun sank, the shadows of the towers grew like elongated fingers across the landscape gradually clawing over villas and hillside alike.

Indigo and Eliza had dressed themselves up. George and I went as ourselves. The ambiance and the food were delicious. After a while, Indigo started talking to her neighbours – she will always be able to break the ice at parties as she loves to talk to anyone, if she was sitting next to a donkey, then only the front legs would be left. They were all impressed by her conversation and her dress sense. Everyone had a very nice time.

On the way home, the girls had some ice cream from one of the geletaria's on the main square who made their own. The place had a thank you letter on the wall from Tony Blair, but George was not impressed and wanted to judge the ice cream on its own merits. It was good and George was impressed.

Day 49
Mileage 3763
Tuesday 11ᵗʰ June 2002
Rocca and Harp

Today we were going to the church but it was expensive and we thought we would see better ones in Rome.

On our way up to the rocca we saw a harpist play soft sounding music
that could harmonise with beast and any sort of anger.
When we got to the Rocca, there was a flautist with a wood flute.

*

Our last day here. I wanted to go and look around the Duomo, but we decided to give this a miss otherwise the children would start suffering from church and art fatigue before we hit Roma. In the square by the Duomo, there was a young harpist. He played very nicely and his audience grew rapidly over the space of a few minutes. The girls were both entranced, Indigo particularly. We climbed up to the Rocca above the town and got a very different view from those yesterday at the top of the Great Tower.

At twelve o'clock all the bells in the town rang including some in a tower. Although we had heard the bells before, we had not seen the ones in the tower swinging.

We found a restaurant for lunch which served nearly 50 different varieties of *bruscetta*. I'm used to only one: tomatoes, garlic and olive oil on slightly toasted bread.

I went off in search of fresh food for dinner that night. Over the hill and down the other side to the fresh fruit shop. We had also seen some door knobs and I was in search of a load to replace the wooden ones in our kitchen. This proved difficult to find. Everywhere had lots of knobs with corks for use as a stopper, but I could not find the ones with the screw fittings. Eventually I found them, but I could only find one which was of a suitable size. Never mind.

Roma
Day 50
Mileage 3809
Wednesday 12ᵗʰ June 2002
To Roma

We moved again this time to Roma the capital of Italy and where there is another country – The Vatican.

It didn't take long to find Roma, but it took twice as long to find where we were staying! When at last mum sighted the hotel she said, "You go and park the car and I'll take the children."

We trooped up the stairs and into the bedrooms and slumped onto the beds.

We got changed into some nice clothes and walked down to Piazza Navona where in the centre there was a fountain called La Fontana Dei Quattro Fiumi. We had dinner at a place called the Piazza Navona the same name as the square, which cost us an arm and a leg according to mum.

*

Today we were off to Roma. I was very excited by this. I have never been to Roma before and was looking forward to it immensely. It took us a couple of hours to pack up and load and then we were off. The journey to the motorway was tedious as the whole road from Siena was being widened to be a dual carriageway. It was hot and becoming hotter as we drove south. Temperatures reached 32°C.

I was a bit worried about finding the Vatican B & B in Roma as we only had a schematic map and some instructions downloaded from the Internet. I'm sure that the Internet instructions were correct, but they gave you the road names and not the signs to follow. We found this particularly difficult, as you could not see the road names until after you were past the roads themselves. Still we managed the drive, only making a couple of mistakes and more importantly realising that we had made the mistakes and managing to rectify them without making things worse.

Parking was exciting. This sort of excitement I could live without. It's like playing musical chairs and trying to avoid being the one left behind without a seat. Except in Roma, the number of players increases over time and the spaces continue to diminish. We ended up double parked while we unloaded the minimum that we thought we needed. Ermina told us there was a place nearby with an underground garage which would do off street parking. We opened our bedroom window and we could see it opposite. I went off to drive to it and left our nice homely double parking space to find it. I wasn't quite orientated yet and thought our window looked out onto another street and I managed to drive around the block several times before finding it. I nosed into the entrance, but I decided it was prudent to check it out before going down the ramp. It was like a large cool cavernous cave down there – a different world from that at street level. There were loads of empty parking niches in every part of the garage. I thought our luck was in. I hunted around the cave for some minutes until I found someone. In my very broken Italian I said *"Parcheggio?"* He said *"Non"*. I said *"Quanto costo?"* He rubbed his hands together gleefully and said *"Non, complete"*. I looked around in dismay. There was loads of room, you could easily fit all the cars needed to transport George's swimming club team on the way to a gala, but Golem, as I thought of him, had said *"Non"* and he was evidently king in his own domain. I left him rubbing his hands together with joy, knowing the struggle I would have finding a space in the real world at street level.

I drove round the block a couple more times waiting for a car to move. I saw one and drove towards it only to see a Roman dive in front. I would have to do better. I found another space but I would have to reverse into it. The road was too narrow for another car to pass and there was so much traffic that if I drove past it reversing may not be possible. I tried and I succeeded. My parking success was being watched by a man working in the ladies hair dressing salon next to the space. He watched me cautiously as I corrected my position, his hands deep into a set of curlers on some woman's head. Without taking his eyes off me, he was rolling up hair and pinning it up. After I stopped, he looked directly at me and barely perceptively his head nodded in approval at my parking attempt. The only problem with this space was that it was not too far away from the Vatican B & B, but too far to carry the rest of our stuff.

We were slightly paranoid about leaving the car on the street with all of our gear in it. Not so much for the intrinsic value, but the sheer inconvenience it would cause if it were broken into. With off street parking we were happy to leave it more heavily laden.

Later I walked to the car to move it. On the way there, there were two traffic wardens examining every car and issuing tickets. I thought it would be just our luck to get a ticket so soon. We were okay. I drove round the block again to find a spot where – double parked or not – we could park to at least unload. Miraculously, well this was Roma after all, I found a spot right outside the gates of the condominium where we were staying. I pulled over in order to manoeuvre. I looked back and the space was gone. A large black Mercedes had guzumped me. I went over, under the eyes of the traffic wardens, and with all innocence I asked if they were just leaving. They looked at me and must have taken pity on me, or maybe it was because of the wardens, because they did leave and relinquished the space to me. I vowed that the car would stay put there until we left.

After showers, we went for a stroll. The temperature had dropped to about 30°C, and it now felt balmy rather than just intolerable. The apartment was round the back wall of the Vatican very near to the entrances to the museums and the Sistine chapel. We walked around the wall towards the entrance to the front of the Vatican. There was an innovation in the Roma pavements: every corner had a small ramp down with a wheelchair sign for easy access. I was impressed, but then a vision entered my head of a group of naughty nuns deliberately rolling a man in a wheelchair off the pavement to his fate in the middle of the Roman traffic. I could not shake this vision and it haunted me for the next few days. Every now and then I would break into an irreverent giggle thinking about it.

We walked along to San Pietro – the cathedral and the piazza. Got fleeced for a very expensive set of ice creams all round. Then across the River Tiber, down some back streets to Piazza Navona. Here, there were lots of activities going on: mime artists, people pretending to be statues, musicians, painters wanting to do your portraits and caricatures.

People were peddling all sorts of tourist tatt, oil paintings, drawing and temporary tattoos. We sat ourselves down on a relatively cheap square side café to watch. It was entertaining and the children were happy watching what was going on, but it was very expensive and not very good. We were playing real tourists and not travellers.

We walked back along a different route and found a whole string of antique shops with wondrous pieces of furniture in their windows. There were lots of spectacular pieces, but some were completely over the top with all their unnecessary adornment that they became hideous and simply ugly. There were maybe only one or two pieces that I would even consider giving house room.

Coming back home around the walls, we saw a *gelateria* where Italians were crowded round like bees around a honeycomb. Ice cream was dripping off children's and adults' faces alike. Cars were parked, nosed dived towards the pavement at rakish angles while parents and children queued up excitedly for ice cream. This, "The Old Bridge" geletaria was worth a try. Amazingly, it even had its own zebra crossing.

We got back to the Vatican B & B, the car was still there and I managed to get all four keys to work in the right sequence to enter the apartment. The gently shoosh of the ceiling fans swirling the air around gave the feeling of coolness. The fans were shaking as though desperately trying to free themselves from the ceiling and massacre the innocents sleeping beneath them.

Day 51
Mileage 3988
Thursday 13th June 2002
The Vatican

Today we went to the Vatican and the museum there. The Vatican is where the pope lives so the country is very religious, probably the most religious country in the world.

Today I found ten things that I found amazing, here are the first few:

The booby woman, she had 19 boobies and a boy at the age of three killing a goose.

The booby woman was a statue of the goddess of babies.

The statue of a boy at the age of three killing a goose, which I think might be Hercules at a young age.

When we had trooped around a bit more we came to the map room and all the maps were made so that the centre would always be Roma.

When at long last, we had trudged the final part of our journey, we had come at long long last to the Sistine Chapel done by Michelangelo. Michelangelo had to be begged by the pope to do the Sistine Chapel because he thought that sculpturing was better than painting. According to a piece about the Sistine Chapel "it still puzzles art historians what caused Michelangelo to do this piece of art work." Michelangelo spent most of four years on his back.

After we found the exit we walked to St. Peter's Cathedral in order to go to the top of St. Peter's – the Cupola. At first we went by lift instead of 164 step. We stopped after 38 steps to look inside the Cupola. It really was an amazing view from up here. Then we carried on up the winding staircase. 100 steps, 200 steps, 300 steps, 335 steps all the way up to the very top. Up here we could easily see for 30 – 40 miles.

When we got back down again we went inside and we saw the statue of St. Peter which you are meant to touch his foot for good luck.

*

The sounds of the Roma traffic rumbled on well into the night. I thought this was odd as we were on a tiny corner in a one way street leading from the main road back onto itself. It must have been that the game of parking musical chairs went on continuously. The sounds varied from the rumble of lorries and dust carts to the chirping and buzzing of mopeds. There were also the whissshing sounds of street cleaning vehicles, but in the day time there had been no evidence of their presence. Maybe the noise had been dredged up from a dream. We were not used to the noises of the city anymore, but I found them strangely therapeutic and calming. Several times during the night I woke. After about one o'clock the noise diminished noticeably and then picked up again from five as the city stirred from its slumbers.

Eliza, George and Indigo slept on. I had to go and get some change for the parking meter as I was too paranoid to disregard the possibility of more traffic wardens during the day. I went to a nearby Hotel and tried to change a ten euro note into coins. They were very helpful and changed the note into two five euro notes. Not exactly very helpful as the parking meters didn't take notes. I went to buy some water from an alimentary. Still not enough change. I went to have a coffee in a bar and at last I had enough change.

I fed the meter and went back to apartment. Everyone was still sleeping.

Eventually we got up had some breakfast and went out.

Until yesterday we had not realised that this coming Sunday was a very special day for the Catholic church: Pardre Pio was being canonised. Now I recognised the figure of the man made into souvenirs of lava up mount Etna. The whole of Roma would be inundated with the faithful flocking to the occasion at Piazza San Pietro. Touring the Vatican today rather than leave it until tomorrow or Saturday would be sensible. The entrance to the museums was about 100 metres from the apartment, so we were quickly in a position to judge the queues for ourselves. Luckily there were none, so joining it was the only sensible course of action. It was hot already, but inside it was air conditioned.

The museums were all awesome. I was surprised by how much was not directly related to religion, but was related to the history of Roma. There was so much to see, even on the short tour, that after a while you just glaze over at all the wonders: sculptures, pictures, the map room, the Raphael room, the room of the conception of the virgin, the apartment of pope this and pope that. Trying to keep George and Indigo interested was quite heavy going. To them it was more of a trudge than of interest, but I was very pleased with their stamina. We found a quiet spot in the Raphael rooms where they could sit and do some sketching. George wound herself up by being upset that her attempts were not as good as the original. The Sistine Chapel was stunning. The pictures could not do it justice and the pictures of how it looked prior to the recent restoration made the colours only more vibrant. This was, however still a chapel and every now and then as the crowd noise grew the tannoy system kicked in to remind people to keep quiet and not to take photographs.

Even the Vatican snack bar was quite tasty.

The exit from the museum was via a spiral ramp which got steeper and steeper as it went further down. First a gentle slope, then some gentle steps far apart, then steps becoming closer and steeper together. Despite the warnings people could not seem to manage this without tripping over their own shoelaces.

After lunch we went to see San Pietro itself and started by climbing to the top of the Cupola. We cheated, as there was a lift to about the mid-way point. There, there was access to the gallery at the bottom of the dome. All around here were large mosaics in the form of cherubs and angels. Their sheer size made them larger than me. It was nice to see some things with feet and toes larger than mine.

Looking down to the floor of San Pietro you could see all the people wandering around looking like small puppets. The route up to the top was between the inner and outer skin of the dome. The sides of the staircase gradually leant over more and more with the curvature of the dome, but the last part was more vertical. George made it 333 steps to the top. Here we were. The sun was baking down and there lay Roma before our feet. The city lay there quietly slumbering at our feet with few people on the streets and little traffic. I could make out the Coliseum and the Forum as well as the Piazza Navona where we had been last night. Then, the quiet that hung over the city was broken. There was an enormous cheer from ground level and car and bus horns started sounding. This was a city in full celebration – almost orgasmic. It could mean only one thing, Italy had scored in the World Cup.

We descended from the top. Eliza and Indigo taking the lift down and George and I taking the stairs down. The ground floor of the cathedral was extremely spacious and full of decorative structures, sculptures, shrines and paintings. At lot of the materials used here had been recycled from the ruins of earlier era Roman buildings. The steps of millions over the centuries had worn the different marble surfaces in different ways. The statue of St. Peter was especially popular, where pilgrims had touched his foot and stood in silent prayer. There was a statue by Michelangelo showing off his full skill at the tender age of 25.

That evening we went to an *Osteria* recommended by Ermina called Tony and Danni. It was only five minutes walk away from the apartment. There we were ushered into the back away from the traffic noise and fumes. There appeared to be no menu and Tony – for it was he – was determined to give us his best. He insisted that we had his *antipasti* and these came out in two parts. We drank his red wine and then we ate his pasta. After all of this we were already bulging, but we were not allowed to get away with leaving just yet. More meat followed and more wine and then a dessert. Watching all the other tables around us we noticed that they too were not being allowed out, but these looked like local clientele who obviously knew what they were letting themselves in for.

Day 52
Mileage 3988
Friday 14ᵗʰ June 2002
Roma and Her Fountains

Today we caught a train to the Spanish Steps. At the bottom of the Spanish Steps there was a fountain like the shape of a boat.

We walked on further until we reached the Bourghese Villa park where we hired a bike for four people, which had a canopy, two sets of pedals and two sets of wheels.

We walked out of the park and down several streets before dad turned us onto another block and out of the blue there was an orange sign invitingly saying "Le Grotte" we went here for lunch because it was highly recommended. Oh my was it worth it even with the walk which was about a mile.

After our scrumptious lunch we trooped to the "Fontana di Trevi" where you throw in a coin to say that you come back to Rome.

Next we trudged to the Pantheon which is a big church with a hole in the top. There were some chairs laid out and mum said, "I hope it doesn't rain." I asked, "Does it have glass on the top?" and mum's reply was "Well, if we see a cat walking across the top we'll know if its got glass on the top."

Then we walked all the way to the Piazza Nuvona where we had dinner on the first night. Me and Indigo both got tattoos. When it was time to go home we went the long way round in search of a shoe shop. Both me and Indigo needed new sandals. At last a shoe shop was in sight: a perfect fit yet again.

*

I had to do my tours of the alimentary and bars again to gather enough change for the parking meter. This morning I was recognised in the alimentary and offered a bag to carry my water. The woman in the bar who served me my *caffe lungo* was as ice cold as yesterday. She seemed to treat everyone with the same frozen look of indifference. The I'm-only-here-to-earn-some-money-because-I-have-to look and I-really-wish-I-wasn't-here-at-all look.

This morning we were off to the Spanish Steps. We were going to try the Roma Metro and I was desperately hoping that it would be more effective than the Napoli Metro. The station was about three blocks away and easy to find. The children were free, but again it seemed like only those who wanted to buy tickets could be bothered to. The Roma Metro only had two lines, but the city itself was quite large. It's only then that you realise how well served London is.

Spagna was only three stops. The early morning heat hit us as we came out of the Metro. It must have been at least 30°C already. At the bottom of the steps there was a boat shaped fountain where people were busy using a stepping stone to touch, drink and collect the water. George and Indigo thought this was terrific fun. Walking up the steps presented you with a brilliant view of the city below, but not nearly as awesome as that from the copula of San Peitro. From here we walked by to the Boughese park, further than I thought judging by the map. Once inside the park and away from the traffic and noise, the large umbrella pines provided a high canopy of shade, stopping the intense sun and making us feel much cooler. We found a place that hired bikes and took one which would carry us all. We sat three in the back and Indigo sat up front in her own little basket. Downhill was great fun except that George had got it into her head that we were going to crash and all get seriously hurt. We didn't. Uphill was a lot harder and at times I had to get out and push. We found various fountains and the Villa Borghese itself, standing there in bright white stone in the hard sunlight. Once more round the park and it was enough.

We walked back down into the city and found a place for lunch. It was a veritable oasis. Cool and quiet inside with some excellent food.

We had hoped to do the Forum after lunch, but it really was too hot and too ambitious with the children. Instead we walked some of the back alleys seeking shade towards home. We found the Trevi fountain: such an enormous rush of water and large statues in such a small space. We all threw coins over our shoulders in the traditional manner guaranteeing our return to the eternal city. I think this was one use of the euro that everyone agreed was good. Considering how much coinage was been tossed away in this manner I cold not help but wonder where it all went. The bottom of the fountain was virtually empty. Had it been designed in such away that the coins ended in a sump and were taken away nightly? Were there armies of scavengers who came out at night and waded into the fountain and picked the coins out?

Further along we found the Pantheon, one of the best preserved ancient buildings in Roma. This was both a temple and church open to the worship of all gods. Next we found some ice cream to keep the children and me happy. It was still very hot and the sun was shining virtually straight along the street onto our backs. We had to keep changing sides of the street to find the small amounts of shade wherever possible.

Further we came back into Piazza Nuova. Here we let both George and Indigo choose a henna tattoo. They both chose Dolphins, but Indigo's was a lot smaller.

We took the metro back and walking back we found a shoe shop, as both the children needed sandals. The poor staff were rushed off their feet trying to serve more than one customer at a time. Inevitably, this meant that we all got bored, and although they weren't too unruly the girls made up games hiding behind pillars, using the mirrors and climbing all over sofas and chairs. The perseverance was worth it as they were both pleased with their new sandals.

On the way back to the apartment, we stopped off to try the ice cream from The Old Bridge gelataria. It was very scrummy and some of the best we have had. It is very difficult to judge the best when all of the home made ice creams were so good. We also bought some cherries, apples, crisps and drinks and went home for a reasonably early night.

Day 53
Mileage 3988
Saturday 15th June 2002
Ancient Roma

Today we went to the Coliseum a Roman gladiator ring. But before we enter the Coliseum let me tell you what it would be like to be lifted off the ground by one leg: you would feel as if someone was pumping vast amounts of blood to your head. I know this out of sheer experience because I was lifted by a Roman Centurion.

Inside the Coliseum I learnt many things. The fighters and the animals were both lifted out of the dungeons ready to fight. The one thing I learnt from here that many people do not know is what arena means. Do you know? Well if you don't it means sand. After gladiator fights, the loser would ask for a pardon. The crowd would vote but only the emperor could decide if he lived or if he died. If he was to die he would remove all his aromer and wait for his oponat to kill him. Romans flooded the Coliseum so that they could have navel battles, but they only did this twice.

When we were out of the Coliseum we went on a restaurant hunt, turning down street after street then we finally stopped at a small one level restaurant, it looked invitingly cool. When we sat down I chose were we sat – under the fan – the lucky thing about it was we had a good view of the TV. Though we didn't realise it at the time, this was a good thing because we watched England completely devastate Denmark; 3 – 0.

After a satisfaing lunch we went to the Forum. Don't think it was a place where gladiators trained there because it was where Roma was run from- all the politics and things.

But when we got there, all we found were broken pillars, broken slates and a hand me down church which had been past down to many popes through the years until finally it had fallen down and stopped to be used.

After we had been to the forum we tried to catch a train back home, but there was no train home so we caught a bus to playtown.

Playtown was very enjoyable. Indigo had missed all her physical activities, she was so glad we had come but she didn't know what to do first she just wanted to do it all. It was brilliant you could barge through bendable pillars as big as I am and bigger ones.

*

Today we went off to see the Coliseum. We went past the entrance to the Vatican museums and today the queues stretched around the walls and out of sight. Rome was filling up with pilgrims to be present and partake in the beatification of Padre Pio. There were groups of pilgrims having impromptu bible study classes and hymn singing on the corner by the hairdressers.

On the way to the metro we went to a covered market. Here were a full range of fresh fruits and vegetables, meats, cheeses, fish and basic household goods. The fruit, as always, was very brightly coloured and really smelt freshly picked. The fresh *porcini funghi* were piled in crates. Borlotti beans in their red and white speckled covers lay neatly in serried rows. Large bright yellow zucchini flowers blossomed in boxes still attached to their children. Long trailing plaits of garlic bulbs were draped across stalls interlinked with the bright reds of chilli and pepperoncini all bound closely like strings of Christmas paper chains. Inevitably, there were television sets tuned to watch the world cup. Today Germany was playing Paraguay and although it was being watched, in both colour and in black and white, there was no emotional buzz showing in the viewers' faces.

The Roma Metro worked well again, but today we had to change trains! The Coliseum was very close to the exit from the metro and very imposing. Nearly two thousand years after it was first built, Romans were still making money out of this cash cow hand over fist. There were Romans dressed as gladiators, centurions, senators and ordinary soldiers. Before long George had an encounter with one. He hauled her up and threatened her mockingly with a long dagger twirling her haplessly above his head with one arm. George emitted hysterical laughter. We knew it was just a show, but it was still very odd seeing these fit ancient Romans smoking cigarettes and talking on mobile phones between short and sharp bursts of activities in their chosen rôles.

Street peddlers abounded selling postcards, maps, guide books, hats, toys, miniature models of the Coliseum, Pantheon, Trevi fountain and David (wasn't he in Frienze?)

We attached ourselves to a group with an English speaking guide and went inside. Most guide books seem to be particularly neutral about the Coliseum neither saying it is worth while seeing or avoiding as if it was both necessary to see yet not very interesting. The guide was excellent and gave a real feeling of what the place could have been like. Just as examples, he described the way the lifts and the trapdoors used to bring gladiators and animals to the surface, he told us that originally the coliseum had also been used to stage naval battles by being flooded. He told us some of the politics behind ancient Rome and how games were sponsored by candidates – the word itself comes from the white garments that they had to wear during elections – and that candidates would often lay on feasts for hundreds and once for 200,000 people. He told us that gladiators were well respected and if they survived they became very wealthy. We found out that the death rate amongst professional gladiators was only about 10%, much less than I expected. Professional gladiators would train for two years before fighting and even then they would fight only once or twice a year. Like boxing today, the higher up the rankings you got the more infrequently you fought. If you fought well and lost you were more often than not allowed to live to fight again another day. However, prisoners of war were obliged to fight to the death and there were times when thousands lost their lives in just a few days. Criminals – guilty and innocent – were brought here and fed to animals as their punishment. There were gladiators who were clowns and "fought" blind and played a slapstick role to entertain the crowd. Gladiatorial bouts originated in Tuscany and not in Rome, but were adopted by the Romans. However, they were still never as popular as historical fiction portrays them. The Greeks and the Eastern Roman Empire deplored the games and even in Rome when there were games for many days a year, the number of days when the Circus Maximus was used for racing far outweighed the number of days that the Coliseum was used.

During games, the Coliseum must have absolutely stunk with the smell of people (both audience and participants) and animals being kept in close quarters for days and weeks on end eating, sweating, pissing, defecating and dying.

Over the centuries, the Coliseum, like all of Rome's ancient buildings, had been plundered, not by invading barbarians (read non-Roman), but by the Romans themselves. Rome was well known as being in an earthquake zone and buildings like the Coliseum were constructed with large numbers of metal supports held in place with soft lead joists. These lead joists allowed the buildings to flex during earthquakes. Like all Roman buildings, the Coliseum suffered more from fire over the centuries than from earthquakes and had been rebuilt many times during its active life. The plundered materials were used by the Romans to raise new buildings and monuments, more often than not these building were associated with the church. San Pietro itself contains marble and other stones plundered from these buildings. Brass and lead work were also removed to fashion newer more catholic monuments.

We left the Coliseum after a couple of hours. This was a long visit considering how compact the building actually is. It was very hot again with temperatures in the upper thirties and with the sun very strong. We sought out refuge in a restaurant where we had a simple lunch. This turned out to be a longer lunch as England were playing Denmark. It was important to see this modern Gladiatorial bout. Here were more young men revered amongst the world at large who were very rich and famous, but now the death rate was a lot lower than 10%. Final score: England 3 Denmark 0 - George was very happy.

It was still and it was still very hot. The walk to and through the Forum drenched us in sweat, but there were water fountains en route and both George and Indigo soaked themselves at every opportunity. The ruins had their own collection of cats.

They languished in various places always just out of the reach of prying children's fingers. They obviously did very well out of tit-bits fed to them from the passing tourists. Nobody knew their exact numbers but they were well into their dozens. The sheer area of the ruins gave an impression on how big the centre of Imperial Rome must have been. These ruins dwarfed anything that we had seen in Sicily or near Napoli except that they were nowhere near as well preserved. Again the descendants of ancient Rome had plundered their ancestors handicraft. By now, we had done an awful lot of walking and tiredness was claiming victory over the children's legs.

Getting back to San Pietro by bus without a bus or street map was not easy. Each bus route said where it was going, but to me these were just a random jumble of street names, which themselves on the most part were named after famous people in history. We eventually asked which bus to take.

When we crossed the river we got off the bus, instead of going straight home we went to a children's play area we had seen yesterday. Bouncing castles, a street theatre and things to drink and snack on made the children believe that they had gone to the Elysium Fields. Somehow, their wooden legs found the enthusiasm to run and jump and play.

On the way back to the apartment later, there was still time to visit the Old Bridge Gelateria once more.

Day 54
Mileage 3988
Sunday 16th June 2002
The Hottest Day

Today we are moving on out of Roma and to the Madonna della Grazie a place with a pool. Before we arrived there we went to the catacombs but this time they were not used like the ones in Naples they were used for burials.

These Christian burial chambers were used until around 400 ad. Down here was much colder than Naples probably because in Naples we had jumpers and here in Rome I was down here in shorts and a vest! The guide explained how they put names on the tomb of the baby or child or adult. I thought that there would mostly be adults but to my horror there where many more babies and young children than adults. The catacombs had three levels and it was all made out of tufa rock.

Outside in Tivoli it was 43 we stopped to have lunch which was very good and then we went to the gardens ... ...

... ... The gardens were very pretty the smell was just lovely. And then there were fountains everywhere a perfect place to splash the cold water over my very sweaty face and a perfect place to soack my hat and letting my back get wet in this heat it was a delight. Just as we were approaching the exit there was a little girl along with two fountains she covered up one fountain so I could get a drink. I did the same thing for her but she was holding it down too. Suddenly I leg go and foom my fountain there was a sudden eruption of water that got me soacked.

When we arrived at Madonna della Grazie the first thing we did was – apart from unpack – go into the coolly refreshing pool. We had a late dinner at 8:00 and I slept under mum and dad – the room under mum and dad.

*

Packing up day again. This was not too bad as we had not used much on this stay. Outside, the game of musical parking places continued. As we were loading I seemed to be continually being asked if I was leaving. The centre of Roma was focussed on events up in the Vatican. Although it was only a few minutes walk away it was very peaceful.

We left and tried to find our way out of Roma. Roads we hoped to use were closed and so we had to improvise. Not the sort of thing I would wish on my worst enemies, but we did have the advantage of nearly empty streets. We found our way across to the north side of the city where we stopped to visit the Catacombs of Priscilla.

These catacombs were very different from the subterranean vaults we had visited in Napoli. These were used primarily for burial. The sheer scale of them surprised me. They were on three levels going down 35 metres and there were 30 kilometres of tunnels. The entrance to these catacombs was in a building attached to a church. The grounds were donated by Priscilla who originally owned them for use by the poor.

Today we started with a nun as our guide, but she quickly handed over to a man who spoke better English. It was cool down below at a constant 12°C. Down below there were niches everywhere for bodies. At this level, the bodies had been removed and re-buried to stop souvenir hunters, but there were still some undisturbed graves sealed with brick tiles. The niches were only about six inches deep and were quite short. Just enough room for a sheet wrapped body to be placed and sealed in with brick tiles. Next to each grave or on the brick tiles themselves were evidence of the identity of the deceased. Sometimes a name could be made out.

Specially decorated tombs were made for martyrs. Some had very ornate paintings which had survived down here since the 2nd and 3rd century AD. Being buried near a martyr's tomb seemed especially popular. Some of the martyrs' tombs had become special places of meditation or worship. In one, there was an image of Mary and Jesus. This is supposedly the earliest image of Mary known to survive.

In another area, there were family graves with portraits of members of the family. In one there was a picture of a woman with open arms outstretched upward in evangelical pose.

There were a large proportion of child graves here. So many children must have died at a very young age. Indigo described one child as "too dead to come out."

Back up to ground level, we came up into the heat of the present day and drove on to Tivoli. It was getting hotter all the time. At Tivoli we had a light lunch where the waitress was complaining about the heat - *troppo caldo*. She informed us that the weather forecast said that it would continue to get hotter until Thursday, which would be the hottest day and then the weather would break.

After lunch we went to see the Villa d'Este, or more importantly, the gardens of the Villa d'Este with her large numbers of fountains. Normally I'm not a Gardeners' World water feature person, but these were simply fabulous. The number and variety and the sheer exuberance and excess of water was splendid especially on this very hot day. I very much liked the fountains and cascades where you could walk behind. Unfortunately, these access paths had been fenced off. There were some little grottos where there were internal fountains. Very refreshing and soothing to listen to. There were long long rows of fountains in patterns, spraying upwards and flowing downwards. There were long stretches of cascades linked from one to the next. These though were not working. Beyond the boundary of the gardens you could see for miles around, but everywhere looked dry and parched in comparison.

To leave we had to go back through the house. The interior just looked neglected and sad. Everyone was only interested in the garden.

We walked back to the car. It was now very hot indeed at 43°C.

We drove off north to Città della Pieve to find our next stop at Madonna della Grazie. This one was very easy to find, well signposted with good instructions. There was a mix up with the rooms which meant that George had to sleep one night downstairs while the three of us slept upstairs in one room, but we had a grand terrace with a view overlooking Umbria and stretching across the Tuscan border. It was lovely. The children were desperate to get into the swimming pool even though the temperature had by now dropped to about 37°C and who could blame them.

Dinner was served outside with the other guests. The food was as it should be and put that of Le Tore to shame thank goodness. The rooms were very hot overnight, but somehow we slept.

Madonna della Grazie
Day 55
Mileage 4113
Monday 17ᵗʰ June 2002
Città della Pieve

Today we just relaxed by the pool swimming here and there splashing and splishing about jumping, running and many other enjoyable things.

After lunch we went to a town to get me a birthday present, we decided some smart clothes seeing as I don't have any.

The clothes I chose were blue. The top was a navy blue with patterns in a golden yellow the shorts were also navy blue but with cream patterns and a cream strip.

The clothes I disliked were red and checkered – I don't like checks.

*

This morning we woke up slowly and we had breakfast downstairs. It was hot but definitely not as hot as yesterday. After a lazy morning getting orientated around the farm and by the pool, we went up to the Città for some refreshments. We had some ice cream in a bar and again were told by the barmaid that it was terribly hot and that it would get hotter until Thursday when the weather would break. To us it was an almost autumnal day with temperatures only up to 37 or 38°C. Shade seeking habits were evolving rapidly in the Horth clan. Ducking down alleyways because they were shady became a chief navigation tool.

We found a clothes shop where we bought George – her choices – a pair of blue shorts and a blue shirt for her birthday. They suited her very well and the designs and patterns are one which I think she will love for many years. Eliza decided that Indigo ought to have some armbands for the swimming pool.

Back to Madonna della Grazie for an afternoon dip. The children were now both in a room next to ours which makes life so much easier. The bathrooms are very small. No baths, of course, but even the shower was tiny and pathetic. The design of the showers was so inconvenient that it was hard to believe that this was deliberate, but it must have been as the building was just a fraction too small. The shower curtain is small and overlaps the toilet. You cannot turn around without wanting to sit down. And the shower just dribbles water.

Best consolation is dinner. This is excellent home cooking which again puts Le Tore to shame. The one drawback is that it is a bit late for the children.

We ask if George and Eliza can go horse riding, but the horses are really too big for George and although Eliza could go she considered it to be unfair on George if she went and George couldn't.

The sunset was perfect tonight. We could watch it as we ate our dinner outside on the marble table. The hills on the horizon were in Toscana. Renato's vineyard of Merlot grapes stretched out below us collecting the last rays of the evening sun. The gibbous moon was visible high up in the sky. As darkness gently folded its grip on the countryside, the mosquitoes would come out and go on their raiding missions. They were quite irritating when they bit, but I did not suffer too strongly. It did mean that on a still night like tonight, the windows had to remain shut and the rooms were too hot.

Day 56
Mileage 4116
Tuesday 18ᵗʰ June 2002
Compleano

Last night was a restless one; no sleep, eyes shutting, yawning and yet I was tired, but as tired as I was I couldn't sleep. But that could be because it is my birthday.

At last someone was awake, it was dad bare in the breeze of Tuscany, at five o'clock in the morning wrapping my birthday presents and the first thing he said to me on my birthday was, "Go away. Happy birthday, but go away." Feeling a little upset I went away trying very hard not to remember the things on the table. I had only glanced at whatever it was on the table, at first I thought they had brought me something like an Italy shirt!

At last I could open my presents. I got books about thinking and puzzles, the book The Lion, The witch and The Wardrobe, the book The Number Devil and a Bear Footin' tee-shirt.

When mum and Indigo woke up I asked if I could be pushed into the pool with a tee-shirt on. When I was pushed in I felt a sudden chill when my toe touched the surface of the water.

For dinner I had pasta, hamburger and cake. The cake was delicas but I could only eat so much. After my second piece of cake I was stuffed.

*

Today George is 10. It is quite amazing for me to remember her birth and think back on her life. I am extremely proud of her. She has been a wonderful daughter and, even though she can be irritating at times she has on the whole been marvellous. I am very happy with the way she is growing up so far, of course we do not know how she will turn out and of course, like all parents, we hope she will do well for herself at whatever she chooses to be.

She was so excited about her birthday that George had woken up a three and then again at five. She crept in to catch me wrapping her presents on the terrace. Everything had been left to the last moment as usual.

When I finished wrapping them I took them through to her bedroom where she proceeded to unwrap them immediately. She had already had some presents and we knew we would be buying her a skateboard when we returned home, so these were just a few bits and pieces. She was very pleased with life and especially happy that she was ten today.

We spent the morning by the swimming pool, playing with the ball and generally splashing about. Indigo's confidence improved very quickly with her new armbands. She now goes in the pool on her own. After a while she took off her armbands and gained enough confidence to swim near the edge of the pool or to me or Eliza. She loves to fling herself into the pool as long as I am there to catch.

At lunch time we went to the television room where we had lunch of fruit and crisps. The Italian family is also here to watch Italy vs South Korea in the World Cup. Italy take the lead in the first few minutes and then settle down to defend their lead. Gradually South Korea become more and more aggressive. They are awarded a penalty which the Italian goal keeper dives and makes a brilliant save. During the second half, South Korea continue to get stronger and stronger with the home crowd behind them until they equalise in the 88th minute much to the chagrin of George and the Italian family. The match goes into extra time with the golden goal rule. Everyone is on tenterhooks and anxious. I am anxious, because everyone in Italy will be happy if Italy win and miserable if they lose. Suddenly, as is always the case with goals, South Korea score and the game is over. The television is unceremoniously switched off.

We need to escape the sudden claustrophobic atmosphere and go for a drive heading off for Lago Trasimeno and Castiglione del Lago. It is hot again today, but we don't care any more. Castiglione del Lago is a very pretty looking town but we don't stop. As we continue doing a circuit of the lake all the views are stunning. The water is very much paler than those we normally see up in the lakes of the deep blues we saw down in Sicily and around Sorrento.

It takes us not much more than an hour to complete the tour, but it was enough. We go back to Madonna della Grazie in time for a long session by the pool before dinner.

George has a specially made burger for dinner and is in heaven. At the end of the meal Maria brings out a birthday cake which she has made. Everyone one sings her happy birthday George is ecstatic with all the attention. As the evening wore on we would go up and talk to the horses.

Day 57
Mileage 4182
Wednesday 19th June 2002
Gubbio

Today we went to Gubbio another mediaeval town to add to our list. Gubbio was quite big compared with San Gimignano, with lots of steps and mediaeval doors and many other thing that could give away its date. The mediaeval doors were huge, oak and heavy with sharp metal suds to stop people breaking in. The steps were carved out of rocks in a circle – almost.

171

After climbing up the almost circular steps to my dismay we had to descend down them again. We found a restaurant just by the steps, where we had a delicious lunch. I had a wonderful scallapine and chips and a portion of spaghetti with pomodoro – tomatoes.

By the time we had our lovely lunch the temperature was 37 – 38 ° C.

We reached the car in the shade. We reached Lago Trasimeano in about half an hour when we got to the beach. There was the worst smell that your nose has ever smelt! Along the water front there were weeds of all kinds growing, there were kids out 20 feet but they were only up to their ankles. So we went back to the Madonna della Grazie.

*

Umbria is laid out before us today and we set off towards Assisi. En route to Perugia, Eliza reads out some things about Assisi which imply that St Francis has been milked for all he is worth by the Catholic Church and the town. Frankly, I don't have the stomach to go and visit another religious cash cow, so we decided to give Assisi a miss. We drive to Perugia. This town has a large urban sprawl, but we head on towards its centre hoping to find its historical roots. Slowly we climb up the hill, but the town looks like any other modern town. We can't even find its centre so we give up and drive on toward Gubbio.

The route to Gubbio takes us through some beautiful scenery along a ridgetop. There continues to be the usual olive groves and up here plenty of bright yellow gorse. It's running hot again outside with temperatures at 37 and 38°C. This time it is easy to find the historical centre, there is no urban sprawl. We wander up to the town and start talking to an English couple who are also on tour. We spend some time getting to know each other, but the focus of the conversation gets drawn towards their daughter who sounds as if she is suffering from ME and/ or Candida symptoms. Eliza tells them about her history and some of the treatments she has undergone.

Climbing further up into the town we find a bar for water, coffee and ice creams. Here we spend the next half hour enjoying each other's company. Afterwards we split up and carry on exploring the town. We go to the Lupo restaurant for lunch for which Eliza had found a very strong recommendation. A bit posh for me, but the anti pasta was definitely worth the drive all the way from Madonna della Grazie.

After lunch it was back towards Lago Trasimeno again. This time we were on some of the more minor roads and again the countryside is beautiful with undulating tree covered hills and gently rolling cornfields, olive groves and vineyards. We see the first sunflowers out for the season. We light heartedly discuss the possibilities of coming out here to live. It is just a pipe dream.

At Castiglione del Lago we parked by the waterfront. Despite its beautiful looks from afar, close up the lake was different. The waterfront was very shallow and stagnant with weeds growing all around the shoreline. Marsh gas bubbled up. There was a group a children splashing around about twenty metres out, but even then they were only up to their ankles. It certainly did not look inviting and even the locals must spurn the lake for swimming as there was a swimming pool just across the road.

We returned to Madonna della Grazie for the pool and dinner.

Day 58
Mileage 4308
Thursday 20th June 2002
Orvieto

Today we went to Orvieto a hill town. To reach it we had to go along winding roads, sharp bends and many tight squeezes.

We went on a tour around some of the caves to escape the heat. In the first cave we saw an olive press driven by an oxen, donkey or horse. We also saw a Tuscan well, which was rectangular rather than a circular one. In the second cave we saw many pigeon roosts where some rich people could come down from their houses and collect a pigeon or two.

After our lunch we went to the Thermal baths. On the way however we past through the dead forest, a forest where all the leaves had fallen off. Then in a flash, a thunder storm was approaching, rain pelting down for all it worth, wind howling like mad trying to blow us off the winding road and at one point it felt the wind was picking us up.

When we finally reached the Thermal Baths the worst of the storm was over but rain was still pouring down but the wind had blown itself out. When all of us had changed, we went to the pool, well it wasn't a pool but a huge bath tub! And it wasn't cold either it was warm.

*

There were some thermal baths nearby at San Casciano del Bagni which Eliza wanted to try. These were only a few kilometres away across the Tuscan border and up in the hills. The roads were white on the map and twisty and sometimes cool under the shade offered by trees. We found the baths and went into see what was what. Eliza and I both decided to have a massage, but would have them consecutively and booked in for the afternoon.

Beyond San Casciano del Bagni lay Orvieto. Again beautiful scenery towards Trevinano. We drove through a forest where the trees were not in leaf. This was very strange and we could not think of a single reason why the forest was not in leaf. In our minds this place became known as the dead forest. We were driving along the crest of some hills through to Allerona and then came down onto the plain. A high railway viaduct stretched from horizon to horizon. The road meandered alongside it and in between its legs. There were towns lying between its legs too, but we saw no place for a station.

Orvieto was perched on the top of a large outcrop, clinging onto the top like a crowned tooth. The Galaxy climbed up to Orvieto and we made our way to the Piazza Duomo – right at the top and the centre of the town. The façade of the Duomo was very spectacular, covered in statuary telling some of the biblical tale of the fall of man and the resurrection of the dead on judgment day. The central door was surrounded by tall columns with very intricate spiral patterns. The sides of the cathedral were layered in black and white brick. Indigo thought it looked like a zebra.

We wanted to go on another subterranean tour as this would take us out of the heat and booked in for one. This gave us enough time for a snack and a (very) brief wander along the streets of the town. While eating our nibbles and drinking our water Indigo started talking to the lady on the next table. It turned out that she was a tourist guide and she was shepherding her party around for a week. We asked her what she thought about Assisi. She told us it was a lovely town, and was much better after the refurbishment work that had been and was still being carried out after the 1997 earthquake. We all said it was too hot again, but that we had heard that the weather was supposed to break today. There was no sign of it happening.

Orvieto is built on top of a volcanic outcrop made up of two materials, tufa rock and volcanic ash. Under the surface of the top town there are 1200 known caves dug into this material. The public tour explored just two of these. They were both very different. The first cave was originally excavated by the Etruscans about 800 BC. It was done with considerable skill and care. The internal ceilings were shaped like the inside eaves of a cottage. The cave was symmetric. In mediaeval times this cave had been extended. You could tell that this extension had been simply hacked crudely out of the rock. Inside the cave there was an old mill and olive press. The technology to crush olives and then press them to extract the juice was basic, simple yet obviously effective.

Further inside the caves there was an area which had simply been used as a quarry. The tufa rock was light yet strong and the ancients found that the volcanic powder could be mixed with lime and water to make a building material similar to concrete and mortar. These caves were a rich source of building material to the early Orvieto inhabitants. More recently however, there have been occasional rock falls and landslips as some of these caves have collapsed, but luckily nothing serious. Since the 1980s work has being going on underground to add support to the caves and to "nail the cliffs together" using long metal spikes up to 40 feet long. We came across a well. The archaeologists say that this well was Etruscan. You could tell an Etruscan well as it is always rectangular and in Orvieto they are always the same size 120cm by 80cm. Roman and Mediaeval wells were always circular. The Etruscans had discovered water 80 metres below the surface and had built these wells in order to access the water. It must have been dark, hot and filthy work digging by hand this far down in such a confined space. Lighting by candle or torches must have been a nightmare for ventilation. I was very impressed by this.

With water available, it meant that the town could become self sufficient for long periods of time as long as they could have enough food to eat.

In the second cave there were a large number of openings covered in pigeon holes – literally – each hole would house two pigeons. These pigeons were free to come and go through openings in the side of the cliff. With access to the outside world, the pigeons were able to feed themselves. These openings also gave very good look out points for the surrounding country. Just in this one cave there was sufficient room for 10,000 pigeons to roost. When the townspeople wanted fresh meat then here was their supply. Entrances to this cave could be seen coming down from the town via a series of steps.

So the Etruscans had their own source of fresh water and fresh meat. When the Romans came north to conquer this part of Italy, they laid siege to Orvieto for more than two years before the town surrendered.

All the other caves are today privately owned and are accessed from street level under private houses. Most of these are thought to be still in use and are individual *crottos* for storing cheese and wines.

Coming out of the caves was like going straight from the fridge to the oven. Inside the temperature stays constant all the year round at about 12°C. Outside it must have been 37 or 38°C. We went for another stroll around the town, this time in search of ice cream. And then it was time to go back to the baths. The roads out of the town seemed half as wide as those coming into the town. It was extremely tight getting round some corners without scrapping paint or stone, but we managed it ok. As we came to the bottom of the town we noticed that the sky had clouded over and there was even the odd spot of rain. We drove back across the plain through the legs of the railway viaduct trying to keep up a fast pace as we were short of time for my appointment. We started to climb up the hills when suddenly the heavens opened. The rain came down with increasing intensity and the road very quickly turned into a river. The outside temperature dropped to 30°C, 28°C, 22°C and finally bottomed out at 19°C, quite an amazing drop within ten minutes. I had to slow right down and at one point I thought I ought to stop, but continued regardless. Eliza and I looked at each other and we both mentioned our luggage, most of it was outside on the terrace at Madonna della Grazie, but sheltered by the walls and the roof. Would it be enough or did we have a catastrophe on our hands? Then the rain abated as fast as it had started as we were driving back through the dead forest.

This was just a respite. Five minutes later either we drove back into the storm or it had caught us up again – it was very difficult to tell which as the roads rewound back on themselves over the hill. George kept on soothing Indigo who by this time was rather frightened. She said there was nothing to worry about and that there was no thunder or lightning. Then there was a bright flash rapidly followed by thunder. Umm. We turned the corner and could see the thermal baths in the distance and we cleared the storm again. At the thermal baths the sky looked threatening and the wind was gusting strongly as we ran for shelter inside.

I went for my massage while the girls went to the swimming pool. Everything inside was clean and clinical. My masseur was a tall and thin lady called Valentina. It must be a very strange job. As the new age music played in the background with the sounds of burbling brooks, twittering birds, gentle harps and wind chimes I could only think that only old, ugly and fat people would come and pay for such treatment and that she probably never got to massage a strong fit and handsome body. It did make me feel totally inadequate. Afterwards, I joined Eliza, George and Indigo in the pool and let Eliza go for hers. There was no sign of the storm, but it was still cloudy and comparatively cool. I wondered weather the whether had actually broken. The waters were very hot and a greenish-brown and were certainly not smelly or unpleasant. Considering that George and Indigo had already been in for an hour, they were still very keen just to loll about in the water and underneath the waterfall and the pressure jets.

Eliza returned looking relaxed and smiling. George told her that daddy always looked sad and never smiled anymore. I vowed to do better.

Today had been a day of celebrity look-a-likes. We had spotted Elton John at the underground caves in Orvieto and then there was David Crosby with a wonderful walrus moustache now working as a car park attendant. The third look-a-like was in the thermal baths. There was a woman who looked the spitting image of Jabba the Hutt. My sympathies went out to Valentina and her colleagues and I suddenly felt a whole lot better about my body.

As we drove down into the valley on the way back to Madonna della Grazie, the clouds evaporated and the temperature began to rise again and reached 35°C by the time we got to Città della Pieve. On this side of the valley everything was bone dry. There had been no cloud, no storm, and no drop in temperature. All our things were safe.

Day 59
Mileage 4389
Friday 21st June 2002
Mount Amiata

I was up and ready to watch England's quarter final with Brazil. Within 25 minutes, England scored. Owen had simply chipped it over the top of the Brazilian goalkeeper. Just before half time a Brazilian player put in a blaster. At half time we played table football, dad won 9-0! After half time Brazil put in another blaster. But England failed to put in another goal.

After the football match we went up mount Amiata which is 1700 meters tall. After a steep walk up a ski run we reached the top of mount Amiata, there before our very eyes was the Italian version of the Eiffel Tower. On the way down the ski run looked like a death trap.

Indigo found loads of ladybirds, about ten million or something like that.

*

George was up to see England play Brazil in the World Cup. She got very excited when her hero – Michael Owen – scored and put England into the lead after 25 minutes. She believed that England could win the world cup. But it did not happen that way. Just before half time Brazil drew level and just after they went into the lead. No matter how much George and the rest of the England fans wished it that would be the final score. George and I played table football in our own little world cup. She played very well as this was her first time on this size table.

The temperature was already hot. We found there were some grottos near by in Mount Cetona which might offer some relief so off we went in search of them. The leaflet and map we had were very vague, but we eventually found a track leading to them. We could not work out whether this track was drivable or was for walking only, so we chickened out. Instead we decided to drive up to Mount Amiata just a few miles further. The road rose steadily as we drove through Cetona, Sareano and Radiofani. It curved its way across the landscape as the Tuscan and Umbrian countryside dropped away. Both parts were very soft and gentle. As we rose higher and crossed to see the view in the other direction, the view dramatically changed. Everywhere was hard rock and looked very barren. There was a lot of gorse growing with its distinctive bright yellow flowers, but the olive groves, vineyards and parchment gold wheat fields were all gone. Rising further we entered woodlands. It seemed the entire forest was spindly chestnut trees. Dappled sunlight crept down through the canopy lighting up tree trunks randomly.

The mountain rose up to over 1700 metres. Near the top was a small collection of restaurants and bars and some ski lifts (closed at this time of the year). It never occurred to me that there would be skiing in Tuscany. The temperature had dropped to a cool 26°C and was definitely a relief from the valley. Motorcyclists and pedal cyclists clustered together in groups. The cars here were mainly Dutch and German. There were very few Italians and we were the only British car.

As we rested here, Indigo discovered that the whole mountainside appeared to be alive with ladybirds and proceeded to collect them by the handful. As we were in the forest, the view was obscured. We could not drive the last couple of hundred metres vertically, but we walked to the viewpoint and the cross on the top. The valley was very hazy today but we could see for what seemed forever. The cross looked like a miniature version of the Eiffel Tower, but the children did not believe we had been suddenly transported into Paris. As this was the highest mountain around, there was also a gaggle of telecommunication transmission equipment near the summit. The ski runs down didn't look too challenging, but I wondered how often they would get snow this far south. I imagined that the locals would make good use of any snow when it fell but that pre-planned trips from the UK would not be worthwhile.

The temperature rose steadily on the way down to the valley and back to Madonna della Grazie reaching 38°C. The swimming pool was a very welcome place.

Day 60
Mileage 4469
Saturday 22nd June 2002
Città del Domenica

Today we went to Città Della Domenica – a zoo. When we arrived we tried to go to the rettilaro – reptile house – but we decided to do this last to cool down because it's very hot outside. So we got our tickets and took a little train ride across swan Lake and guess what? ...we saw turtles! The driver was a clown and she was very funny she laughed and joked with us. I liked her, she liked me.

We went to the Africa Zone where we saw a dismal looking camel, bored looking lions and well anything else you can think of. As weird as it may seem in the Africa Zone we saw sheep being sheared.

We went to find the maneggio – a riding ground, but on the way there we found the witches' forest and her house. Then we found the riding ground, but you didn't ride them properly, you were just put on and taken round by an adult.

We wended our way back through a playground. I had lots of goes on a car and beat mum and dad at races!!!!!!

Then we went to the reptile house. I liked this best because I saw dull looking crocodile – he was bored so he looked dull – poisonous snakes and so on.

*

Indigo was up unusually early this morning and we spent some time exploring the farmyard. There were two very large horses, a bay and a chestnut, who were glad of some company even if it was only us. Down the other end of the farm, were some chickens, ducks and geese all crowded together in a single run. They too looked as if they had been suffering from the heat and had obviously been fighting and pecking each other.

It was time to take the children to a park for them and not for us. They have been very good at following us through all the ruins and sights with only minimal resistance and grumbling. Here was a park with animals and rides and we expected some light relief for us all. It was near Perugia and was about an hour away. I was worried that it might be too hot, but we decided we ought to go.

On arrival the whole place looked deserted. There was an enormous car park and we must have been the fifth car there. In typical Italian style, there was no one about directing anyone; there were no signs as to where to go. We wandered around aimlessly for a few minutes before find a small *ingresso* sign to follow. We paid our money and went right on in. There was a train which went around the park and a zoo in the park. We wanted to take the train to the zoo, but finding out how long we had to wait was impossible. The train went every half an hour, but no one seemed to know how long it was since it last went. And anyway the train didn't go to the zoo. We walked, it was not far and the woodland offered us plenty of shade even so it was still very hot. George spotted a baby fawn wandering around the woodland and indeed we saw several other deer and fawns later on wandering around freely.

The zoo was described as an African experience. Its walkway took us past several enclosures with rather sad looking animals in them. They all had plenty of room to wander around, but they just looked bored. They had pools and water features to play in, but these looked tired and green and half drained. We saw a very dreary looking camel whose coat was half moulted. There were some mountain goats with very long and twisty horns, some zebras, lions, yaks, ostriches, emus, llamas, sheep and so on. The village feel was rounded off with a couple of African style huts with model warriors standing around looking gruff and with drumming and tribal chanting coming out of the huts.

As we left the zoo and walked around in search of the horse riding we came across the Sleeping Beauty Castle and the Wicked Witch's House. The horse riding was simply American style. George was very disappointed and refused to go, as it was an affront to her skills as a horsewoman to be led round a track without any control. Indigo, however liked it. It was expensive especially as Eliza had to do all the work and leading herself. We then found the Pinocchio Village and the Indian Village with the Apache Fort. There were some trampolines and a bouncy castle. George wanted to have a go at the Archery, but it was for adults only. She did have a go on the carts and after one go, both Eliza and I raced her round. Indigo had been very patiently watching and now wanted a go on a little electric boat round a small lake.

We tried to lose them in the Labyrinth, but without success and then we were back at the entrance.

The lady clown who had greeted us on our entrance was pleased to see us. She asked if we had a Ford Galaxy car. We said yes and then the barman handed over the keys. I had left them in the door (Dave 2, Eliza 1). We sat inside and drank, cold water and then more cold water. Although we had enjoyed ourselves, the whole place was rather sad. The park would have been more fun if there had been more children around. The staff told us it was quiet because it was very hot. Everyone would go to the sea or the lake or the mountains on days like this.

Outside the park there was a *Reptilaria*. Here there were crocodiles, iguanas and snakes. Their boredom factor looked even higher than the lions in the zoo. Only a few showed any signs of movement. I think it was a game for them only to move when nobody was looking as often when you looked back they had indeed changed position.

We got back to the car to find it unlocked, but nothing was missing.

This time we decided we ought to go to Assisi after all. It was not far from Perugia as long as we could find our way to the Perugia by pass we would be fine. Assisi was on a hilltop rising suddenly from the wide plain below. You could see the skyline was still full of cranes. The town itself was squeaky clean and reflected its mediaeval image of the home of a saint. It was very much a tourist and pilgrim stopping point. There were bars and restaurant and expensive shops to buy icons, ceramics, toys, wooden gifts and so on. We bought some ice cream and cake – which were both nice. To us Orvieto was a more natural town, as there were shops that residents might actually use.

Casanova
Day 61
Mileage 4559
Sunday 23ʳᵈ June 2002
To Toscana

Today we are moving on but first we went to Citta della Pieve to look at the flower festival. Purple flowers, blue flowers, bright red flowers, light blue flowers and green flowers, every colour you can think of was there somewhere.

We stopped at a small looking place for lunch, it looked small and welcoming. But when we went to our horror it was massive! And we sat down someone gave us a menu and we had to write in what we wanted!

When we arrived at Casanova all I wanted to do was to go in the pool. Swim, swim, swim, swim, splash, splash, splash, splash.

*

Indigo and I went for a swim before breakfast this morning. George joined us after a while after struggling with her journal. Packing up was continually interrupted by chatting and breakfast and trying to keep the children amused.

Eventually we moved on, but first stop was just to Città della Pieve where there was a flower festival (*Infiorata*) today. Last week we had seen all the pictures outlined on the streets and had seen a notice for the flower festival on the Saturday before we arrived, but this date was just for the picking of the flowers. We thought the place would be crowded for parking so we stopped outside the city walls on a spot opposite a garage. The garage had created a bench out of half a dozen brilliant polished, but slightly bent chrome bumpers. We walked up into the town along Via Roma – every town seems to have one. In the middle of the town the main *chiesa* was just emptying its flock onto the *piazza*.

The bars, *gelateria* and *pasticceria* were all buzzing. Down one street all the houses were draped in red and white flags. There was a group of people round each picture who were responsible for adding flowers to the design. The finished designs were printed in colour on a stand next to each outline. They mostly represented different areas of the City and the surrounding district with either a set of symbols such as a castle and a tortoise, or a religious (what else!) scene such as Jesus carrying the cross. Areas around this design were covered with tessellating patterns of squares, stars, crescents and curves. These pictures were still being worked on and flowers were being strewn onto the designs with a good degree of accuracy. There was not much space between the displays and the walls of the buildings. People had to squeeze past each other, taking care not to damage any of the pictures. I don't think that the flowers had been dyed in any way, but had obviously been dried since last week. The yellows and the whites were the brightest, but there were also browns, greens, purples, oranges and reds. There were old men going round with sprays casting fine mist over the works to help keep them in place. I would hate to think how difficult this would be if there were any wind at all. There were about 50 pictures and the whole display was about half a kilometre long. That's an awful lot of flowers.

I could not imagine something like this happening in England. The weather is far too unreliable. But I could imagine the intense rivalry that each team would produce. The English should stick to their village fates or carnival parades.

Later in the day it looked as if these pictures would be judged (on what criteria?). Who would "The Best Display of the Flower Festival 2002" go to? What about the "Innovative use of colour and texture award"? Or "Most consistent use of tessellations without the aid of a template"? What about sabotage? Did this ever happen?

What would happen to all the flowers at the end? The road was closed to traffic, but would open up later. Were the flowers simply left for cars to drive over and the displays left to deteriorate and rot over the days to come? Or were they all carefully swept up by some specialist machine?

We didn't stay to find out and we left the Città to the locals to enjoy their day.

Once across the border to Toscana we followed the direct route to Siena despite the signposts continuing and annoying insistence on directing us back to the autostrada. Near Montecupliano we stopped at a *fattoria* for lunch. It was quite big inside, but Indigo insisted on sitting on the terrace. All the Italians were inside hiding from the intense heat, and all the tourists were outside sweltering. There were mutterings all around us about how hot it was and how lovely it was, but in reality it was uncomfortably hot. It was just that no one wanted to admit it. The *fattoria* had some lovely food, drink and oils to take away and would have been very handy if we were about to load up to go home to England. We just bought some wine for day to day drinking later.

The countryside around here had much less olive and grape and much more wheat than around San Gimignano. The wheat was already being harvested and the sunflowers were beginning to come on strong.

Around five o'clock we arrived at Casanova di Larniano. By then both George and Indigo were desperate to go into the swimming pool. The apartment was relatively cool, but not air-conditioned. There were no mosquitoes here, but there were plenty of flies.

Day 62
Mileage 4666
Monday 24ᵗʰ June 2002
Not Moving

Today we went to Volterra for the supermarket to fill up our stores. Going this way turning all about oh we did look funny.

When we got back we started to unload Posie – the car – almost dragging everything in. As soon as we had completely unloaded the car we changed into our swimming things and made a mad dash for the pool. We stayed in there all day.

When at last it was time to get out we went in merry and hungry. Indigo was so tired that while she was eating her honey sandwich she fell asleep!!!!

*

Lots of sorting out and unpacking went on first thing, as we would be here for three weeks. It took us a while to get out of the house and then we were off to Volterra to find a *supermercato* and buy some supplies.

Volterra is another hill top town and like the Grand old Duke of York we had to go all the way up and then all the way down the other side to find the supermercato. We seemed to spend an age in here – well it was air-conditioned – and spent a good deal of money. By now the children were drooling for food, but when we got back to Casanova they were more interested in getting into the pool than eating. We had asked Cattia whether the apartment had an oven and she had gone out to buy one especially for us. Altogether different treatment from Le Tore. The apartments here were also much more spacious. And we have proper full size showers, but no baths. Eliza and I have an en suite, but just to confuse us we discover that the hot and cold are plumbed in the wrong way round in our bathroom.

All afternoon Eliza is playing washerwoman, while I entertain the children in the pool. I do some household chores in the evening by doing the ironing.

Indigo has done so much swimming in the pool this afternoon that she falls asleep on the sofa half way through a honey sandwich.

Day 63
Mileage 4697
Tuesday 25th June 2002
Pisa

A swim before breakfast started the day off. Cold but refreshed we trooped in for breakfast.

After we got dressed we headed off up north to see the leaning Tower of Pisa. On the way there we saw a mass of brown cows moving in the opposite direction that we were going, but it looked like the cows were coming out of a church! There was a church in the middle of the field don't ask me why!

Still moving steeply north me and Indigo were thinking of Chinese food – home food fantasies and what it would be like to see Flex – our cat – again.

When we arrived at Pisa we saw everything what I called the Marble Square. Everything was the cleanest white you've ever seen, but it wasn't just white because everything was glinting in the sunlight like a white gold sparkling.

After dad (with difficulty) managed to get tickets up the tower, but to my dismay not until 5 o'clock. So mum said, "Why not go on a horse and carriage." So we went on a horse and carriage which I very much enjoyed.

On the ride the driver pointed out the Botanical Gardens which proved shade and nice breeze. It seemed a nice place to stop off and spend time there. We sat under a big umbrella tree according to Indigo. I looked up and saw huge ropes holding up the tree, I hoped the tree would hold out for ½ an hour.

At long last it was time to go up the tower. Excited, me and dad went off saying, "See you at the top of the tower." Walking happily to the tower. When it was time to go up the tower we found it strange because some times you found yourself pushed out to the outer wall and sometimes it pushes you to the inner wall. At the seventh floor we go out and spotted mum and she was waving frantically.

*

An early morning swim before breakfast could become a habit. This is fine by me. After breakfast, we headed off north along the smaller roads of Toscana and drive towards Pisa. As we drive along there is a chapel standing alone on a small hill in the middle of a field. What makes this different is that it is surrounded by about 50 deep brown coloured and horned cows who all appear to be walking away from the chapel at the same time. It looks like the cow service has just finished and they are now all coming out for their *passegiata*. Just like the crowd at Casteldaccia. However, today there was no sign of the priest and no sign of whether the cow/bull priest was robed correctly or had her/his horns removed. The chattering distraction about the cow service somehow made me miss the road to the *superstrada* and we wind up taking the back roads almost all the way to Pisa.

Today it happened. Quite suddenly and out of the blue George said "I would really love a Chinese meal." All of a sudden the children were talking about food fantasies. What they would like to eat when they got home. I've experienced this before on long trips as a student, but that tended to be because we could only afford to eat bread cheese tomatoes and fruit. A nice diet, but it still gets boring after a while. George went on dream like "Nice egg fried rice. Mmmmm. Lovely crispy duck and pancakes. Mmmmm. Baked beans." Indigo started by adding she wanted to have Ribena. I said "Fish and chips and pickled onions." Not that I ever eat those when I'm in England anyway.

At the outskirts of Pisa, there was a plethora of varying signs to the Duomo, Torre Pendant and the Piazza dei Miracoli, all of which are the same place. Sometimes the signs are in white, sometimes in brown and sometimes in yellow. This confusion (but not proliferation) of signs makes it quite hard to navigate and we need both Eliza's and my concentration. This unfortunately, is constantly being broken by George and Indigo wanting things and asking questions. Soon we were at the gate of the Piazza dei Miracoli and through the gate we saw our first view of the leaning tower. All we had to do now was park. The traffic was slow and dense and the temperature was hot. The nearest car park was very expensive so I tried going round some back streets. We found a *supermacato*, which was useful, as we wanted to get some stuff later, and parked there. This was only five minutes from the main square.

My memory of Pisa from the early eighties was that all the major attractions were in this one square. Of course, with any city of this size, there is more to it than one central square. Never mind, we were here as tourists and would not have the time or the strength to explore further. The Basillica, the Cemetery, the Duomo and the Torre were all built with gleaming white marble and they looked radiantly beautiful in today's light. Down one side of the square there was a road, for taxis and bicycles only with a collection of stalls selling postcards, guidebooks, models of the square and the tower. Between all the buildings was verdant green grass where it was absolutely forbidden to walk. On the whole people left the grass alone. All alongside the road was the classic view of the leaning tower. This was also the place where you could pose to make it look as if you were holding the tower up. You could look along here and at any time you could watch half a dozen groups of people standing strangely with their arms and hands bent in odd directions posing.

Further along, at the right angle the tower almost looked straight. I overheard two or three groups complaining that the whole thing was a fraud and that the tower was not leaning at all.

The children were already restless, bored and hot. This year the Torre was open to the public. George desperately wanted to go to the top. Of course it was the most expensive thing to see, but I was surprised that there were not more people on the tower and that there was no queue.

After a light lunch we went to the ticket office to buy some tickets. As we headed that way George and Indigo were leering longingly at the line of horses and carts waiting to whisk tourist off on a tour of the city. We were as resistant as ever. We got to the ticket office and I got into the long queue. I arranged to meet Eliza and the children outside. There are very complex combinations of tickets available depending on what you wanted to see, so although this was adequately explained on a large board in Italian, French, German, Dutch, English and Japanese, the clerk selling tickets seemed to have to explain it individually to everyone in the line. Just as I got to the front of the queue, the cash desk closed. I asked, "Are you closing for lunch?" "No." "Well, what are you closing for?" "Accounting." "How long will you be closed?" "We don't know. Use another ticket office."

Frustrated, I went down the road to the main office opposite the cathedral. Here, there was no queue. But they sold tickets for all the attractions except the Torre. "Go to the ticket office by the Opera Museum" I was told. "But it is closed." "Why is it closed?" "For accounting purposes." "That is no reason to close." "Well they are." "I am sorry, but we do not sell tickets for the Torre from here." "Where can I buy some?" "There is another office the other side of the cathedral."

All very bizarre.

I walked around the cathedral and found the other office. This looked more hopeful, as they were advertising trips up the Torre. The queue was long, but the office was air-conditioned. The queue slowly made its way forward and I could see that the tours up the Torre were every forty minutes or so and that the times were gradually being crossed off. I wondered when we would be able to go up. Children under eight were not allowed up the Torre so it would just be George and me. Two tickets for 17:10. Okay, we had just under three hours to wait.

I hurried off to find Eliza and found them wandering around looking at the stalls. I told them the news. With so much time on our hands we decided to take the horse ride. But it was hot and we needed some cold water. I went into the Bar Duomo and the staff were just unable to see me. Now, I'm not exactly skinny, but somehow they were looking straight through me serving Italians only. I went to another bar across the road and picked up two bottles of water out of the fridge and went to the cash desk. I paid and left. Eliza, George and Indigo were climbing up onto the cab of the first horse. I asked Eliza if she had agreed a price – she had – and I instinctively checked for my wallet. Not there! We called for the driver to stop and I went back to the bar. Some lady said that a waiter had found a wallet. I found the waiter and he had my wallet, but he wanted a reward for finding it. I gave some money, but he wanted more. I gave him some more and got my wallet back. Everything was there alright, but I was furious at the waiter as I suspected he had lifted it in the first place and that this was a routine supplement to his income. Never mind.

Once on board the horse and cart, we moved off in a stately fashion. As soon as we were moving, the circulation of the air brought us relief from the heat. We all enjoyed the ride and I must say it was much better than I had expected. We went around some of the other famous buildings of Pisa and other landmarks that we would not otherwise have seen were pointed out to us: the botanical gardens, the university, the house where Galileo lodged, the students lodging houses. And, across the River Aude, the old Commune Palazzo and some old churches. Indigo was delighted being pulled by a horse, but it was all over too quickly.

We decided to go and look at the Botanical Gardens for a while. The entrance was around the back streets and it was free. The gardens offered shade, but even here there were green houses. We weren't allowed in but we could stand at the entrance and feel the furnace that was inside. Thank you very much but 36°C was ample. The gardens were attached to the University and were used for research so we were quite surprised at how little was actually growing there. There were serried ranks of beds most of which had gone to pot and were just dried up weed beds, but there again, that's what they might have been researching. There were some splendid palm trees which were at least fifty years old rising elegantly and straight into the bright blue sky and some very old examples of plane trees with their peculiar variegated and spotty bark. As we sat under the canopy of one of these trees, I happened to look up and notice that there were a whole series of wires supporting the tree and pulling it in different directions. I just hoped that they were adequate for the next half hour.

We came back to the Piazza dei Miracoli around the back streets and wandered down to the supermercato to do our shopping now rather than later.

Soon enough, it was time for George and I to go up the tower. We left Indigo and Eliza at the Bar Duomo. I hoped that Eliza, as she was definitely more attractive than me, would not remain invisible to the staff. We went to where the tour was assembling. Everyone had to leave all their bags behind in security lockers, but we were allowed to take cameras as long as they weren't in bags. Another classic example of laying down the rules and then finding a way to break them. The tour consisted of escorting us to the Torre, checking our tickets and showing us the entrance.

The entrance was below ground level as it had sunk over the centuries and had been excavated in the 19th century. The tower itself was two marble cylinders with a staircase in between. It was the most peculiar sensation climbing up as the lean sometimes forced you to the outer wall, sometimes the inner wall, sometimes you felt you were falling forward and sometimes backwards. The marble stairs had been eroded over the centuries into the pattern of easiest footfall. Every now and then there was a viewing point to the outside, but this was barred and you couldn't walk around the outside column. This was just as well as there was no guard rail and I am sure that the tourist drop off rate would very quickly kill the attraction. At the seventh level we could get outside where there was a guardrail. It was still extremely eerie and gave a distinct feeling that one was going to fall off the edge. At this level there were seven giant bells whose clangers had been replaced by modern electrically controlled clangers, so I assumed that they must still work. We could see Eliza and Indigo and they spotted us and we waved to each other. We found our way to the top of the eighth level and gazed out over the piazza, the entire city and well beyond. From here, I can look down through the bells and just make out Eliza and Indigo sitting at the bar.

George and I started down and stopped at an opening through which we could see Eliza and Indigo. Eliza appeared to be looking towards us so we waved frantically. No matter what we tried to do we could not attract their attention. Two floors up though, directly above the Bar Duomo, the window was open and a group of nuns had noticed our waving and were now busily waving back. Still Eliza had not noticed us, so we carried on down and out of the Torre and went to meet them directly. Eliza had bought Indigo a model of the Torre to make up for the fact that she couldn't climb the tower. She is so proud to have her own leaning Tower of Pisa and is already very much attached to it.

Getting out of town was almost as bad as getting into town, except that now there were jams everywhere as we merged with the Pisa rush hour. A slow crawl took us out onto the autostrada. Although this was faster than the road we used this morning. In reality there was not a lot to choose between them.

We went back past the cows and their chapel just as they were being recalled into church for their next mass.

Day 64
Mileage 4697
Wednesday 26ᵗʰ June 2002
Semi-Finals

Today I'm allowed to watch the semi-final Turkey vs Brazil. I also watched Harry Potter with my right eye and with my left the semi-final. Final score 1-0 to Brazil.
Afterwards we splashed around in the pool to cool off.

*

Dawn crept up quietly. I was the only one stirring. Even by nine o'clock there was no evidence of life from the bedrooms. The flies in the kitchen were doing their dances around the tables and the curtains. With a quick use of the anti *mosche* spray the flies were soon doing swirling dervishes and break dance routines around the floor.

It was a hot morning and eventually the bodies in the other rooms stirred. Eliza decided that her tan needed a top up and this would be a good day to do it. George and Indigo played and played and then played some more in the pool without any thought of getting tired or bored. Indigo and George made friends and played with two of the Dutch children Carine and Woutek.

George and Indigo came in at lunch time to watch Brazil beat Turkey and they insisted on watching Harry Potter at the same time. One eye on Harry and one on Brazil. Harry Potter certainly was more entertaining.

The rest of the day passed off quietly.

Day 65
Mileage 4775
Thursday 27ᵗʰ June 2002
A Meal With Cattia

*

It was Indigo's half birthday today. She was very proud to be four and a half at last. We gave her a magnetic shape toy which she could use in the Galaxy. She was very happy.

This morning we headed off to see Siena. Although Siena was beginning to sprawl it was very easy to find the way up the hill to the old town we parked in the new underground Duomo car park. The downward ramps seemed very spacious and I thought this must have been designed by an architect who understood how large cars were becoming. But this was an illusion. When we got into the parking spots they were very tight. Everyone had to get out and I took several attempts putting the Galaxy into a spot. I could get out but only just. Then I found I could not get past the wing mirror to join Eliza and the others (I had reversed in). Mmmm. Round the back of the Galaxy, the wall was not quite perpendicular to the Galaxy so I was able to push myself through against wall and bumper. It was lucky that my bum is soft in all the right places.

The car park was still so new that it was clean, no rubbish, no dirt and no oil. But also, all the exit signs led to building sites. Only by climbing the stairs blindly and following the ramps did we emerge into the sunlight. We followed the signs to the Duomo and Il Campo only to find that that both were signed in two opposite directions. We found our way to Il Campo where preparations were already underway for *Il Palio* next week on 2nd July. This meant that the central portion of Il Campo was boarded up and that temporary seating was being constructed around all the outer ring of the piazza. Sand had already been laid on the racetrack. My recollection of Siena was of a beautiful and unspoilt city, but I hadn't expected this. I know that *il Palio* is the most important event in the Siena calendar, but from our perspective the preparation had completely spoilt the town itself.

We had thought long and hard about staying in Siena for *il Palio*, but had decided against it, as it would be impossible to keep the children amused and entertained for long enough during the day itself to be enjoyable. As they were so small it would be impossible for them to be able to see anything unless they were right at the front and then they would have had to be very patient for several hours.

In the museum on *il Campo* we enjoyed the paintings and the artworks. I especially loved the man with the hangover. He reminded me of a party invite from college days showing the effect of Horth's Best Bitter.

Here on the second floor there was a solitary chair by an open window looking down onto *il Campo*. I wondered who would be sitting here next Tuesday and what favours he or she had called in for the right. I couldn't believe that only one person would be here.

After lunch we wandered up to the Duomo. The children just wanted to sit as they complained about the heat. I went inside to have a view. It was similar in style to the duomo at Orvieto in as much as there were alternate layers of black and white bricks. Most of the floor was protected (hidden from the public view) from the ravages of thousands of visitors' footsteps by hardboard. Those that were visible were interesting, but again nothing special that we had not already seen on our travels.

Because our stay in Siena had been so short we decided to drive through Chianti Classico country up to Rhadda and around that area. Once we found the right road we were surprised at how much woodland there was in the area. I thought more would have been cleared for vineyards, but obviously, the vintners' interests were better served by containing their cartel and ensuring that the wine production stays limited.

Up in the hills were some very small *fattorias* selling wines and olive oils at their shop. Even Eliza was astounded at how much they were trying to charge and realised that they were using their own name to up the price. We drove away empty handed and stopped at a small house advertising *miel*. George and Eliza went to do some tasting and came back a few minutes later to say they also sold olive oil and that we had been invited in to taste some Vin Santo and *cantucci* biscuits. I just wanted to go, but it seemed rude so I was dragged indoors. The old farmer and his wife had a smallholding and were proud of their products. The oil looked very green and had the cloudy look of oil from a cold press (good). The bottle was unlabelled but we took it at half the price of the oil up the road. Both Eliza and George had picked the *castagna* honey.

Eliza took her hand at driving as we wended our way back west toward Casanova. The roads were very tortuous, narrow and bendy. On one stretch a four-wheel car was driving round a corned far too fast and clipped our wing mirror. BANG! We were shook up but no real damage; just the glass in the mirror was cracked but still serviceable.

We crossed over the Florence-Siena autostrada and continued cross country. Now the sun was low on the sky and the ripples of the hills in the distance were smearing out with haze.

I was getting queasy from the map reading and the winding drive.

This evening Cattia and family laid on a Tuscan feast for all their guests. Cattia's husband, Livio, and their son Nicco aged 15 were there and Cattia's parents were there too. There were two other Dutch families in residence. One was just two middle aged ladies and the other was a family with three children.

Cattia's family showed us around their apartment inside. It was very well laid out and the main room had a vast fireplace for the winter. Although it gets cold here the temperature only dips below freezing a few times in January or February and there is only occasional snow. The Italians do feel the cold after the summer heat. Originally, the building had been old farm outbuildings and at one time had probably been cattle sheds. They had done a wonderful job on the refurbishment and conversion.

We all mixed together in our seating and talking in a mix of pigeon Italian and pigeon English. The Dutch spoke very good English.

There were vats full of *ribollito* soup – a real Tuscan bean feast. After this there was some pasta with meat sauce. Followed by *crostini* – chicken livers, *tartofu* and tomatoes all separately on toast, Palma ham and melon, fresh and aged *pecorino*. All served with homemade red wine grown from the grapes around the back.

Afterwards there was watermelon and homegrown *albiccoci* and Vin Santo and homebaked *cantucci* biscuits

Indigo was dressed up in her black sparkly dress and silver glittery shoes. She really loves these occasions and spent time talking to everyone. George was wearing her new clothes and although was quite talkative and enjoyed herself she did not circulate like Indigo. She did have rather a large amount of melon of both sorts and I thought she might make herself sick, but didn't.

The evening was very warm, the hospitality generous, the company gregarious and occasion seemed to go on forever.

Day 66
Mileage 4894
Friday 28ᵗʰ June 2002
Fruit Trees

*

Everybody was sleeping late after last night's extravaganza. I decided that we needed some bread and milk and went off in the Galaxy in search of some shops. I didn't want to go to San Gimignano or to Volterra, but drove off on the road towards Pisa. There were some small villages and the odd town, but I did not find a food shop anywhere. After a while I gave up and went back to the apartment. I realised when I got back that I had been driving for just on an hour. It would have been expensive bread and milk.

All were still asleep, so I went for a walk down to where Nicco had said the apricot tree was. Here there was a whole row of fruit trees, not just apricots. There were plums, apples, pears, nespole, cherries, walnut and sharon fruit. The apricot tree was just hanging with fruit, not over ripe just yet but would be soon. I picked some for breakfast.

Later we went off to San Gimignano. Indigo needed a dentist. Although she wasn't in any pain, one of her milk teeth did have a hole in it. Our dentist in England had treated it and said that there was nothing to worry about, but we were concerned. The tourist office helped us to find one but we would need to make an appointment next week. Both George and I needed haircuts and Eliza wanted her legs waxed so we were also pointed in the right direction here. George had a severely short haircut which she thought was brilliant. I had one not quite so short. Eliza's legs had to wait until later in the afternoon. We had lunch and then went up and down the shops. Ice cream on the square and then back to the Galaxy and home.

An hour cooling off in the pool was what George and Indigo needed. Indigo's swimming is still getting better, but she refuses to do a width non-stop. She is getting more confident of going underwater with goggles on and is now trying to sit on the bottom. George just does everything.

Back to San Gimignano and I drop Eliza and the girls off at the hairdressers while I go and check on my e-mail.

Day 67
Mileage 4945
Saturday 29th June 2002
Castelfiorentina

*

We decided just to go around some of the more local towns not on the major tourist trail today.

Before we went off we bumped into Cattia. She gave us a fresh set of linen. I wished her luck with her cleaning today as she had three apartments to clean. I said she would learn to hate Saturdays by the end of the season.

We set off towards Gambassi and drove through Castagno. There was only a bar/restaurant at Castagno which had been recommended by Cattia. In Gambassi there was a small town centre compact, but nothing special. We drove onto Castelfiorentina which is bigger and parked for a look around.

There was a Saturday market round the town and it was busy with Italians. I'm sure there were some other tourists around but they were definitely in the minority. One end of the market was laid out for food including fruit and vegetables, fish, alimentary stalls. There was a *roastecceria* which sold hot meat cooked on the spit including chickens, turkeys, beef and pork as well as various types of potatoes, deep fried vegetables and fried sea-food. Another rival stall was selling whole roast pork. The pig had been boned and rolled and then roasted whole on the spit. He was being sliced up and handed out between slices of bread as a hot sandwich. The head of the pig remained on this roll as the last piece. On the fish stall Indigo was amazed by the whole octopus on display. No way were we going to buy some *sparnocchie* after our Sciacca experience, the rest of the produce on the fish stall looked decidedly dull. Another stall was selling live chickens, chicks and ducklings. Next to this a stall was selling roosters and eggs. I thought that the eggs would have been laid by the chickens and not by the roosters.

The other end of the market was reserved for clothes. Although the Italians do tend to dress up, even to go round the market, the style of clothes on most of these stalls seemed to me either to be aimed at children under two, with amazingly bad frilly dresses and babygrows, or at underwear for the over sixties. There were row upon row of cheap shoe stalls and belt and jewellery stalls. There were some stalls aimed at older children and teenagers, the fashion seems to be for camouflage shorts and trousers and tops – which interested George – or for skimpy tops for girls which were asymmetric and were guaranteed to show off enticing midriffs and belly buttons.

We needed to top up our phone card and found an Omnitel shop. Our phones had been cutting out and we could not work out why. The man in the shop said it was our phone and after some deliberation and dithering we bought a new hand set.

Suddenly it was one o'clock and everywhere was closing. We struggled to find somewhere for lunch and eventually found a *trattoria* with an open door. We peered inside and yet there was no one around. No customers, no waiters, no staff, no one. We called out and after a couple of minutes a lady appeared and invited us in. It was like being invited into someone's sitting room. We were shown to a table, but the family heirlooms were on display. A large dining table with six ornate straight backed oak chairs and a sideboard with extravagantly carved doors and posts. It was hot inside, but there was a fan directly above us hanging motionless. The food was good though and another couple of tables filled up while we were there.

Back outside in the heat the nature of the whole town had changed. The market had packed up and gone, all the shops were shuttered, no one else was on the street, some litter was chasing its own tail as it was blown about in the wind. There was the steady clang clang clang of the automated level crossing indicating the approach of a train. I half expected tumbleweeds to come down the high street and the strains of a solitary harmonica to echo across the piazza.

We found the Galaxy, baking in the sun and drove off. We went back through Montaione chasing some Germans and Dutch cars along the hill tops. This too was another small quiet and currently ghost town. Then back on to Casanova to spend the afternoon enjoying the peace and quiet around the pool.

We decided to go out to Il Castagno for dinner and set off at about half seven. When we had driven past the place earlier it had looked insignificant so we were surprised to find the car park overflowing. The tables outside the restaurant spread over a large area, half were already occupied and the other half were reserved. We got a table inside.

The menu was full of local Tuscan dishes. Our friend Vilia had recommended that we try the *Zuppa di Farro* and the *Chianina Fiorentina* steak. The *Chianina* is a type of cow that is only bred in this area and were probably brown and went to church in the morning. We knew the steak would be expensive and large so we ordered one between us, but it was not on. Eliza had the *Zuppa di Farro*. We both ended up with different varieties of *Cinghiale* – wild boar. This really was the wrong season for these dishes as they were hearty winter dishes. Nevertheless they were thoroughly enjoyable. The father of the family on the next table had ordered an ordinary (not *Chianina*) *Fiorentina* steak and it was massive, but looked super. We resolved to come back again and try one.

Day 68
Mileage 4977
Sunday 30ᵗʰ June 2002
Rain

*

And then it rained.

We had been watching the weather forecasts over the previous week or so wondering when the weather would break. Since our downpour in Orvietto last week there had been no sign of any change here, yet according to the weather forecast the whole of North Italy was having severe thunder storms or the whole of South Italy was experiencing rain, but not here. We heard about the strong monsoons in India, about 2 inches of rain in the Balkans, but not here.

San Gimignano had run out of water and it was being brought in by the tanker load. Even here at Casanova, where they had their own private well, a tanker arrived.

But today it rained.

In the early morning pre-dawn you could here the thunder rumbling. Eliza got up and brought in the drying towels and swimwear. I opened the windows to listen to the noise of the thunder and the patter of raindrops on the ground. George and Indigo slept on.

The children eventually woke and came into our bed. I asked if anyone wanted to go swimming in the rain. They just thought I was nuts. It was now coming down very heavily but with no thunder. I got changed and went into the pool. The hardest part was stepping out of the door straight into a cold shower. The pool felt very warm and the noise that the droplets made on the surface was like the sound of a dozen drums being stroked with wire brushes. There was so much surface splashing that I could not see and had to go and get some goggles. The children watched from the bedroom window convinced I was mad.

When I came back in the children were huddling on our bed under the blankets hiding from me and the storm. They welcomed me under. "You're mad, Dad" said George, "Absolutely bonkers." I freely admitted it but said that being crazy made me more interesting. It was much more fun being mad playing tents with my two children under the blanket and pretending we were hiding from bears.

Nobody wanted to go anywhere today, but one of us needed to go to the *supermercato* in Volterra. After much deliberation I went to do the shopping. We discussed what we needed and George said I would forget unless I had a shopping list. How well my daughter knows me. I set off. The rain had abated by then and I was glad because I had not brought a coat from England. The outside temperature had fallen to 13°C, but started rising again as I headed away from the storm. The rain came and went in patches as I drove towards Volterra. Although everywhere else too had obviously had a drenching, as the road rose the extra height took it above the main, very low, storm clouds that continued to hug the landscape. I drove carefully as the roads looked very slippery.

The *supermercato* was full of foreign visitors trying to find their way around. Even with a list it seems impossible to spend much less than an hour here.

The way back was clear both on the road and in the sky. Water was steaming off the road and the whole atmosphere had changed since the rain had stopped, but became cloudy as I approached home. The television was on when I got back and the World Cup final had already started. So that's why there were no Italians in the store and the staff were so eager to close promptly.

While George watched the football, I started to cook roast lamb. This time we had an oven that worked and I was determined to make the most of it. The only trouble was that the electric circuit was not strong enough to power both the oven and the cooker. Unlike in the UK the electricity standing charge is ranked according to the rating of the circuit. Most Italian holiday homes appear to be rated at 3Kw.

Hardly enough to boil a kettle and for the most part in the summer this is totally adequate, but it does make you conscious of whether all the appliances can be run at once.

It made the cooking of lunch a challenge, but everything was fine. We could even eat outside as the sun had now come out and was burning down.

Brazil beat Germany. Everyone on Thursday evening had expressed sorrow that Italy, Holland and England had been knocked out. But still nobody wanted Germany to win. Everybody wanted Brazil to win.

I changed the beds and spoke to Cattia and Livio through the windows telling her that today it was my turn to work. Cattia was very surprised when I told her later by the pool that I had changed the beds and not Eliza. She was even more astonished that I had cooked lunch as well. She said Livio just does the garden, but inside the house does nothing.

The children played and played, both in the pool and all around, and had a very relaxing day. George struggled to catch up with her journal.

Day 69
Mileage 5008
Monday 1ˢᵗ July 2002
Monteriggioni

We decided that we would go to the dentist today in San Gimignano to get Indigo's tooth fixed up. It took us quite a while to find the dentist because it was somewhere we haven't been before!

When we arrived there it looked very dismal, well, at least the people inside did. We thought it was just a dentist's but it was a doctor's as well. There wasn't a receptionist and nowhere to get an appointment so we just had to wait our turn.

At last it was all done, but Indigo couldn't eat for 2 hours. As mum had promised we went to the toy shop. Indigo got a Polly stretch – a fashion thing. And I got a ball.

Next we went to Monteriggioni, an old castle with a round wall and high turrets all the way round. By now Indigo could eat so we went to find somewhere to eat. We found a restaurant called The Little Castle restaurant, but they were so rude we walked straight out again! So we ended up going to the place across the road.

Before we went we saw the steep hill back exit. Not a very beautiful exit, but one of the steepest hills you've ever seen.

We stopped again at Chianti Classico. A place where only the people of Chianti Classico grow special red grapes to make special Chianti Classico wine. Chianti Classico's residents have put laws down to stop people anywhere growing the special grapes.

Then we went down some very narrow road where (for a change) we got lost but we found our way to the main road anyhow.

*

The hole in Indigo's tooth seemed bigger this week. It still has not been giving her problems, but we are worried about it. The prospect of a four and a half year old with toothache was not an envious one to have. We went to see the dentist recommended to us last week. We found our way to the surgery and was surprised at how full the place was. It was both a dentist's and a doctor's waiting room. There was no reception and we couldn't discern a queuing system so we just sat down along with everyone else. Everyone thought the children were beautiful and charming.

After a while we got to see the dentist and I sat outside with George. Indigo was very good as the dentist checked out her tooth. "She gave it a good pick," said Eliza, "and Indigo was very cooperative." There was obviously no pain in her tooth. The dentist gave her a temporary filling which should last until we got back to England.

For her bravery, we let Indigo choose a toy. She chose a fashion doll with changes of clothes. George got a consolation football and we also got an inflatable boat to play with in the pool.

We went off to see the hill-top town of Monteriggioni. This small hill-top town had not extended beyond its castle walls and was very compact. Inside it was pristine and quiet.

There was a Piazza Roma with some small stone houses, a couple of bars, a couple of tourist shops and that was all. The place was much more restful than some of the other towns we had been to and was off the main tourist trail. In the tourist shop there was a young man who's main occupation seemed to be deciding what music to listen to next. The Doors were busy playing over the CD player.

While we were trying to decide where to have lunch a coach load of Japanese tourists were ceremoniously led across the square from the City gateway and straight into Il Piccolo Castello restaurant. This was the only place that did pasta, but we decided to give it a miss.

We walked to the back gate of the town and looked out at the very steep hill and across the landscape. The cicadas were all out today and making their famous chiic chiic chiic chirrup in all directions.

We went back through the town and down to our Galaxy. The Japanese coach was still there waiting for their load to come down from lunch. I imagined them being escorted in single file down from the town by their guide.

Off we went to Chianti Classico country following yellow and white roads across the map. The white roads were really white roads with stone chippings as their base. Yesterday's rain appeared to have washed the top layer away leaving dried up rivulets across the road. We found ourselves in Vagliagli, where I had stayed once nearly twenty years ago, and stopped to buy some wine from the Aioli Fattoria. We drove on and took a turning; unfortunately, this road was definitely not the road we were expecting to be on. It got narrower and steeper and the stone chippings got larger. It was not nearly as rough as some of the places in Sicily, but this was not right. We found somewhere to turn and came back down again. Although we had a specialist large scale Chianti map, this white road was invisible on the map. We found the right road further on and drove up to Castellini in Chianti where we stopped and bought some more wine.

We drove back to Casanova through Poggibonsi and via San Gimignano.

Back in the pool the children enjoyed the boat, but complained that it had no oars. The Dutch girls thought it was great fun too. There was lots of laughter and splashing.

Day 70
Mileage 5074
Tuesday 2nd July 2002
Vinci & Limoncello

We were out of the house and in the car by nine which was a good sign because we were getting up later and later every day, but today we were up and dressed by 8:45.

Slipping down the back roads only took about an hour. The museum was meant to be open at ten. The town clock struck, dong, dong, dong, dong, dong, dong, dong, dong, dong, dong, the museum hadn't opened mum found a lady and asked her and she said that it would open at 10:15. Another example of an Italian 10 o'clock.

The museum was full of small working models made from five hundred year (old) documents made by Leonardo. Most of his drawings couldn't be made (at that time) because skills and materials were not available. A pure genius.

We went and had lunch on a balcony over looking olive groves. I was suddenly wetten by a sudden shower. I was the only one to get wet. Mum and Indigo were covered by plants and dad was under the canopy.

We went upstairs after lunch to the second museum. In this one you weren't allowed to touch the model. The thing that amazed me most was that Leonardo invented the bike chain and the bike. He also invented the steam paddle boat as it works by the same prncipool. Jesus could walk on water and so could Leonardo, or I think he might be able to, with his big wooden water skis.

*

Gradually our getting up time had been slipping over the weeks, but today we made an effort to get up earlier and we were actually out of the house and in the Galaxy before nine o'clock. We wanted to visit Vinci, a small town to the west of Frienze made famous by Leonardo. The drive up the back roads took about an hour and we got there before the museum had opened.

This museum was full of lots of small models made up from Leonardo drawings. A lot of things Leonardo had only imagined as there was no possibility of manufacturing them at that time. Neither the materials nor the engineering skills had developed sufficiently. His understanding of mechanics, movement and light was quite outstanding. The mere fact that he could conceive of things and design solutions to the problems they brought up centuries before their manufacture was even possible was outstanding.

George particularly liked the device that predicted the phases of the moon. There was a globe painted black on one half and gold on the other. You turned the handle and the phases of the moon would progress from one day to the next through a series of cogs and wheel. It took between 29 and 30 turns of the handle to complete the cycle so it was accurate. It demonstrated not only a good knowledge of astronomy, but also a mind able to calculate the gear ratios needed to translate one turn of a handle into a number between 1/29 and 1/30, and then to draw this accurately enough on paper to enable a working model to be built nearly five hundred years later.

Indigo loved the hall of mirrors, an octagonal room with mirrors on each wall. You went inside and stared at the large numbers of clones of yourself.

Eliza liked the re-designed Archimedes screw and the working striking clock. The poor woman at the ticket office must have been driven crazy by all the tourists forcing the clock to chime.

I liked the working olive presses and the coin minting devices and loved the early chip maker.

This museum was really good because you were allowed to touch and feel the exhibits, making it much more obvious as to how they worked.

We had a little lunch sitting on a balcony overlooking a hill full of olive trees. Our lunch was dampened by a sudden shower. George got the worst of it as Eliza and Indigo were sheltered by some foliage.

There was a second Leonardo da Vinci museum above the first one housed in the tower on top of the hill. Here there were some huge life size models of some of Leonardo's inventions including a glider, a bicycle, a paddle steamer, and a spring driven car amongst other thing. George and Eliza in particular were amazed and fascinated.

A few kilometres further north we came across the house where Leonardo was supposedly born. Going there was probably the nearest us hopeless unbelievers would come to a pilgrimage. The setting was very picturesque in fields and fields of olive groves. These were not just olive groves, but really ancient olive groves. The trees were small and very gnarled. Olive trees were supposed to live for hundreds of years and I just wondered, just wondered if some of these trees had been alive to witness Leonardo's birth. We climbed further up the hill and found a very impressive view-point followed by a very steep narrow hill coming back down again.

This was a marvellous antidote to the dozens of old churches and museums that we had seen. Here was somebody who added to the practicality of life around him both during his own lifetime and for generations to come.

Back at Casanova, George and Indigo headed straight for the pool to play with the Dutch and their boat.

We had bought some lemons and some sugar to go with the neat alcohol we had found in the supermercato. I was going to have a go at making *limoncello*. Today was also the day of *il Palio* in Siena. This was the horse race around *il Campo* run by the competing districts of Siena. Historically, all 17 districts used to compete, but recently this had been reduced to 10 in an effort to lower the fatality rate. This horse race had been an event for several hundred years and takes place twice a year.

We were so glad we did not go. The television showed all the pomp and processions of the horses. It showed all the districts going through their flag waving rituals. This seemed to take forever. Even the television show got bored with the process and kept cutting out to interviews with previous years' winners and showing previous years' races. We would have missed all of this by going there. Of course, negotiations had been going on for weeks and months before hand identifying horses and jockeys, paying bribes, training and god knows what else. The race itself was just the climax of a lot of work and Siennese politics going on behind the scenes for a lot of people. It was an honour to take any sort of part in *il Palio*. None of the jockeys were local. They all had to be kept isolated from each other and from everyone else as it was suspected that they were susceptible to bribery.

Il Palio was such a force in the town that, even now, Siennese members in the armed forces were allowed special leave to attend.

The race itself was due to start at 7:30. The ten horses were ridden by jockeys dressed in the colours of their district. At the starting line the names of the districts were drawn and called out to give the positional order of the horses from the inside position outwards. It was the rôle of the outside horse to start from behind the others and signal the start of the race. The horses were ridden bareback.

I started on my *limoncello*. Here is the part of the recipe that I did today:

> **"Classical Italian Limoncello.**
> **Ingredients:**
> **10 lemon's skins**
> **1 liter of alcool**
> **1 Kilo of white sugar**
> **1 liter of water**
> **1 carafe whit ermetic shutting**
> **Process**
> **Put the 10 lemon's skins whit the 1 liter of alcool in a carafe whit ermetic shutting for 4 days in a dark room."**

It was nice to know that the grocer's apostrophe has managed to be exported. I thought that buying Alcool would be a bit of a problem, but Cattia told me that you can get it in any supermercato and so you can: 95% proof pure *buonogusto alcool* for the making of alcoholic beverages and soaking fruit under alcohol. Easy really.

As I peeled the zest of the lemons (I was told that there should be no pith left), I settled down to watch *il Palio*.

The tactic of the starter horse appeared to be to wait until all the other riders who were jockeying for position to be distracted and then start. When the horses got too restless waiting for the off, they were led back out of the starting positions, walked around to calm them down again and then back for another go. We watched this ritual being carried out three times.

By now I had finished peeling my lemons and the liquid was set to mature.

Then there were two false starts with further time spent walking the horses around and around. The race finally took off at nearly 8:30. The horses sped around the track and it appeared as if the leader would stay that way up to the end, but he was caught and overtaken with about half a lap to go. The winner looked amazed and stunned and was mobbed by the crowd.

I got the distinct feeling about *il Palio*, that it was very much like the Emperor's New Clothes. I am sure that if you were Siennese and you understood the city politics and local rivalry then *il Palio* was extremely important, but to me there was not a lot there. Yes, some fancy flag waving with men dressed up in colourful tights, clothing and wigs. Yes, some horses galloping around in an amazingly dangerous manner reckless to themselves, the horses and, if the barriers were not there, then to the crowd too. Yes, it is an historic tradition that now contributes huge amounts of money on its own right for the town. But, quite honestly, to me as an outsider, what a waste of time.

Day 71
Mileage 5136
Wednesday 3rd July 2002
At Rest

Today we sat around the pool occasionally getting up and going for a swim or having a nice lovely long dip. Jumping in with a splash and soacking everyone around the pool. I was playing with Wolther a 17 year old boy who was Dutch and Indigo with Carine a 14 year old girl.

*

Another long and slow day by the pool after our day trip to Vinci. The children are really enjoying the pool and over the past week have made good friends with the Dutch family's children, the two girls , Carine (14) and Merel (18) and the boy, George's favourite, Woutek (17). No matter how much water gets spilt over them or how many times their inflatable canoes or boats get capsized there seems to be no loss of energy or enthusiasm. The younger girl Carine is very good with Indigo who especially enjoys the individual attention that is lavished upon her. She still doesn't have the confidence to swim a width unaided, but can do most other things. She loves to walk on the bottom under water with goggles on and making faces at you. She thinks this is like walking on the moon with the deliberate, exaggerated and slow movements that astronauts make.

George and Woutek's favourite game is in the pair of canoes, which are now showing signs of wear and tear. Chasing each other and tumbling both in and out of the canoes. Woutek has learnt that he can make quite big waves in the pool by standing in the middle of the pool and plunging the canoe up and down at the right speed. He has found the fundamental resonance frequency of the pool. Everyone finds this extremely funny until the waves threaten to spill over the sides.

We spend a pleasant couple of hours with Be and her husband Ruub sitting in the shade of the umbrella pines, drinking some wine and watching the children play and the grapes grow. We all decide to go to Il Castagno for dinner together on Friday.

We have decided which hotels in Firenze we would like to try and stay in and have to telephone them, but we do not get a signal here. So we decide that we should go to Il Castagno, have some coffee and book our table for tomorrow and ring from there.

Day 72
Mileage 5141
Thursday 4th July 2002
Lucca and Grotta del Vento

Today we went to Lucca a very large city in Tuscana. A long 2 hour drive took us to one of the main car parks which as you can imagine on a Thursday morning it was full. Half an hour took us to another car park next to a castle. Someone left so we went for it. Stretching we all climbed out of our giant car.

We came to many secret passages that all lead "right into Lucca." One of them had a big oak door – most likely – we saw two large iron pins.

On our way to the main square in the town we heard some drums, boom, boom, boom, boom, boom... When we got there there was a big parade or protest going on.

We were on our way through a dark shadowy tunnel and then there was light at the end of the tunnel me and Indigo ran for it. The light was getting nearer and nearer, brighter and brighter, then I found myself in bright sun and it's rays beating down on me. When dad arrived he told me that we were standing in a Greek Amphitheatre. You couldn't tell that it was a Greek Amphitheatre because houses were build on top of the outside ring.

After our trip back through the tunnel dad spotted something that would make my heart jump, if I had seen it. The lantern was dangling down from the roof, it was a Chinese restaurant. It was the best meal I had ever had. For pudding I had Red Bean Cookie! Not what I expected. Red Bean Cookie was not a cookie but pastry with red bean paste.

We went up winding roads to the cave of wind. A little girl about the same age as Indigo discovered the cave of wind when the cave was very small, no bigger than 50cm tall.

The cave of wind had many stalactites some of them miniloins of years old.

We got to a point where we came to a door. When the woman opened the door a cold chill went down my spine, the door she opened stopped the wind coming in and freezing me to death.

When we got out we went to look at the shop, to my amazement none of the things came from here or around.

*

First thing in the morning it was cloudy and gloomy and we thought we were in for an English Wimbledon summer's day, but without the strawberries and cream. We managed to get up and out of the house early again today. We drove off north towards Castelfiorentina and near to Vinci where we went on Tuesday. We pressed on toward Lucca and arrived with the sun intermittently shining through a semi-overcast sky.

We managed to find a parking space under some trees near the San Pietro gate, but we noticed that all the locals were following a path to some hidden corner in the wall. Playing tag, we followed. The path led to an open door and a short, but dark tunnel. Traversing the tunnel we found ourselves in a small grassed courtyard with another entrance on the far side. We went in and climbed some steps to find ourselves on top of the city wall. I knew the wall was supposed to be a wonderful sight, but I had no idea just how wide it was. As we went over the wall and down into the town, I wondered how hard it really was for marauding foreigners to have got in this way.

Along some of the back streets we could hear an incessant drum beat and headed for it to see what was going on. At a small square there was a union march going past with representatives from public unions, workers and pension groups. Lots of red flags were in evidence. Most of the people on this march were in their thirties and forties. No student radicals here.

After the march had passed we wandered along to the Piazza San Michele and found San Michele in Foro. The cathedral façade was truly special with layer upon layer of pastel coloured stones rising into the sky and finally topped with the Archangel Gabrielle spearing a dragon – enough to put St. George to shame. We wandered up Via Fillungo – the main drag. Here were shops which were not stuck into the mediaeval mind set but were in the designer mind set. We passed the clock tower, but the children did not have the enthusiasm for climbing. Off this street was the entrance to an oval open space which used to house a Roman amphitheatre but now houses shops, cafes bars and restaurants.

Lunch was looming and I spotted a Chinese restaurant. After George's outburst on the way to Pisa the other day I thought we ought to satiate their desires. They really wanted crispy Peking duck with pancakes and hoi sin sauce, but they had to compromise. There really was sweet and sour Ravioli on the menu, showing once again that Chinese food adapts to local culinary habits.

Back to the Galaxy we noticed that of all the cars parked in this area under the trees, ours was the only one not in shade. Luckily today was not too hot only about 30 – 32°C. We were going off up to the Garfanganga Valley toward the Grotta del Vento. The change of scenery from the flat plain as we drove up the valley was quite dramatic. Although the mountains were not very high where we were they were completely covered in trees with very few buildings visible up the slopes. The river valley leading up to the grotto was very deep and narrow and had been dammed. The lake behind the dam was very green and inviting. Alongside the lake were two or three villages where the houses clustered along the shoreline. We knew when we arrived because there was a car park. It was quite busy which surprised us as we had not seen any other traffic on the way up or down in the last few kilometres.

There were one, two and three hour tours of the grotto. We opted for the one hour tour, as we did not know how Indigo would cope with the walking. As the group gathered in the entrance there was a palpable sense of anticipation. The Grotta del Vento had two entrances and the temperature difference between the outside and the inside provided the driving force for a wind. In the summer the wind came out of the mountain and in the winter the wind entered the cave. This had been known about for several centuries, but the way in was only discovered when a four year old girl was persuaded by her elder friends to enter the cave above a river.

I'm not sure what happened to the river, but it certainly isn't there now.

There was a door just inside the cave which was kept shut to stop the wind. It was opened to let the tour group in and you could immediately understand the grotto's name. Today was not very hot, but apparently it can blow up to 40kph when it gets very hot outside. Inside the caves there were lots of magnificent features. The speleologists that first opened up the caves in the mid 1960s were stunned by the beauty of the caves. They had left some ladders behind from these early expeditions leading off into chambers that still have not been fully explored. The water dripping down from the roof was more than I expected with a very steady flow. Some of the growths were pure colours and some were striped more like streaky bacon. The caves went up over 35m from the entrance and we followed the route along concrete paths and windy staircases. It was narrow and dank in places, but the route was well laid out and I had no worry about hitting my head. After the rise there was then a steep descent with a drop of about 80m. We were on the short tour, and the top of the rise was the end of our tour. Those on the longer tour headed onwards and we went back the way we had come.

Back down the valley we made a stop by a classic old bridge which had a wonderful asymmetric shape. One of the arches was several times bigger than the others, I assume to let craft with tall masts through. This arch was not central and the bridge had become known as the devil's bridge.

Day 73
Mileage 5309
Friday 5ᵗʰ July 2002
Il Castagno

Mum and dad started to pack as we are moving into where Woltder and his family were staying.

While mum was packing, me, Woltder and Carine made a Leaning Tower of children! I stood with my legs apart Carine went through them and stood up. I was now on Carine shoulders at first it felt strange. Then Woltder went under Carine's open legs and then as quick as lightning shot up into the air holding me on top Carine middle and himself bottom. At first I wobbled and fell off the top. Secondly when I was on top I fell off and felled on top of Carine and she fell off as well. It was terrible funny.

*

The long driving days are taking it out of the children more and more. The allure of the pool and the ability to wake up late was also making an impact. We spent quite a lot of time tidying up today as we were moving apartments, but staying here, tomorrow. George, Woutek and Carine have discovered that they can make a three person high tower in the pool, but this is very unstable and they called it the Leaning Tower of Children.

In the afternoon we went off to Volterra in order to find presents for the Dutch children, Carine, Woutek and Merel who all had enjoyed looking after and playing with George and Indigo. We were looking for some jewellery for the girls, but did not know what to buy Woutek. Eventually George spotted a Formula 1 Ferrari Calendar, the perfect gift for every young man who dreams of owning a Ferrari. Indigo found a necklace for Carine and we also found a small alabaster box for Carine and an alabaster candle holder for Merel.

Indigo rushed back to the Dutch family apartment when we got back. I told her that the presents were a secret and that she mustn't tell. She is such a chatterbox that I doubted there would be any secrets at all.

We had to go and fetch her for showers and to get ready for dinner. As usual Indigo treated going out to dinner as something to do in style. Eliza had found her black dress with a large pink rose on the front. She looked special and knew it. Driving to Il Castagno, Carine came in the Galaxy and George went with the Dutch family.

We were outside tonight at Il Castagno and the temperature had dropped to 22 or 23ºC, but nevertheless it was wonderful to be able to sit outside. Indigo handed out the presents with a great gleeful smile and everyone was very happy. This time we managed to order a *Fiorentina Chiani* Steak between Eliza and I. It was magnificent, in size, colour, texture and flavour. We could not easily choose what Chianti Classico wine we wanted so we just went for the one below the Aiola that we had had last week.

All the children were down the other end of the table enjoying a party of their own. It was lovely to have such a happy gathering tinged with the fact that tomorrow they were leaving. As usual we exchanged addresses. Would we meet again? I don't know.

We went back and the adults shared another bottle of wine as we talked into the night. It was late when we went to bed, but not too late.

Day 74
Mileage 5344
Saturday 6th July 2002
Volterra

It was early in the morning and everything was quiet until a very loud drumming noise could be heard which woke me up with a start. Jumping out of bed I raced into mum's room where the noise was very muffled. The noise was the fly spray (a big machine to kill all the flies).

When I went outside I found that Woltder and his family were gone. But there was another Belgium family had arrived.

Me and dad went to the swimming pool and played football. Then the Belgium boy came in and played too. This was very good fun until I shivered and got out.

*

I got up for a wander around and saw the Dutch family leave, but they did not see me and no word passed between us.

This morning the outsides of the apartments are being sprayed to try and control the flies. We had been warned and all the windows were tightly shut. A large van came round and plagued vast amounts of insecticides over the umbrella palms and around all the other foliage. It does seem rather over the top, but the flies have been getting to us and – no matter how hot it is – the doors and most windows are kept firmly shut. Hopefully, this will make a difference, but I am yet to be convinced.

Moving apartments, even if it is only 20 metres is becoming more tedious as the tour progresses. Eliza does another sterling job with the packing.

Cattia, Livo, Nicco, Nonna and Grandfather are all busy cleaning and gardening the whole complex. Although we have to wait until our new apartment is cleaned before we can move, we still seem to have plenty of things to pack and do.

Eventually we are allowed into the new apartment and Nicco brings the tractor and small trailer around to cart off our baggage. Both George and Indigo love to ride on the back when it is empty. It must go all of two miles per hour, but who cares at least we're riding and not walking. By lunch time we are in the new apartment and I prepare some lunch.

Afterwards, we go to Volterra again. We need to confirm our reservation in Frienze via the internet and deal with any mail. Instead of a cyber café we find a cyber wine bar. So sitting with a terminal and some glasses of very expensive Brunello and pecorino makes a wonderful change.

The world seems to be going on as usual. Corporate America is currently producing the worst scandals and every day more such news seems to hit the streets. Afghanistan is still up there with accidental deaths at wedding parties and the assassination of a vice president. The Middle East rumbles away unnervingly, but the news about Pakistan and India has all but fallen out of view. News from friends continues to dribble in. Everyone says the weather in England has been appalling.

Volterra is full of alabaster and claims to be the alabaster capital of the world. I do love the texture and the transparency of the stone, but know that we do not have the room to keep anything fragile safe in our house. Most of the items on sale are unbelievably ornate to such an extent that they have lost there beauty and become hideous. There are large selections of chessboards, jars – of all sizes, imitation fruit, clocks, lights, plates, small animals, large animals – especially horses or horses heads (did they get that from the Godfather I wonder or was it the other way around?), eggs of all colours, bottle tops, cheese knives, ash trays and goblets. I hope I haven't offended any alabaster artisan by leaving out their particular area of specialism, this was only a fairly generic list!

We check out the Alabaster museum and find even more examples of exquisitely ornate and yet overwhelming hideous objects, but these are on a grand scale and you simply have to admire the delicacy of the artisans touch here. In the museum there are statues and busts and fleetingly I wonder about the sorts of lives the owners of these faces must have had. We find a cupboard full of porcelain teapots (in an alabaster museum?), but these teapots are each with their own stand and room for a candle or oil lamp underneath to keep the tea warm. I think we will stick to the tea cosy when we get home.

Day 75
Mileage 5373
Sunday 7th July 2002
Peccioli Dinosaurs

Today we went to a theme park of prehistoric animals – Parkco Perastorico. Huges modles of terrifying monsters from times long ago. First there was a model of a philosoraptor, then a skull bashing dinosaur (I forgot the real name for it – sorry) and a diplodicos, then a tirsaratops and all sorts of things. The brontosaurus was in the Guinness book of world records!

I was amazed at the real detail and I was surprised that all the models weren't in the book of records. The detail was real, the raptor had its claw that killed it prey. It was baking as much as it was awesome at the theme park!

We stopped at a place for lunch, but just before we sat down for our lunch, dad said, "Look, I think there's a bike race or something like that." And sure enough just as he said that bikes by the hundreds were in front of our eyes! What luck we had just seen the start of the race.

We settled down for lunch at a place where there was a wonderful children's menu. I had a peter pan and so did Indigo. A Peter Pan is made up of three courses; no.1 a small portion of pasta with tomato sauce, no.2 a beef steak with chips. no.3 a portion of ice cream, chocolate or vanilla.

Perfect timing to see the end of the bike race we saw the beginning of before lunch.

Mum said if we had planned it it wouldn't have worked.

I know perfectly well what I'm going to do to finish my day off. I'm going to go into the swimming pool and then have my tea.

*

There was a park nearby full of models of prehistoric creatures. We decided that being Sunday we would avoid the main tourist towns again and headed off once more into the unknown.

Well it was familiar territory to start with, as this was the route we took to Pisa. Today we weren't going so far. We turned off towards Peccioli and climbed into another town. As we entered the town, they were erecting crash barriers along the main street with signs saying *Agripeccioli*. We thought that later they would be having a town festival or something. Just outside the town we found the *parco prestorico* just beyond the Fransican monastery. The park was still and empty, we were the fifth car to arrive. Both George and Indigo ran around from model to model going "Wow" and "Come and look at this" and "This one's just like a real xxx". The models were quite good and their sizes were impressive. The man at the *cassa* had told us that they were real size.

They were all dinosaurs except for a couple of models in the "Grotto" which included a rotating woolly mammoth, some Neanderthal men and a grizzly bear. There was a world map in the grotto showing the range of the various dinosaurs and a chronology of when they lived. I loved the way that the map showed Italy as the biggest bit of the Mediterranean. It was so big that all of the Balkans and Greece had to be removed to make room so that Italy ran right up to the Bosporus.

Next to the Stegosaurus there was a water, tunnel and volcano feature. Our presence triggered the volcano and a large number of different coloured tennis balls were thrown into the air in the crater accompanied by a deep rumbling effect. George thought this was great fun, but Indigo was frightened at first and then just laughed remembering that she had seen a real volcano erupting.

George particularly liked the Velociraptor and the Brontosaurus, which was simply very large, and, we were told, it was in the Guinness book of records – so there!

As we drove out of the park, a pair of bright orange and blue wings dove in front of the Galaxy. Then there was another pair and a third. A whole host of kingfishers were nesting in a sand bank.

Back up to the town it was now a hive of activity, but we did not really understand about what. We managed to find a place to park on the town square and Eliza went to investigate a nearby restaurant. While she was away we could see there was a bicycle race underway. Everyone was standing around watching down the road – waiting in anticipation. We joined them. After a while a car came by with flashing orange lights, then a bit later some police motorcyclists, then some more cars, then after another gap even more cars. All of a sudden a group of about fifty cyclists came round the corner. They weren't going as fast as I would have imagined, but this was near the top of the hill and they were hardly breaking a sweat and all looked relaxed in their rhythm. They were all women. They swept past in less than a minute and then they were gone. They were followed by more cars, more motorcyclists, ambulances and other support vehicles with spare bicycles and wheels. All the cyclists were in one pack; we took that to imply that this was the beginning of the race.

The restaurant was really nice. We were able to sit down in peace and quiet and have a very civilised meal. The children spent most of the time under the table playing with the packs of model dinosaurs that we had bought from the *parco prestorico*.

Back out in the heat and the bright light, the cycle race was still going on. I had thought that the race was just passing through, but it was doing several laps of a circuit. We stood at the top of a wall to watch. A solitary car went past. After another minute a motorcyclist went past, then another and then round the corner came a dozen or so cyclists. Now they looked tired and they were concentrating hard coming up the hill. The crowd offered them water, some was taken. One man insisted on spraying them, and astoundingly loud verbal abuse came rattling back. There was a large gap. A few more cyclists and then lots of cars and motorbikes. A lone cyclist was struggling here and George said, "They're cheating" as she pointed to a hand coming out of the window of a car pushing the cyclist. She was, however, the last one so she probably needed all the help she could get.

All the people watching did not move. There was obviously more to come. Within a minute, the lead car came around followed by some motorcyclists. Three of them were standing up trying to cool down. Then the leading pack came past. A small group of nine, all working hard and sweating, concentrating intensely on the road in front and the cyclists around them. The sudden noise of the swish, swish, swish of their wheels going past and the heavy rhythmic bellow of their lungs pumping rapidly in sudden contrast to the gently purr of the motorcycles and the relaxed look on the faces of their riders. The crowd gave a smattering of applause and cheered to give them encouragement.

The next pack were a minute behind and although they were working hard, the look of hard concentration was not in their faces. After this pack the crowd began to move down the hill. We followed to watch the finish.

The winner's podium and the press block had been put up since we drove into town this morning. There were about twenty guys hanging around with cameras with substantial telephoto lenses, all trying to position themselves for the best shot of the winner coming up the hill and crossing the line. There was one very wide photographer who had the biggest telephoto lens of the lot. His blue sweaty tee shirt barely covered his ample middle while his bulging pockets were full of other lenses and a flashgun. Standing on the podium were two young girls in bikinis and stilettos – Italian eye candy for the winners, but wasn't this a women's race and therefore shouldn't the eye candy be muscle bound men? There was a commentator relating what was happening in the race, but I could not understand a word.

Some cyclists came up the hill struggling and were greeted by the bell at the line. These stragglers continued for some time, probably glad not to suffer the ignominy of being lapped. There was some ragged applause, but the photographers ignored them completely.

The lead car came up the hill so we knew the leaders were on their way. The police outriders came next, all of them standing this time wishing that the chequered flag was for them. The photographers were jostling for position very much like the jockeys at *Il Palio*. The fat man was getting quite agitated by anyone else getting in the way of his lens. The leading bikes came into view as they sprinted up the hill. Lots of shouting and applause encouraged them up the hill. They crossed the line and it was very close, barely a wheel between them. The winner had her arms up in triumph and broke into a wide grin. The woman in second place had eyes black as daggers and her face set in stone.

Within a minute the riders who had finished were all looking very relaxed as if they had hardly broken any sweat. It was likely that this was just a single leg of a bigger race.

When all had finished, the presentations were made. The eye candy handed out flowers, cups and jerseys. There must have been about a dozen presentations made and the usual vigorous shaking of magnums to spray the crowd. Pictures were taken: smiles and poses all round. And then everyone started to dissipate and we went back to the Galaxy. I was amazed at all the hangers-on that were part of the race. Not only were there the press and the photographers, but also the back up vehicles, the team managers, the jury, the dope controllers and so on. I would say that there were at least three times as many camp followers as there were cyclists.

Back home it was time to do something with the *limoncello*. The next part of the recipe reads:

"Process
After 4 days add in the carafe 1 kg of sugar and 1 liter of water and wait the sugar's dissolution; after that mix it all then filter it and bottle the Limoncello"

Well that seemed very easy and it was. Adding the water to the existing liquor turned the clear liquid into the traditional opaque yellow that I expected.

We didn't have any glass bottles, but we did have some spare water bottles. We didn't have any way to funnel the liquor into the narrow neck of the bottle. Oh well, I just ladled it into a small saucepan and poured it. What a very sticky yellow mess, but I filled an entire 2 litre bottle. There was a small glassful left and very tasty it was too.

Day 76
Mileage 5420
Monday 8th July 2002
Big Rides And Jellyfish

Today we were up and out of the house early, because we went to Marina Dicastagneto. It took us an hour and a half to get to Marina Dicastagneto, but in that time the scenery changed so much.

When we arrived I spotted in the distance a huge, blue mass – the sea. I couldn't wait to get there and get into the refreshingly cold water. At last we arrived and now I could see quite clearly the huge mass that stretched as far as the eye could see.

When we reached the beach we plonked down on the soft sand. I changed straight away and went splashing into the water and straight away I got stung. It hurt badly, I staggered along back to shore and when I showed mum where I was stung there were burns.

I started to feel hungry so I asked mum if we could have some lunch. She agreed so we got up and she strode past the rest of the beach. We got in the car and drove a mile or so. We all hopped out and dashed into the restaurant, ordered our food and relaxed with icey cold drinks.

After lunch we went to a park full of allsorts of rides to go on. I think that me and mum went on all the rides in the park! One of my favourite rides was the water jet – clik in the metal bar to keep you in and pull the string to start the ride and you're off.

Up a 10m, 20m, 30m, 40m, 50m, ramp and as soon as you get to the top you are sent zooming down the ramp and onto the water with exstreamly fast.

The other ride I liked was the fantasy Mouse. In a cart you are cranked up a steep ramp and you are thrown about in your carriage.

The ride I liked the most was the water log – going up a ramp and down it twice as fast; going up the big one and going down everybody got wet.

*

The morning came. It was time to go to the Mediterranean coast and go and see the sea. There was an amusement park that we hoped would act as an antidote to all that mediaeval stuff that we've been inflicting on the children. The drive was to Volterra and then we struck out west to Cecina. It was definitely becoming busier now on the roads with plenty of Dutch and German. There were also the odd smattering of Poles, Czechs, French, Swiss and Brit. Down from the hills surrounding Volterra the countryside was far flatter and the road did a zig-zag tango with the railway.

We were going to Marina di Castagneto-Donoratico, what a mouthful, south of Cecina. It looked like a specially built resort. We passed the park on the way to the front it looked like a deserted rather dilapidated adventure playground. I dropped the family near the beach and went off to park the Galaxy. We rendezvoused on the beach. The place reminded me of why I didn't like these types of beach holidays. Rows upon rows of ranks of umbrellas and deck chairs. Battery tourists basting in the sun turning every twenty minutes desperate for a tan. A narrow strip between the end of the umbrellas and the sea itself was devoid of people sitting so we squatted down here laying out our towels. The sea was very calm and still, changing colour from green to deep blue about half a mile out. George eagerly started digging holes as if she had some very important bones to hide. A young man came up to us and mumbled that we could not sit here. I asked why not and was told that this was a private beach. I asked how much it cost to hire an umbrella and chairs and was told 20 Euro. As we only planned to stay a couple of hours this was extortionate. I asked where we could sit and he pointed up the shore to the free beach. We wandered down a couple of hundred metres to the end of the private beach. The next private beach started about twenty metres on. For squatting it all looked the same.

In the sea off the private beaches there were posts no more than ten metres out which marked the area of "Safe Water". As these beaches had life guards on duty I assume their liability would finish along this line. Where we sat there was a single post which simply said "*Peroclosi*" – no life guard.

The water was warm and shallow and even Indigo could stand up for quite some way out. We enjoyed floating on the waves and made pretend that these were a lot higher and more dangerous than in actuality.

When it got too hot we came off the beach and went back inland to the Galaxy, had a snack and drove to the park. The park was almost deserted, but definitely looked more fun than Città della Domenica in Umbria. We took the train (an electric road vehicle done up to look like a 19th century wild west steam locomotive) to the main attractions. There were some good water rides and as all rides were free and there were no queues we were kept busy all afternoon.

The Colorado River featured floating logs racing down large rapids.

Eliza managed to get soaked on this ride, but miraculously nobody else did. We changed places in the boat for the second trip and again Eliza got soaked and everyone else escaped. George and Indigo got their faces painted: a tiger and a butterfly.

We discovered a roller coaster. I have never liked roller coasters, but I knew I would be letting the side down if I did not go on it. We all went and then I remembered why I hated these things. I got off and let the others go around again, and again. We did lots of everything. Most of the rides you had to set going yourself and were completely unattended which surprised me.

Outside the park was an aquarium with some good specimens. There were large eels, lots of camouflaged fish disguised as rocks, plants and sand, small rock life such as shrimps and mussels, some piranhas and other colourful flesh eating fish.

We drove back to Volterra as dusk was falling. The countryside was littered with the lengthening shadows from row upon row of tall pointed cypress trees. A soft orange blanket overlaid the ripe corn fields. As we climbed up to Volterra the set sun was forced to rise again. We saw three or four successive sunsets this way all from different viewpoints. It was almost dark when we got home and we had to carry two children asleep to bed.

Day 77
Mileage 5519
Tuesday 9th July 2002
San Gimignano

*

The children didn't want to wake up at all this morning, but we needed to get some general food shopping and decided to go to Sam Gimignano. By the time we got there, it was already nearly midday and I wanted to go to check on any news from home.

We walked up and down the main shopping street looking for souvenirs and presents. I bought a couple of bottle stoppers for my *limoncello* amongst other bits and pieces. *Bruschetta* and white wine for lunch was very refreshing and tasty. Indigo, followed by George, spent half an hour chatting to some English people on the next table.

We went for some ice cream and then went off to do some food shopping. I went off to fetch the Galaxy and Eliza took the children by foot. I was surprised that I got to the supermercato first and even more surprised that they took nearly another half hour! Finding the supermercato was obviously not easy.

Back at the Casanova, the children went into the pool and made friends with the two English girls, Lotti and Rio and a Belgium boy. We watched them playing as the afternoon went on enjoying the rustling songs of the trees and vines. Swifts queued up on the telephone lines that stretched across the vineyard and took turns in swooping over the pool just low enough to catch some water.

I transferred my *limoncello* to two clean wine bottles and corked them proudly with my new stoppers. Eliza soon told Cattia that I had bottled my *limoncello* and soon after Cattia had tasted it and approved of it, all the family started dropping round for a taste. I was surprised myself at how good it was for a first attempt and they all said they were impressed.

Day 78
Mileage 5529
Wednesday 10ᵗʰ July 2002
Market Day

Today we had breakfast in the car because we were going to Siena for market day.

It took us a while to find the market and on the way we found a McDonalds.

The market was huge. We could easily get lost in this mass! Most of the stalls were clothes stalls! If I was a S and E this would be a great place to buy nice clothes for cheap prices. Indigo got a blue flower dress, half an hour later I got red Hawaiian shorts – at last I got my hands on something Hawaiian!

Just before lunch I got this wild stinging pain in my ear. Painfully I got up and told mum. She too stood up and told dad that we were going to a farmacia. When we got there guess what? It was closed! Luckily there was another one down the road when we got there the nurse gave me some drops to put in my ear. It seemed to work rather well because pretty soon after mum put it in it worked.

We trod our way back to McDonalds. Sitting on the table was a warm bag with six chicken nuggets a box of chips and a large drink. I ate ravenously until there was not a chrum left.

*

Cattia and her son were flying off to London today to see Nicco's doctor in Harley Street. He had had an operation two years ago on his back and was just going for a check up.

Cattia had told us that there was a large market at Siena. Despite trying to leave early, it was gone 10 by the time we left. This time, I dropped the family at Porto Marco and left them at a small playground while I drove down the hillside to find a parking spot and walked back up the hill.

We wandered into the walled city via a different route than before, following our noses towards *il Campo*. The symbols of the different districts were easier to spot today, but the flags had all been removed. This time, *il Campo* was cleared of sand, barriers and extra seating. The natural beauty of the piazza was suddenly clear and its classic scallop shape there to be seen and enjoyed. The whole town was alive and no longer focussed on a single event. The Italians and tourists mingled together as the town got on with the business of living.

The market was over the other side of the town near the fort. The route we took there went along the main shopping streets of the town. It was easy to find the market, just follow the crowds. This market was colourful and typical Italian, but just a lot bigger. We stopped for some *porchetta* in a *panini* with some *crusto*.

There must have been a couple of hundred different stalls, but the numbers of stalls did not reflect the variety of goods available. About three quarters of the stalls were cheap and cheerful clothes, shoes and leather stalls while the rest were mostly fabric stalls with a smattering of food stalls: *maceleria, frommaggi, roasteceria, salumeria, ottofruita* and *venduria*. George fancied some camouflage shirts and/or shorts, but couldn't find any that would fit and were to her taste. She settled instead for some bright red Hawaiian shorts.

George and Indigo were finally treated to a MacDonalds just near the market. A slow walk back in the heat via some more shops to the playground and then a drive back to Casanova.

Day 79
Mileage 5590
Thursday 11ᵗʰ July 2002
The Marble Mountain

Today we went to the Marble Top Mountains. It took us two hours to get there, when we got there we went out to stretch our legs and guess what? It was like walking on the moon!

From where I was you could see all the different types of marble that had formed there thousands of years ago. Do you know what makes marble different colours? No? Well, its different types of minerals. In mum's opinion she said that was more spectacular than some of the churches we've seen, and some of the churches we've seen are spectacular.

We wondered around looking at the way people in roman times used to get and transport the marble. Even Michelangelo went there to choose the marble for David his masterpiece.

After a while we went into the shops and me and Indigo both got nine marbles. Eight small ones and one bigger one. In other words we bought marble marbles!

We had another long dose in the car to get back, but the thought of the pool made me feel better.

After a couple of hours in the pool me, Rio and Lotty got out to get ready to go out to dinner.

*

We had read about Michelangelo travelling up to the mountains to pick marble for his statues and had heard that the mountains were simply dripping with marble. His statue David was made out of Carrara marble. I had thought that David had been made out of a block of marble chosen personally by Michelangelo, but it was sculpted from a block left over by another artist who had started work on the block but never completed it. David was carved out of a second-hand block!

We set off to find them. Carrera is north of Pisa going towards Genova. We were much more successful in finding the right roads towards Pisa, familiarity helping with geography and navigation. Once we arrived at Carrera we had to find the marble museum at the quarry at the top of the mountain. Driving round the town we suddenly saw the wondrous sight of the marble mountains. Great swathes had been carved away, making the whole area barren but bright white in the sunshine and sparkling.

The landscape became more spooky and unreal as we climbed. We found the museum and parked. My sandals settled into a centimetre of soft white marble dust as I stepped out of the Galaxy. Lorries were going past carrying vast single blocks or a small number of still large blocks. You could see the lorries coming down the mountain in a convoy, tackling the steep slopes and hairpin bends with a steady very professional manner.

On display in the museum were the tools that had been used since Roman times apparently right up to the middle of the eighteenth century. Tools for drilling holes in the mountain and for cutting blocks with wire, sand and water.

A pair of marble oxen were kitted out showing how they were used to pull blocks of marble.

A miner's cottage had been mocked up showing how they might have lived. A single room was enough for a whole family, with a double bed for two adults and three children all sleeping together. Certainly this would have been a sufficient contraceptive. There were some children's toys there including two pieces of wire shaped into spring clips which could be used to shoot small stones, like a catapult, and a small wooden cylinder that could be used to squirt water several metres. A selection of hand tools was also on show in the cottage. Without all of today's luxuries such as air conditioning and running water, it must have been a tough life.

There were some old photographs showing a team of eighteen pairs of oxen pulling a single marble block. This same block was shown pictured on board a train for delivery down to the port at Carrera. Most blocks appeared to be pulled by a single pair of oxen so 18 pairs emphasised the enormity of this particular load. The trains used to run across a pair of ornate viaducts. These bridges were still there and the entrances into the mountains could still be seen. It was difficult to tell if these routes were still used or were now just scars etched into the landscape.

Just up the mountain road you could see into one of the sides of the open quarry. A large collection of blocks had been hewn out ready for loading and transportation. The mountainside looked like a natural cathedral – magnificent in hue, awesome in size and glorious in natural sunlight – without any of the religious trappings of all the man-made cathedrals down in the cities.

I felt that this landscape was very different, but also very similar to that up Mount Etna. This time the landscape was white rather than black. Here the rock faces showed there was smoothness, whereas Etna was always craggy. The marble stone were very dense and heavy, but the black volcanic ash was full of air and light as sponge cake. Etna was totally barren, but Carrera had some vegetation. Etna was covered with a swirling mist which made the whole place eerie and quite, whereas here the bright sun and brilliant blue sky were accompanied by the constant sound of men working and the drone of lorries taking the mountain away piece by piece.

Back in the museum there was also a gift shop and we decided to buy some slabs of marble to take home to make into a tabletop or two.

We drove back down and followed the coast road for a while. The sea was very inviting and blue, sparkling through the trees and beyond the sand, but the march of the umbrellas and sunbeds was ubiquitous with red, blue or white the favourite colours. Surprisingly, even though this was the middle of July, the vast majority of these beds were empty and so the beaches looked relatively quiet. High season had still not reached here, but in August, I am sure that every spare square centimetre will be sold off to an Italian, Brit, Dutch, German, Belgium or other white European seeking sunshine and sea for solace during a two week break from their daily toil. I'm also sure that the great majority of these people would have a really good time, but this would not be for us.

We drove back to the Casanova and, as driver, I could see the leaning tower of Pisa and the Duomo. We listened to a lot of Harry Potter on tape on the way back to keep the children amused. It kept the adults amused too.

We went to Il Castagno for the third time tonight with the English family and again had another great meal.

Day 80
Mileage 5770
Friday 12ᵗʰ July 2002
Volterra

*

A lot of today was spent in packing and washing, making sure everything was put away for tomorrow's drive. The children either slept or played, making the most of the swimming pool and of the Tuscan sun.

In the afternoon, I took them off to Volterra for some quite time and to try and buy my niece, Sue, a small present. We approached Volterra from a different direction than normal and were rewarded with a great view to the west over the soft landscape. The wheat had almost all been harvested by now and the land was scattered with large circular bales of hay. Some farms still had the more traditional rectilinear shaped hay bales, but these were few and far between. I thought about how much fun it would be to roll all these bales down hill and wondered whether bale rolling could ever become a traditional harvest festival sport.

We nosed around several shops looking for the perfect gift. No such thing for anyone. Indigo and George were particular helpful and picked out several items. We chose one from three or four shops to keep in mind on the way back. I was also on the look out for some wine for Eliza, but could not find it anywhere and decided to go upmarket and buy some Brunello. It was cheap for Brunello but amazingly expensive for anything else.

As a treat, we sat in a bar and had some gelato. I watched the tourists and the Italians wander up and down simply enjoying the town and the cool its shade offered. We bought Sue a white and grey alabaster sphere that opened up to give a hollow dish – George's choice.

We drove back the way we normally approached Volterra, down the winding roads to the plain for the last time. The roads had definitely become familiar over the last three weeks and it felt sad knowing that we were leaving this landscape behind. However, it was definitely time to move on and not get stuck in the Tuscan rut. The landscape had become so soft to our eyes that we longed for the more challenging vistas of the mountains. We could very easily understand why Northern Europeans get drawn here. It is a place full of pleasurable things, good food and wine, beautiful landscape and weather, artefacts and history. You could spend a lifetime simply exploring and understanding the area and its history. There is no need to move into the future and when you are so comfortably cocooned in the past, there is very little to bring you back into the present.

The English in particular buy property here, whereas other foreigners who want to stay a long time simply rent. The Italians can't understand why the English buy property and then leave it empty for most of the year. For the Italians property is not an investment. The value of property if anything tends to drift downwards over time.

This evening we shared another meal with Cattia and her family. Eliza had struck up a real friendship with them and I think they will remain in touch. Their son Nicco hopes to come to England to study English, we might see him again.

Cattia runs the business on a day-to-day basis as well as having a full time job as a clerk in Poggibonsi, but her father, Vasco, is the big boss – *il grande capo*. Livio is a furniture salesman which takes him all around the region.

Their trip to London had been successful, but London was very cold. Everyone we had been in touch with in England had said that this summer had been unremittingly cold, dull and wet. Whenever we caught the weather forecast we saw that the London temperature was stubbornly stuck at between 18 and 25°C. Once it had ventured up to 26.

The evening finishes with everyone drinking my *limoncello*. I am told I must make and sell it when I get back to England, but it would be fraught with so many problems and regulations that to do so was totally impractical.

Frienze
Day 81
Mileage 5801
Saturday 13th July 2002
To Frienze

*

Packing the Galaxy was the chore of the morning. Although most of the work had already been done yesterday, it still seemed to take a long time to get everything loaded. After three weeks, it was surprising just how much rubbish we had accumulated and we threw out an amazing volume.

Trying to keep George and Indigo amused all this time was quite hard work. Trying to stop Indigo unpacking boxes that we had already shut was even harder work. Both Indigo and George did spend a bit of time with Lottie and Rio next door. They found a lost nestling of a bird and eventually picked it up and released it in the trees beyond the terrace. Indigo later spent time trying to find it again, but luckily the bird had hidden successfully. Whether it survived who knows.

This time an Italian 10 o'clock worked in our favour and we were ready to leave by 11. There were only two changeovers today so Cattia was not frantically at the bit trying to get into our apartment to clean. We all said our goodbyes, Nicco and Livio cleaning the pool, Grandad Vasco over the fence tending the vines and last of all Cattia shook our hands smiling broadly. We thanked her for everything wished her luck for the rest of the season and then we left.

We were going to drive to Frienze through the back road via Castelfiorentina and over the hills into the city. It turned out to be a great decision as these roads were practically empty and the scenery continued to be gently rolling in the usual Tuscan manner right up to the last minute. As we came across one hill we suddenly saw Frienze at last spread before us. The Duomo and the Campanile were the two obvious landmarks. Although this was a city it was fairly compact and you see it all in one go in complete contrast to Roma which sprawled beyond the horizon even from the top of San Pietro.

We drove to Piazza Michelangelo with its grand view over the city. I remember coming here on my last trip to Frienze nearly forty years ago on a day trip with my parents. I don't remember much else except this view.

We followed the signs to *centro* and found our way surprisingly easily to the Hotel Casci. I had never before stayed at a hotel which was just on the second floor of a building. We were all in one room, but it was clean cool and had a bath. We took out the bags we needed and handed over the Galaxy keys for parking. Wonderful, we would not drive again for five days.

After settling down we walked the short distance down Via Cavour, stopping off for ice cream at almost the first possible opportunity as the children were wailing desperately, and then came right to the front of the Duomo. It was very wedding cake, decorated principally in white, pale green and a soft rose marble. The dome itself was stunning with it bright terracotta orange tiles with six ridge sections in white. The top was crowned by the *laterna* which let light into the roof of the cathedral and a single golden orb on the apex.

Also in the Piazza del Duomo were the octagonal Battistero and the Campanile tower. Both were in keeping with the style of the cathedral, especially the Campanile.

We wandered further south and came to the Piazza dei Signoria, dominated by the Palazzo Vecchio and the Loggia dei Lanzi. Here the piazza was simply littered with sculptures including a reproduction of David who used to stand here, but was moved to the Galleria dell'Accademia in 1908. The two wings of the Uffizi stood before us and we strolled between them. Here were a variety of street artists and painters and hawkers selling their wares. We saw a gold Egyptian mummy standing still and only moving occasionally exactly like his friend in Piazza Nuvona in Roma. Indigo thought it actually was the same person. There were two men in gold both with very large gold sun masks and a wicker chair to allow you to pose as king, queen or princess for a moment for a euro a go raking in a fortune. Another photo opportunity was laid out in the form of pictures of some of the famous pieces of artwork with the faces removed allowing you to pose.

Looking back from here up towards the Piazza dei Signoria you got a wonderful view of David and Neptune in profile. They made a beautiful pair standing in the golden afternoon sunlight. I wondered how much of Frienze's history had been played out under their feet within their sight or within their earshot. It was perfect that they should dominate this Piazza.

Down to the Fiume Arno and then we could look across at the Ponte Vecchio. On the bridge all the shops were jewellers. The place was simply dripping with gold and silver and gems. Lots of people were looking in the windows, but the shops themselves were empty. It had not always been this way and originally the shops sold produce. The butchers' shops were supposedly the worst and really stank. Above the bridge there ran a corridor, which connected the Palazzo Vecchio to the Pitti Palace going through peoples private houses. It was when this was built that a decree was laid down banning the butchers' shops and turning all shops on the Ponte Vecchio into goldsmiths and jewellers – at least these didn't smell.

It was now very hot again and Indigo was beginning to whinge for shade. We decided to go back to the hotel and chill out for a while before going for dinner just round the corner to a lively street where we could sit outside and watch the crowds on their *passigiata*. The food was very disappointing, but the children's pizza was good. Afterwards we joined in the flow of people and wandered across the city centre down past the Duomo and found an ice cream shop to satiate our desires. This one did chocolate and orange as a single flavour which instantly become our favourite.

Day 82
Mileage 5842
Sunday 14ᵗʰ July 2002
Uffizi

Today we went to the childrens museo. The men in the playroom told me to think of something I really wanted and I said a skateboard. I made my skateboard out of two pieces of cardboard together with a stick in the middle and then 3 levels of packing tape with corks as the wheels and my emblem in the middle.

Afterwards we had a lunch which was far from lovely, but some horrible lumpy stuff and mum made me eat it all! Yeck!

We arrived at a tour guide's house for a tour to the Uffizzi art gallery. I learnt that a gold background means that the scene is set in heaven, and all the people that are meant to be in heaven wears a gold halo. The girl who took us knew a lot about art. The pictures were all very beautiful to look at.

After a while we decided to go out for dinner. We found a very good pizza place and we loved the pizza to bits.

*

We wanted to avoid all the queues that we knew built up around the museums, and we also thought it would be good for us if we had a guide to take us round. The hotel had handfuls of leaflets advertising tours by foot and by bike and advertising day trips to other parts of Toscana. We had had our fill of Toscana and there was no way we were going to do a bike tour so we were left with just a couple of agencies. We decided to try the Walking Tours of Florence Company which seemed to do some interesting and specific tours and so we booked on the Uffizi tour for the afternoon. Most of the art galleries and museums were closed on Mondays and we wanted to ensure we did something today.

Eliza had read about the children's museum in the Palazzo Vecchio and we decided to give the children a museum antidote before we started. After breakfast we walked down to the Palazzo Vecchio to find out more. We had to pass through security control on entering the building into an internal courtyard. George loved the little fountain in the middle and I loved the amazing detailed faces and vines climbing up the four columns. We found the ticket office, but there was no sigh of children's museum. We asked once we had got to the front of the queue and were sent elsewhere. Eliza managed to find someone who thought they knew something about it but their English and Eliza's Italian left us very much in the dark. We found out that there was a young man who ran some activities and he was happy to run a workshop for us there and then, but we first had to buy tickets at the ticket office. They gave us a special form to show the ticket office what sort of ticket we needed. All very Italian in its total confusion.

We were taken to a playroom where there were lots of toys and models which had been made by other students. George and Indigo were going to make a toy. This is certainly not what I had came to Frienze to do, but the children enjoyed being able to play as children and mess about with oddments and paint and glue to make something. Indigo spent her time making a doll out of an old water bottle and old clothes while George wanted to make a skateboard. She wanted to make a real useable one, but in the end realised she could only make a model, as even the strongest cardboard would not be able to support her weight.

Our tour around the Uffizi was at one fifteen and we found ourselves in an awful rush trying to grab a snack for lunch. We decided to try a self-service restaurant on the Piazza dei Signora which looked inviting. We were disappointed with food and surprised at the high cost. We had a miserable time trying to force feed George who had insisted that she wanted a whole portion of pasta rather than just sharing a portion. Oh the woes of parenthood!

Just round the corner we went to pay for our tour and meet our guide, Catherine. There were about ten other people on the tour so it was quite intimate. We walked to the "tour" entrance to the Uffizi and joined the short queue to get in. Unfortunately we had arrived just a few seconds after a large youth orchestra from Oz stepped into the queue. This delayed our entrance for quite sometime as they all had backpacks and each and every one of them had to be opened for security. Never mind.

The picture galleries were on the fourth floor. They had started off as just one room in the Medici's offices and had gradually spread. At the demise of the last Medici, their entire art collection was left to the city of Frienze on condition that the artworks never left town. The entire ceiling of the two corridors were painted with friezes, each ceiling panel was different and each contained five red and one blue ball as a clue to the Medici's coat of arms. You could have made a study of each of these panels if there were enough time and if the crick in your neck allowed you to. The corridor also contained statues and portraits of family members and the rich and famous who were known to the Medici. All very imposing. The tour was focusing on the progress of Florentine art through the period leading up to and through the renaissance.

Catherine was very interesting and obviously knew her art history. I have only got a fraction of what we saw and heard, but I hope this gives a flavour.

She talked us through some of the symbolism that was used on the paintings. Each painting had a story to tell and most individuals who saw the pictures were illiterate and used symbols to read the pictures.

Here a gold background was used to signify that the setting was in Heaven and not on Earth. People who were in Heaven always had halos, whereas those who weren't or who may not have been did not.

In the pre-renaissance works, the people in the picture were all the same size except for the central characters, so the Madonna looked larger than life and baby Jesus was always a large baby (but because he was a baby he was never the largest person in the picture). All other faces in the pictures were looking around vacantly in different directions as if trying to work out what their purpose was. A lot of faces looked the same and they were often stylised in a fairly simple manner.

There was often no sky or landscapes in these pictures and faces were stacked one on top of the others to the top of the frame. Halos were also shown as solid gold circles, later halos were shown as simple gold circles and these became elliptical when shown from different angles.

Specific saints were always shown with a specific object or item of clothing to help identify them. John the Baptist was shown carrying a cross on a long stick over his shoulder and normally wearing rags or animal cloths.

Later works showed the faces in the picture taking an active interest in the central action of the picture drawing your eye to it. Later still, there were figures making eye contact with the viewer. These tended to be either a self-portrait of the artist themselves or a portrait of the patron who commissioned and was paying for the work. These two figures never had halos!

At this time perspective was beginning to show in pictures as figures became more lifelike and smaller over distance. Some pictures were still "stacked" to the top of the frame with no thought for skyline or horizons.

We saw the famous pictures of Duchess Battista Sforza and her husband Federico. They were posed in complete profile, an innovation in itself, the man had lost his right eye in battle and therefore presented his left (best) side only to the viewer. The details in his face were now being painted as realistically as possible including his warts and the nick in his nose. Nobody knows how his nose became this shape; one theory states that it happened at the same time as he lost his eye, another states that it was deliberate mutilation in order that he could gain some peripheral vision on his right hand side. His wife was shown as being very pale. Pale faces were very popular with the aristocracy at the time as to have been exposed to the sun was what the peasants and workers did. But for this lady, she was pale because she was actually painted when she was dead. She had died suddenly at 26 after the birth of her ninth child, but I don't know if she died because of childbirth. The painting was done from a plaster death mask and hence there were no eyebrows. The line of the death mask was also quite visible.

High foreheads were taken as a sign of intelligence at the time and her hair had been plucked quite far back. Blondes were especially in vogue too and this was achieved by dying the hair in urine with the ammonia acting as bleach. We heard the same story in Pompeii where they used urine in the laundry nearly two thousand years earlier.

Botticelli's Venus and Primavera were very special. These pictures had been found accidentally between fifty and a hundred years after they were painted in one of the Medici's private residences and no documentation was found to describe them. So art historians have had a field day with these pictures trying to interpret the figures on them and who they are and what it means. There are at least three competing theories regarding the Primavera picture all of which are plausible to me as a simple laymen, but the most intriguing to me is one that has all the figures from ancient Greek and Roman mythology except for one who represents the Madonna and that this picture hung in the private Medici residence as a conversation piece to help extricate and bring out people's political persuasions (you're either with us or against us).

Michelangelo's pictures were also quite stunning although I hadn't realised that he had only done a few. The medium he loved was sculpture.

In one picture where the work was split between Michelangelo and his Maestro, the faces of the figures painted by Michelangelo were very much more lifelike. The face of one angel painted by the Maestro looks adoringly at the angel painted by Michelangelo. After this picture was completed the Maestro gave up painting altogether as he was overwhelmed by Michelangelo's brilliance.

One picture he had been commissioned to paint as a wedding gift showing the holy family (Joseph, Mary and Jesus) as a group. This he had painted as a round picture and had himself also made the frame where there were five carved figure heads emulating the figures sculpted on the doorway to heaven at the baptistery opposite the Duomo. It was a stunning picture with bright and vibrant colours used by the Florentine school.

The story goes that Michelangelo had agreed to undertake this work at a price of 70 ducats. When the painting was finished Michelangelo sent a messenger to the patron asking for his money. In return he was sent 40 ducats. Michelangelo wrote back saying that the man did not have to buy the painting, but if he wanted the painting now then the agreed price was 70 ducats. The patron wrote back saying he was only willing to pay 40 ducats. Michelangelo wrote back again saying that the man did not have to buy the painting, but if he wanted it now then the price was now 140 ducats. The patron ended up paying Michelangelo's new asking price. Michelangelo had also wanted to show off his skills of painting the naked form and had added to the background of this picture five naked men in various poses.

Wow. This was a whirlwind tour, but absolutely fascinating and brilliant. Catherine left us in a bemused group allowing us to wander through the other rooms we had not seen. Outside it was raining. It had been a lot heavier as we were going around, but it had now eased off. We did some more exploring of the Uffizi on our own and saw three more rooms that we had not been in before. Downstairs we left the gallery and the rain was now just a few drops. All the people who had been busy performing for the crowds and most of the crowds themselves had gone. We had managed to escape the effects of the rain completely as we went to the open air market round the back of the hotel.

Later we found a good looking pizzeria called Il Lupe for dinner. These were good after the Tuscan pizzas.

Day 83
Mileage 5842
Monday 15ᵗʰ July 2002
The Indoor Market

Another rainy day started. The first thing I did was staring out the window rain was coming down in sheets. "Another wet day mum. What are we going to do now, the rain is coming down in buckets." I said grinning.

Hiring an umbrella mum strode into the hall and said, in a cheerful tone, "Right then, come on." Squeezed together to keep under the umbrella me, mum and Indigo strode along the street looking for one or two more umbrellas for me and Indigo. At last we stopped off at a hopeful looking stall. Dad spotted some children's umbrellas and brought out a pink one. The stall owner opened it up and guess what was on the top? A pink ballerina. The next umbrella was bright yellow with a chicken on top and the last one was a royal blue with a dog on top. I almost chose this one, but I spotted a bright red one that was plain.

After a while walking around the market I spotted a stall with football shirts and my heart leapt when I saw one shirt; 10 Owen England. Michael Owen my idol. I showed the shirt to mum and asked the price it was 8 euro the cheapest I've seen.

We found an entrance to an inside market and decided to explore inside – it had the look outside that it wouldn't stop raining (nothing missed there then!) Mum pointed out some weird white stuff, guess what it was? Tripe! "Yuch! Cow lung!" I mumbled, "This lot is making my stomach turn."

We followed the path round and found a restaurant. I only wanted bread. When dad came back I grabbed my bread and as soon as I bit into it I found out that it was salted "Yum!" I suddenly exclaimed out loud.

After a lunch that I enjoyed – I didn't have to eat anything! It was warm outside when we came out, it had obviously cleared up very quickly and the sun was beating down on us, I soon became very hot under its hot rays. It was so hot we were allowed to get an ice cream, I got 3 flavours.

243

Next we went to the Science Museum. In there included Galileo's middle finger from his right hand! When we arrived we found his finger. An old, wrinkling, rotting finger in a condensed glass case.

There was an optical illusion machine. You would spin it and it would appear to move up hill, but its not, its going down!

Cousin Sue came round at 7:30 and we had a wonderful chat before marching into the hall. Down went the lift and opened at the ground floor, leaping out I bounded towards the big front door.

We had booked a table for five at a "posh" restaurant – but not as posh as the one near Le Tore. We showed her the fine place and she gasped with amazement.

As we sat down I picked up my glass and put it back down, but as I did my glass stem cracked in my hand!! I was very embarrassed and went red in the face.

By the time we got home it was 10 o'clock. It was 12:30 before Sue went home and 1:00 until we went to bed.

*

It was raining again this morning. It was coming down in great swathes, but it was also showery and there were gaps between these downpours. Our diet was suffering from a lack of fresh fruit so we decided to explore the central market area, which again was very close to the hotel.

We were all umbrella less and all our wet weather gear was in the Galaxy. Rather cheekily we asked reception if they had an umbrella we could borrow and amazingly they obliged. With a single large umbrella we set off. It was now hardly spitting. Where before we could shelter from the rain in the eaves of the buildings, now the eaves were the worst places as the buildings themselves were dropping water. The uneven pavements had collected puddles making it even more difficult. Both George and Indigo discovered that the stone benches – built around the outside of some buildings as waiting rooms for people coming to plead before the town officials – were the best places to avoid the water. We were soon in the outdoor market with lots of pitched stalls.

Just like those nature programs describing deserts which lay dormant for years while the weather conditions are bone dry and then after a single rain storm, the whole environment blooms. So Frienze was like with umbrella hawkers. Suddenly they were everywhere. George wanted a sensible folding red umbrella, while Indio wanted a bright pink one with a ballerina on the top. Oh well. As we walked, you could see all the faces turning and talking about Indigo's umbrella. Whether she was aware of all the interest she was causing I just don't know.

We quickly found the indoor market and ventured inside. Downstairs there were dozens of shops selling mostly food. The usual displays of fresh meats and fish as well as cheeses, breads, salamis etc. Upstairs, there were fruit and vegetable stalls in a much more informal layout with no actual shops. As we wandered round I caught a glimpse downstairs of two bright red anoraks each with a large pair of wide red thighs exposed. Eliza and I looked at each other and said, "Don't look now." It was eerie to be reminded of this film – set in Venice – just before going there. The soft fruit was good-looking and very inexpensive. We bought some *albiccochi*, *prugne* and *banane*. We all started to wolf these down. They tasted as good as they looked. Fresh apricots were definitely my favourite fruit. There were two or three stalls selling dried fruit including apples, pears, pineapples, melons – both water melon and honeydew – papaya, mango, star fruit, strawberries, raspberries, cranberries, coconut, passion fruit and lychees; a real dried *macedonia*. I loved this stuff and bought some to nibble.

As we came downstairs we caught sight of the "Don't look now" twins sweeping round a corner. We decided not to follow on principal and came across a wonderful food counter – The Narbone – selling cheap hot lunches. We settled for roast rabbit and beef and potatoes while the children had some pasta and rolls. We sat to eat at some marble tables where there was a bit of a free for all for seats. It was very tasty and the wine was very palatable too! Behind the counter there were two scenes in tiles of working men drinking, smoking and eating, evocative of a bygone era.

Now we were ready to tackle the market and the rain again.

Outside, although it was grey, it was not raining. Indigo still insisted on carrying her bright pink umbrella open though, just to attract the attention. There were some outside restaurants which were looking bedraggled and empty, their trade had simply been killed off. The market stalls were still quite busy, even the "Don't look now" twins appeared to be buying!

Beyond the Uffizi, we spent a couple of hours in the Science Museum. Here there was a large collection of scientific instruments mostly dating from the sixteenth century. There were some wonderful examples of early telescopes for observing the heavens, some of Galileo's own instruments were there including – in its own glass bottle – the middle finger of his right hand. It was not at all clear how his finger came to be in the museum and whether it was "donated" before or after death. Could this be evidence of how the church operated to suppress his support of the solar-centred universe? I didn't think so really, but we did wonder. Further round there were some large globes including a working (alas no more) model of the earth and heavens according to the old Earth-centred model with the moon and the planets all shown circling the Earth and the sky and fixed stars beyond.

I was really pleased that the staff actually demonstrated some of these simple yet effective experimental instruments. George was most fascinated by the ball rolling down a slope. There were bells spaced along the slope and had been spaced so that they sounded at equal time intervals. The spacing went up as the square of the time: 1, 4, 9, 16 and 25.

Near the end of the exhibits were balances and weighing machines; some with chairs to weigh people. There were some medical tool and gadgets which simply looked barbaric and some waxwork models of some of the problems of childbirth. Indigo was particularly interested in these as it showed babies growing inside and being born. She already knew that babies grew inside mummies, but had not really visualised it before.

Back at the hotel, we found a new use for a bidet and washed out the remaining fruit that we had bought in the market in it and left it there as a fruit bowl. Indigo, especially, would be in the bathroom frequently picking up an apricot or a plum.

That evening we met my niece, Sue, who was out in Italy preparing for a television programme about the Medici family – The Godfathers of the Renaissance. We all had an excellent meal together with some great Florentine food and wine. The children were really pleased to see her and we all swapped news about the family and other friends. We talked about her programme and how she was busy trying to arrange shoots at galleries and interviews with various dignitaries.

Yesterday's tour came up and amazingly, we were telling her things she did not know and that her researchers in London had not found out. It was great fun talking with her and listening to her enthusiasm about the subject. After dinner, we carried on talking back at our hotel well into the night.

Day 84
Mileage 5842
Tuesday 16th July 2002
La Specola

It was sunny when we left the hotel. We strode along the streets to the Old Bridge so we could get to the other side of the river to go to a Naturale History Museum – or in mum's opinion a museum of weird things.

When we arrived there the museum started off with shells, insects and that sort of thin. Then came the stuffed animals and then the stuffed mammals and so on and then the wax works of human bodies. It really was very detailed; they didn't forget one artery, a single vein and missed no muscle.

After having the feeling my stomach had been turned upside down and been turned the right way up again, we went out and had the most delicious lunch I've had for a long time.

After our lovely lunch we trooped off to the Bobili Gardens, where we just walked about anywhere until as quick as lightning a clap of thunder shook and chilled the air. "Lets get going before the heavens open." Mum decided quickly.

We all dashed for the exit and only too soon as soon as we got out we had to dive into a bar. It soon calmed down and we had our chance and we took it. We went as fast as we could down to our hotel.

*

It was still grey today, but it was not raining. Eliza had discovered La Specola, the zoological museum, where there were lots of stuffed animals and waxwork models. George had expressed great interest in seeing this rather than more churches. We found our way there beyond the Pitti Palazzo.

The rooms were organised by biological family: shells, molluscs, insects, spiders, birds, mammals, reptiles. Some taking up more than one room. George liked the giant bats and the brightly coloured butterflies. Each room was brimming with dead and stuffed animals.

Among the exhibits were walruses, hyenas, tigers, lions, leopards, starfish, scorpions, koalas, kangaroos, even a full grown hippopotamus, alligators. A large python hung along the wall above the other glass cabinets.

The mammals looked the worse for wear as their fur looked worn and thin. Even though there were large creatures, their eyes were never quite right peering vacantly in different directions and it felt more as if they were sad old and neglected teddy bears whose owners could not bring themselves to part with them. Certainly all the mammals looked like they needed a cuddle. There was a group of primates in one room and here there was an empty case with two footprints at the bottom for "Homo Sapiens". George and Indigo posed here.

A right pair of old monkeys they looked too.

Beyond the animals, there were the human waxworks models. These were what made the museum famous. The collection had been started as a means of teaching doctors about anatomy without having to go through the gruesome process of dissection. The details on these waxworks were quite stunning today. I do not have the expertise to tell if these were accurate enough, but they certainly looked correct. Heads were show where the skin had been removed to show the muscles, blood vessels and the eyes. Bodies were shown with their torsos opened and their entrails simply spread – intestines here, kidneys there, a heart over this side and so on.

The artists, not content with showing the insides correctly, wanted to show off their prowess and make the outside of the waxworks beautiful and correct too. You have to imagine a beautiful young naked woman with hair trailing down from her face and being lightly held in her hand quietly smiling up at you. Her hands and arms, and legs and feet are all intact and elegantly relaxed as if this was a pose that she undertook every day. Her belly and breasts, however, have been ripped opened and her insides had been carefully laid out around her on full public display. The visible man and Damien Hirst were beaten by a couple of hundred years.

George thought that this was well gory and both the children were feeling quite squeamish by the time we left the exhibition.

It had been drizzling while we were inside, and as we walked back towards the centre the rains really threatened and we took shelter in a small bar/restaurant for lunch. George's squeamishness soon evaporated when the idea of pasta was presented to her, but the residual horror will last for some time and will compete with the Torture Museum in San Gimignano.

After lunch we walked to the Pitti Museum, the sun was back out again and the heat was rising. The children had itchy feet after the morning and were in no mood to look at yet more art. We went into the Boboli gardens for a stroll. This was a big disappointment. All the main points of interest were either under reconstruction or simply not interesting. The amphitheatre was closed, the grotto of Neptune was dry and had scaffolding all over it, the cheeky fat dwarf (my rôle model and the antithesis of David in physique) had been removed and replaced by a poster, and the nature trail where you could see lots of different birds was empty. The only flying animals were mosquitoes. We all got bitten very severely especially on the legs. I must have got one stuck up my trousers as it obviously decided to eat its way to death rather than try and escape.

The distant sky was rumbling and grey. We decided to beat a strategic retreat. On the way out we discovered two enormous baths, from the ground you could not see into them, but from above you could see that a full rugby team would have no trouble fitting into them.

We hastened down to Ponte Vecchio with Indigo on my shoulders. The threatening skies started to splash heavy droplets in quick and sudden short bursts as if a wet brush were being shaken dry. Across the Arno we headed to Piazza dei Signora and past the Duomo onto Via Cavour and the Hotel. I was keeping my eyes out for the "Don't look now" twins, but luckily we didn't spot them again. The rain was beginning to come down more consistently, but we got home almost dry and ventured upstairs for a well-earned rest.

In the evening, we walked the opposite way from normal and found a simple trattoria around the back from our hotel.

Day 85
Mileage 5842
Wednesday 17th July 2002
David

*

We just had to see David. We had wanted to do this every day, but today was our last day here and it would be impossible to have been here and not go. The Academy was only about a hundred metres from the hotel, but we were up late and the queue stretched around the building when we got there. Oh dear. I sent Eliza up the front to see if the queue was actually moving and how long it might be. She came back a few minutes later and said that the lady in charge at the front said that she was letting in thirty people every half an hour, at that rate the queue was about three hours long. Oh dear oh dear. We had been doing so well up to now. We were trying to work out what to do when the queue moved and suddenly we were around the corner. This was much quicker than we thought and maybe Eliza had misunderstood what she had been told. We decided to stay put and we were inside within half an hour.

After our Uffizi experience with a proficient guide we were a bit at a loss with just a guide book. The route round the Academy was laid out for you, but the guide book was laid out with David first and then all the other rooms in an order I couldn't fathom. We were able to understand the symbolism in the paintings a lot easier and could distinguish the period of a painting better. All of which surprised me. The central sculpture of the first room contained a plaster model of three entwined figures that had originally been done purely as an exercise. Only much later after the artist had died had it been given the name of the Rape of the Sabine Women – there must have been marketing directors about even then as this name on its own would no doubt have pulled in the tourists. We had already seen the original marble version was on show at the Loggia on the Piazza dei Signori opposite the Palazzo Vecchio. There were a lot of earlier paintings on show, all looking very flat and with lots of gold heavens. There was an exhibition of old musical instruments which was fascinating and there were interactive CDs where you could hear examples of how these instruments sounded. This oral animation breathed life into the exhibition.

David himself was awesome. The sheer magnitude was impressive, his elegant and relaxed pose and his perfect musculature and facial expression were just so. At over 4 metres tall, I took to wondering how big the giant that David slew would have had to have been on this scale and would Michelangelo ever have been willing to have sculpted him and if so where would they have housed Goliath?

You could see where his arm had been broken. According to Sue by, a piece of furniture thrown out of the Palazzo Vecchio during an uprising against the Medici.

David had only been moved to the Academy in 1906 after nearly 400 years exposed to the elements.

David had been carved from a single second hand slab of Carrera marble which was flawed and in which another artist had already started a sculpture. In order to sculpt the piece, Michelangelo could not afford to make any mistakes. He first sculpted a smaller version and then sat this in a bath of water. Every day he would drain the bath by a small amount and use the newly exposed portion of the model to carve the full sized version. This painstaking process ensured that the flaws in the marble slab were not stressed and the piece remained solid.

Alongside David, there was a row of unfinished sculptures by Michelangelo that were known as the prisoners. These figures were in various states of completeness and looked like they were trying to escape from the marble. The figures looked so natural, that it was almost as if they had always been in the marble and Michelangelo was simply releasing them.

The weather remained unpredictable and we had promised George and Indigo some football shirts from the market so we made our way over there and went back to the Narbone for another great lunch.

George was very pleased to have Owen on her back. Indigo had to settle for a very small Italian player. We thought that Totti would get misinterpreted in England and she ended up with Vieri. I got a couple of belts and George got a camouflage belt too.

We wanted to go back and do the secret passageway tour with the children's museum at the Palzzo Vecchio as our final piece of culture in Frienze. On our way there just by the Duomo, there is a pub JJ Cathedral with a first floor balcony with just one table on it. I had noticed this before and now it was empty. We decided to go upstairs and grab it and have a quiet drink as we watched the scenery go by. Not only did we get the balcony and table we were the only people upstairs. It was very romantic just sitting there with a bottle of *prosecco*, people-watching with the afternoon sun bathing the Duomo and the baptistery. George opened the bottle with a flourish – the cork flying skyward onto the square and just missing a pair of pigeons. Later she went down to the square to take our photograph and to retrieve the cork.

No one was running the children's museum today, but there was a secret passageway tour just starting in Italian. The tour concentrated on two or three rooms only, but access to these was limited to staircases within the walls themselves. They were not at all obvious. From the ground floor you could go up two floors and find yourself in a secret bedroom. Eliza said this was where they brought up their consorts, but I thought not as it would not have remained secret for very long. Next there was an entrance into a small very highly decorated room showing family portraits and mythical scenes of the seasons and the four elements – earth, air, fire and water. From here was an entrance onto the main hall of the palace plus two further hidden doors behind painted panels. These led up some more stairs to yet another small very private chamber. This one was much simpler in its decoration and it was where the family stored some of it most prized possessions.

My Italian is hardly existent so I was very pleased to glean as much as I did.

Back in the main hall of the palace we were left to tour the rest on our own. The room was huge, but it had been changed from the original hall – the ceiling had been raised by seven metres. You could easily stand our entire house, including the roof, into this one room at least four times with room to spare. It was built to impress and that it did. It was full of paintings and there were a few sculptures around the sides. There was a balcony around the back – all that remained of the room that once was above.

Upstairs, the private quarters were a lot smaller in scale, but were still very sumptuous. Everywhere there were exquisite pieces of furniture and pictures. How many of these were here when they first moved in and how many had been accumulated since over the centuries – even after the end of the dynasty was impossible to say. Indigo and George tore around the large open spaces despite our continuous cries to "Calm down," and, "Mind what you're doing." The inevitable happened and Indigo took a heavy tumble. We stopped the tour there and then, missing out the top floor and the balcony views of the Duomo and JJ Cathedral.

At the bottom of the stairs, Indigo was still crying and complaining. "I've broken my arm," she sobbed. "I didn't mean to trip her up," said George feeling very guilty, "She fell over my feet." We tried to soothe them both. We told George that it wasn't her fault and not to feel guilty. Indigo was cradling her arm and her fingers were all scrunched up. It was the same arm she had broken last year on the ferry home. She would not or could not straighten them. I had visions of finding a hospital and spending time getting X-rays and plaster casts. Where were our insurance forms? Would we be able to leave tomorrow?

Instant medicine was around the corner in the shape of Vivoli gelato. With Indigo on my shoulders, George and I set off to find Vivoli and Eliza went back to pack. George was amazed that I could find anywhere without a map, but after a couple of wrong turnings and going a touch too far we found what we were looking for. We all sat down with our ice creams, but Indigo couldn't hold it and had to be spoon fed. She was still cradling her arm remembering the sling she wore last time.

I carried a sad, tired injured Indigo to the hotel although she was more cheerful for her ice cream, the placebo effect had not worked. On the way she saw some American ladies that she had made friends with at the hotel and cheerily waved at them. "I've broken my arm," she said proudly holding it aloft. "Oh, have you," they chorused not sure whether to believe her or not.

Back at the hotel we looked at her arm again. It had not swollen up, nor was it disfigured in any way. Indigo was not in actual pain, but felt sorry for herself. We emptied the bidet of fruit and persuaded Indigo to let her arm soak in cold water for a bit. Within five minutes we had a miracle cure. She came out of the bathroom. Eliza asked her to hold out her hand and try to move her fingers. She could, without complaint. She stretched them all and looked down at them with amazement and then she was shaking both arms, hands and all her fingers in the air saying nothing was broken and everything was fine. She laughed and whooped loudly jumping up and down on the mattress very pleased with herself. I was very relieved, but we would check again for any swelling tomorrow.

For our last supper, Vasco had recommended a restaurant near the centre called Il Latini. The proprietor was an old friend of his and we were asked to pass on his regards.

Finding it was straightforward – this time I used the map, but after all our excitement we were quite late, the place was heaving and there was a queue outside the door. We had about a quarter of an hour to wait. They obviously had queues very regularly as they offered us wine and cheese to keep us all orderly. The outside of the building said "*flesetaria*". Inside the ceiling were hung with large numbers of whole *procuttio crudo*. A man by the front counter was continuously slicing either ham or salami for customers. Tables were not discretely kept apart but were thrown together in long rows where everyone mucked in together. Soon, we were found four seats together. We had chosen what we wanted by watching the food being distributed and I had *procuttio* with *melone* and Eliza had *crustini misti*. The girls, who were by now very tired had pasta and *ragu*. There was no need to choose wine as a 2 litre Chianti straw-covered flagon was unceremoniously plonked on our table with a large bottle of mineral water. We decided to have a Florentine steak between us. These looked especially succulent.

The service was very effective. The kitchens must have been well organised to cater for such a large crowd quickly. We found Vasco's friend and managed to exchange pleasantries and make ourselves understood. He was pleased to hear from his old friend and was pleased to know that his new agritourismo venture was working successfully.

We had a wonderful supper here and were full to bursting when we left. It was warm and still with no sign of the earlier rain as we walked the back streets to the main thoroughfares for the last time. We had very much enjoyed Frienze and had only scratched the surface of what it had to offer culturally and only tasted the joy of its cuisine.

Everyone sunk heavily and happily onto their beds once back at the hotel.

Venezia
Day 86
Mileage 5842
Thursday 18ᵗʰ July 2002
To Venezia

*

We were packed and ready to leave not too early, but not too late. We paid our bill and asked for the Galaxy to be brought round from the garage. This wait took an interminable time and we were getting itchy feet after a wait of about forty minutes.

The driver was obviously not used to driving a right-hand drive car as he had parked in such a way that he could not get out of the driver's door and nor could we get in! This meant that Eliza drew the short straw and had to climb over the front seats to drive.

Getting to the Hotel was easy because all the one-way streets were in our favour. Getting out was harder because all the one-way streets were against us. "We can't go down here," said a startled Eliza, "this is where the market is!" "We have no choice everywhere else is 'No Entry'." I retorted. The streets were narrow and full of pedestrians and bicycles who actually owned the streets, so progress was slow. We managed to spiral ourselves out of the small streets only just avoiding entering the multi-storey car park by the covered market and the two police women in their crisp blue uniforms and white helmets.

The ring-road wove its way around the fort – which we had not explored nor even realised existed – slowly edging our way to the autostrada. At last we escaped and were on our way north, when suddenly the traffic slowed to a halt. We crawled for what seemed like forever up five kilometres of road. Desperately, we looked to see where the next exit was and whether it was feasible to travel off the autostrada. The next exit was in twelve kilometres. We could not understand why there was such a weight of traffic at this time of day. It had to be either an accident or road works. Eventually the road narrowed to one lane and we could see that the traffic was free flowing later. Yes, road works. All of half a dozen cones and two men repairing a concrete crash barrier on a bridge. Had someone gone off recently? We shall never know. The hold up meant that the inner lane was now totally congested with a long line of lorries, now moving as if in a very large convoy. The autostrada rose up into the hills alternating between tunnels and viaducts. The old road was firmly attached to the ground and very twisty. After we had made our way over the pass the terrain flattened towards Bologna and the vast Po valley was spread in front of us. We drove up to Padova and were then approaching Venezia. Again we met very heavy traffic and were caught in some serious congestion until suddenly we were through it. We crossed the long bridge to Venezia and arrived at Piazza Roma to park.

We were worried about leaving the Galaxy with most of our stuff on board, but there was little choice. I went off to check the water buses and taxis and the cost of car parking. A water taxi was very extortionate and the buses although cheaper would charge for every piece of luggage. We had not prepared very well as we were going to take quite a few bags. We settled on the communal car park and were sent up to the roof level. On first inspection the place was full. Cars were also parked in the most obscure corners making manoeuvring very awkward. Second pass we saw two cars leaving and had a choice of spots.

The view of Venezia from the roof of the car park was great. "Look!" said Indigo, "The leaning tower of Venice." She was right, there was a tower that was distinctly astray from the vertical. I looked some more and thought the whole city was leaning, there was not a vertical building in the place. Pisa seemed very much a con after seeing this.

Down the lift and across to the water buses. We hopped onto a number 1 bus and were pulled in to the enchantment of Venice and its canals. The bus went under the bridge by the railway station and then carried on down the Canal Grande stopped every few hundred metres criss-crossing from one side to the other. As we approached the Rialto bridge people were sitting on the sides of the canal dangling their feet in to keep cool. The constant lapping noise of the water was very soothing and would replace the background hiss of motor traffic for the next few days. We got off at San Angelo and went in search of our hotel in the back streets.

Despite the fact there were no cars it did not mean that there were no road works. The detailed description of how to get to the hotel was thwarted by a closed bridge. A temporary footbridge had been erected around the back of some other houses closing some canals or *riva* to water traffic. We found our way all the same and got to the hotel only to be told we were actually staying in the annex. Access to the annex was back over the temporary bridge. I was glad we had reduced our luggage to a minimum.

Inside the annex, opposite the entrance, water was lapping the steps of another door. This was a fully functional canal entrance to this building; very weird for us, but I am absolutely certain not unusual here.

Our local square was the Campo Santo Stefano. It was such a real pleasure to see the whole place traffic-free and laid with white stone. I knew San Marco would be big, but I had thought the rest of Venezia was simply small alleys and squares. I was very wrong. We found our way to the Ponte dell'Accademia, the third and final bridge across the Canal Grande and meandered down towards the next waterfront. We all felt very relaxed although throughout our stay I remained anxious about Indigo falling into the water. Most bridges and canals had barriers to prevent slips, but these were designed with adults in mind and small children could easily slip between the bars. Some canals and bridges were unguarded.

The sun was low in the sky, but it was still early and very warm. We went back to the Ponte dell'Accadmia by a different route and ended up having pizza on the waterfront.

We crossed the bridge and found our way to San Marco. I quickly realised that the maps were mostly useless. Not all the street or bridges or canals were marked. The lettering was so small as to be illegible and the way to the major landmarks was well signed. San Marco was very large indeed and full of tourists and pigeons. Cafes spread around the edges were playing classics for pleasure from strings and pianos. At the other end was the Duomo with its distinctive low and oriental looking domes fronted with the famous four horses. The bell tower was tall and erect and did not look as if it was leaning too far. There was the famous clock with two figures posed to strike the bell on top – except this was under restoration and the clock was covered in scaffolding and a cloth covered in a clock replica. We went round the square alongside the

Doge's palace to the waterfront where the two tall pillars stood – the Molo.

We delved into a café for an expensive gelato and strolled along the front and back into the maze of little streets for home. Indigo was falling asleep on her feet and ended being carried home to bed.

Day 87
Mileage 5999
Friday 19th July 2002
The Duomo and Rialto

It had been hot overnight and the air-conditioning was not working. We all had bites and were quite itchy. Upstairs at breakfast there were only four places laid. We had the place to ourselves. The television was on, showing an advert for hair removal cream. This was nauseous enough first thing in the morning, but it was being demonstrated not only by women, but also by hairy men on their chests arms and legs. Italian weirdness coming to the fore again. The whole advert appeared to be on a loop and kept repeating itself. Somewhere, there had to be a remote control to change this! We found it and just watched the news. More and more stock market falls around the world.

The Doge's palace was first on the list of things to see, so we strode off to San Marco along a now familiar route. The square was already busy and the line for the Duomo stretched all the way to the water front. When we found the entrance to the Doge's palace there were a few people huddled around the outside, but there was no queue at all. We very much wanted a guided tour and found that there was not one in English today and would have to come back tomorrow. Could we book? Of course not, their computer systems couldn't cope with the fact that you wanted to book for another day! I would come back early in the morning and book.

I left Eliza in the long queue for the Duomo while I went off with Indigo and George to feed the pigeons. They both thought this was great fun and whooped as the birds climbed all over them and ate from their hands. The queue for the Duomo actually moved very quickly and we were inside within twenty minutes. Entrance was free and we managed to join a free English tour. The place was simply dripping with gold, but a large amount of the objects had been looted from Constantinople. There were mosaics all around showing bible stories including the creation, the eviction of Adam and Eve from the Garden of Eden and Noah and the flood.

The altarpiece is supposedly one of the most valuable objects in the world. Made of solid gold, it was completely covered in fabulous precious pillaged stones. Normally, the altarpiece was set up to face the rear of the church, but there was a special rotating mechanism to allow the congregation to see it on special occasions – how nice.

Upstairs were the four bronze horses although these were now only copies and the originals were under restoration. The view down to San Marco was good, but I think even now when it was crowded that there were more birds than people. St Mark himself lay in the main part of the cathedral and his remains had also been looted by the Venetians from Egypt wrapped in pig meat to avoid detection by customs. His body had been lost twice over the centuries. He had been hidden inside a wall or column and the only people who knew where he was had died without telling. It was only when the building started falling down that his arm came to light. "A miracle," they all cried!

Time was getting on and we wanted to have a look at the food market by the Rialto Bridge before it closed. En route we were hijacked into Burger King for lunch by the children. The Rialto Bridge had been designed in a competition and certainly two other designs had been turned down. Michelangelo's design had been too ornate, and the eventual design had been picked because there were 24 shops in it and the Venetians had become rich through trade (and stealing and pillaging of course, but no one says that). The bridge was busy, full of tourist tatt – glass trinkets and beads, postcards, necklaces, tee-shirts and bags. The far side of the bridge was much the same and we came down to the food market which was closing down. Lots of fresh fruit and vegetables were there as always in the rich Mediterranean colours, but all the fish and meat stalls had gone for the day. The rush of local people had by now passed and there was only the stray tourist, like us wandering about and admiring the colours and the fragrances.

Near the Rialto bridge was a clock tower with a twenty-four hour clock face. After we crossed the bridge we decided to get a 24 hour family ticket for the boat and get some fresh air on the water. The boat took us away from the crowded streets, but it too was busy. When we landed we wandered some more back streets in search of a snack for us. En route we came across the Gondola Factory and nosed inside. Gondolas didn't appear to be made here any more, but there were signs that repair work was carried out here.

Further on, we found a bar which sold Italian food and was run by a Chinese lady. The décor looked as if it was a Chinese restaurant until recently. Refreshed, we ventured back to the waterfront and waited for a bus to the Lido across the water. The ride was faster than the bus around town and both the children enjoyed the motion and hung over the side the whole time trying to catch some spray on their faces.

The Lido was dull. A ten minute walk up and down the main street away from the jetty was enough for us. We stopped for gelato on the way back and then caught the first boat back to Venezia. I'm glad we went though otherwise I would never have been sure.

Back at San Marco we went up the bell tower. George was disappointed that we had to take the lift rather than the stairs. I had expected to be able to climb right to the very top, but no, we could only go about 60m up. Although you could see quite well, the angles made it difficult to see straight down. It was nearly six o'clock and we waited to see if the enormous bells would strike. All around the city church bells started ringing out on the hour, but these remained silent. Down in the square George spotted a young man lying on his back covering himself with bird feed and letting the pigeons clamber all over him.

We went back to the hotel and all had baths and got ready for dinner. We caught a bus to the other side of the Canal Grande and made our way to Campo S. Margherita. This campo was very lively when we arrived and there were a couple of musicians playing odd stringed instruments together with a drum and a kazoo. George and Indigo just sat on the stone floor and enjoyed the sounds and the rhythms.

We sat in a restaurant – the Antique Chicken – just next to them and wanted to order some half portions of the menu, but here the waiter had an electronic order pad and refused saying that the notepad would not allow him to take such an order. This was the last straw for us as the restaurant was quite expensive anyway and did not really have what we wanted so we walked off. Only a few yards away we found ourselves in Due Torri where the first thing we asked was whether they could do half portions. "Of course, we do," came the reply, "This is a restaurant, we can do whatever you want."

The food here was excellent and had a definite Venetian twist with calamari in black ink and locally caught deep fried little fish. Strolling back through the night streets we were feeling very happy and enjoying the warmth of the evening and the noise of the water, but not enjoying the biting insects that seemed to follow us about.

Day 88
Mileage 5999
Saturday 20th July 2002
Redentore

We dashed back just in time to literally step aboard our gondola before it was pushed out and our adventure began. At first it felt so wobbly that I thought it might capsize! Just needed getting used to.

After a while I got used to the wobbling and started to admire the absolute talent to drive one of these things. I also started to arrive at the idea that perhaps I would like to do something like this and it also made me absolutely sure I wanted to go to Hockerill School of languages.

We slowly moved into the water around St Marco's square. Half an hour went swiftly by with out any sign of the fireworks. Then with the sound of a gunshot the first firework had been set off, but everyone in our gondola and the one behind jumped out of their skins.

And soon the air was full of large, white and continuous bellomming fireworks, which sounded as if someone was shooting non-stop into the air. Next came the screamers, which were all the colours of the rainbow and screeched very, very loudly.

My favourite part was the grande finale, there must have been twice as many as all the ones in the Newport show. Some looked like Saturn, some were hearts and some were just like flowers with half their petals one colour and half another.

*

I was up quite early and out of the hotel to go and get the tickets for the Duomo. At San Marco, the early tourists were already about. There were groups being led by ladies carrying umbrellas or small flags; parties of schoolchildren identically dressed in yellow hats and bright red uniforms each with a rather large and cumbersome backpack. They all looked cheerful in the sunshine. The bells stuck nine, including those on the bell tower that were silent last night at six. I got to the Doge's palace and bought our tickets and booked our guide. Back at the hotel, everyone else was just about awake. We caught the water bus around to San Marco. It was very, very busy. There was a group of thirty American school children swamping the boat with all their luggage. After their stop, it was much more civilised.

There was now a queue to get into the Palazzo Ducale so we went through the gate marked for pre-booked tickets. For some reason the electronic gates refused to let us in and we had to fight past the queue of people trying to book tickets to enter. I could not see what we had done wrong! Inside the courtyard was large and grand and all was quiet from the busy throng outside. The four sides of the courtyard had been built at different times and although similar they were also different from each other. Our tour guide met us and explained what we were going to see today.

We made our way up to the balcony level of the courtyard where we could see down in to San Marco and across the waters. Here we posed for pictures. Our guide explained that between the two large columns called the Molo was where people were taken for execution. Thus no Venetian would walk between the pillars, only tourists would do such a thing. She also told us that the air smelt salty today and that meant that Venezia smelt sweet. When there was no salt in the air the smell from the drains was pungent.

Venezia had been founded on these islands as people had come here to escape from marauding soldiers in about the seven hundreds. Over time it was recognised that these islands – often no more than muddy marshes – were safe from invasion. The high ground around Rio Alto was the first to be settled. Wooden stakes were buried into the soil and then heavy stone was laid on top. The wooden stakes did not rot but were petrified by the pressure on top of them. The stone was impervious to water and formed a stout defence against the lagoon. Houses built on top were made light, in comparison with more traditional methods, by using a lot of wood. At its largest Venezia had a population of about 150,000. Now it was much smaller, but for every resident there was in the region of 200 visitors a year.

Up on to the fourth floor were the main historical governing offices. Here the Doges were elected by the Senate for life. Once elected the Doge and his family would take up residence. To be elected he would have to be very experienced in many factors of the city life and – like presidents in the US today – he would also have to be personally wealthy. Because such power was in the hands of one man, the Venetians never elected a young Doge. The average length of rule was about seven years. Also the Doge's power was often reduced to a casting vote on committees. There were three arms to the government, the Executive, the Judiciary and the Legislature: all were independent from each other. The Venetians believed that this helped to keep in check the power of each branch of government. Each branch had its own room and each had the Doge as its chairman and casting vote. In two of the chambers were two large clocks with twenty-four hour faces. The number one was where we now expect nine to be and the numbers increased anti-clockwise. These clocks no longer worked which I thought was a real shame. In one of the rooms was another clock face with only the signs of the zodiac on it. This dial was moved manually once a month.

The government also had a system of denunciation where three "good standing" individuals could denounce another for some crime. This written denunciation would then be posted into a box through a lion's mouth. The box could only be opened on the back with three separate keys held by three separate individuals who acted as witnesses for and against each other. The denunciation would be handed over to the secret police to investigate. If they found evidence then the individual concerned would be presented with the evidence and offered the choice of confessing or torture to reach a confession. If no evidence was found or somehow the individual was pronounced innocent then the denouncers themselves faced prison or worse. Being a nation founded on trade and money, the Venetians could always escape jail by the payment of a heavy fine.

On display in a room of armour and weapons, there was a gift of a suit of armour from Henry IV of France. Before he became king he visited Venezia for the purpose of buying a ship. He had expected to wait three months for a ship, but was told that a ship could be made ready for him within three hours if he requested. Venetian shipyards were turning out three ships a day at that time.

There was also a box of pistols on display which was used as a diplomatic gift to an enemy. It was booby-trapped and would explode on close examination. So much for diplomacy.

In the large senate room – where up to 2,500 senators might gather – there was reputedly the largest painting on canvas in the world. The painting was religious of course with Jesus in the top centre surrounded by faces. In all there were over two thousand faces. At the time the pictures cost according to the number of faces it contained, so the artist added as many into the picture as he could. He was not alone in painting the picture and members of his family all helped.

This room was very large and had no supporting pillars. Instead a framework constructed like an inverted ship's hull supported the ceiling from above. All around the room, just under the ceiling, were portraits of the Doges. I am not sure if this represented the entire history, but I believe so. One however, had been blacked out. He had been beheaded, but I do not know for what crime. This room was where overseas diplomats would be presented to court. It was seen as important that anything they said would be heard in open session with the senate.

When Napoleon came to Venezia, this was also the room where he was given power. From this building and others Napoleon took over 26,000 works of art back to Paris. This probably balanced out the looting of Constantinople and other places carried out by the Venetians.

Venezia had two very famous sons: Marco Polo, the good son went off to China, and Casanova, the bad son who had such a famously good time. To celebrate 1,000 years of Venezia, the senate inaugurated continuous festivities for six months. Everyone took to having a good time and people took to wearing masks to disguise themselves. Ladies who wanted to be paid distinguished themselves from ladies who were just after a good time by wearing yellow.

From here we went across il *Ponte dei Sospiri* to the "new" *Prigioni*. Here prisoners were kept either awaiting trial or execution or undergoing their sentence. Not much time was spent here waiting as Venezians prided themselves in swift judgement. Nor would all sentences be carried out here. You could be sentenced to house arrest or refused leave to leave Venezia or worse banished from the city. There were 104 cells here each capable of holding four prisoners. The city supplied bread and water, but it was up to your guild and/or family to supply anything else. The windows all had at least two layers of bars and each layer contained a lattice of vertical and horizontal bars interleaved together. No one had ever escaped from this prison. There were only two ways out of the prison. Through the prison courtyard after your sentence was completed or back across il *Ponte dei Sospiri*. Going this way you may be able to catch a glimpse of your family as you were taken to execution between the pillars of the Molo; we were led back across the bridge, but luckily sentences were no longer carried out.

Outside the palace we went to catch a boat to Murano, an island just north of Venezia where glass manufacturing had been going on for several hundred years. We arrived at the island and very quickly found a manufacturer who was demonstrating their techniques. It was very hot with a furnace at 1,300°C. There were two people working the furnace, a father and son. The son did all the preparatory work, such as collecting the glass bundles and ordering them and then carrying out some of the preliminary heating work on them. The father, his maestro, would then take these to extend, roll, blow, cut and shape. His dexterity was amazing to watch and the children sneaked back for more after our walk around the shop. The trade and techniques passed from father to son down the generations.

To my eyes, most of the glasswork they did, although very intricate and colourful was garish, but there was one set of glasses that caught our eyes. This was a set of six different single coloured glasses with stems but without bases. They came in a large vase where they could be rested. We were quickly spotted eying these up and were given the full sales treatment. It was interesting to watch and hear the spiel and the price fell several times without any effort on our part except mild resistance. We ended up buying the set because they were so very simple and elegant and were different from anything else we had seen. We were told that there were only one or two other sets made like these in the world, but I somehow think they say this to everyone.

I needed some air after all this expense and heat, but the children still wanted to see the maestro at work again. I went out and wandered up and down the canal side for sometime before being joined by the rest of the family. We strolled towards the other side of the island, over bridges and along empty quiet lanes. We had a snack and found a very old church. The island was very peaceful after the frenetic crowds on Venezia.

On the boat on the way back to Venezia, George and Indigo got chatting to a Hindu lady who lived in Geneva and was visiting for a weekend. It was always amazing who these two ended up talking to. Indigo in particular had not met many non-whites before and was interested in where she came from and what she did and ate.

Tonight was the culmination of Redentore with fireworks at midnight. Redentore – the Redeemer – was to celebrate the end of the plague in 1556. Every year, Venetians would build a bridge of boats from San Marco across the water to a church where pilgrimages were then made. Each family had its own boat and would pile up the boat with food and drinks to last the evening.

The Venetian waterfront was filling up with boats, mostly large and here just for the evening. People were jumping and diving into the water from these boats and swimming around. Not a care about the state of the water.

Back on Venezia we wanted to work out what we were going to do this evening. Indigo and George had been eying up the carnival masks ever since we had arrived. It was no use saying that carnival was in February around the same time as our pancake day: they wanted masks. The masks came in all shapes and sizes. A doctor had developed a mask with a long nose, inside which he put herbs and spices as a protection against the spread of plague, which was thought to be airborne. The masks proved to be very popular, but were, of course, totally ineffective. I liked the masks which had three faces including three noses and three mouths, but only four eyes, each face had a different expression. Shop after shop were dedicated to making and selling these masks. We bought George a harlequin mask and Indigo a black mask with black feathers and a crystal. They wore them all evening, except when they were eating or in the bath, and caused much amusement to the crowds.

Wandering around San Marco it was already getting very crowded and there would be nowhere to sit comfortably and watch. We found a travel agency offering a luxurious dinner on board a boat at €320 each – including the children. Thank you very much; this was *troppo caro* for an adult no matter how good the food. We ventured further and found some gondolas hawking themselves for the evening. This too was expensive, but only about three times as expensive as the normal gondola ride, which we had already promised the children. After much dithering we decided we ought to do this and booked. It would serve as a lifetime memory for us all and we were just tourists anyway.

We went off in search of some drinks and snacks to take with us and then back to the hotel to get changed for dinner.

At about half past ten, we set off in search of our gondola. There was a tidal wave of people making their way towards San Marco. Where had they all come from? Venezia was full. I am quite sure that there were more than 150,000 people here tonight to see the fireworks.

We found our gondola and were very soon whisked away from all the noise and bustle down some tiny backwaters. It was dark by now and the sky was clear so we could watch the stars pass overhead between the buildings. George was fascinated by the gondola and the gondolier with his traditional blue and white striped jersey. This was another skill that was passed from father to son – there were no lady gondoliers at the moment. We spent about an hour drifting the backwaters and the Canal Grande before taking up position near the fireworks.

There was an air of expectation amongst all the boats. We opened our *prosecco* and pistachios and offered some to our gondolier. George and Indigo stuck to Sprite. The gondolier struggled to keep us still for so long as there seemed to be a strong current. Looking around all the other gondoliers were on their feet working. Indigo needed a wee. This was interesting, we couldn't just stick her bottom over the side, she may well fall in. But we did find a plastic bag without a hole in it and with the help of a plastic glass we managed without making a mess.

Suddenly there was the sound of canon fire. This was the signal for the beginning of the fireworks. And they were spectacular. From our low position in the water we got a brilliant view. The sheer scale of these fireworks was breath taking. There were enough of them to fill most of the sky and they were sufficiently coordinated that they were not just a mess of colours but came together in groups. Some high and loud exploding across the sky with brilliant reds, blues, purples and greens, some with gentle showers of orange and white cascading down like waterfalls continuously replenished from above. Indigo was sitting with her hands covering her ears, but in the end gave up.

We kept thinking that the finale had been and gone. Even the gondoliers all started to stand and get ready to be off, before the next batch made them all sit again. I had given up all pretence of trying to concentrate on whether this batch was nicer and how it differed from the last batch and just let the whole occasion overwhelm me. Indigo was now laughing continuously and I could not help but join in. I started doing a real long belly laugh and whooping at it all. The fireworks went on and on. I was no longer amazed, but absolutely stunned by the experience and would not forget this for a long time. Then suddenly it was quiet and dark. Three canon shots signalled the end. The silence was broken by a ripple of applause which grew in intensity for several minutes. We found ourselves moving as the gondolier took us back to shore.

We paid and got off. Eliza carried Indigo and I carried George. They were now both fast asleep. I cannot remember the last time I carried George like this, asleep and heavy. I suspect this might be the last time.

It had been a glorious and expensive day. Well worth every minute and every eurocent. We slept very well and contentedly.

Day 89
Mileage 5999
Sunday 21st July 2002
Window Shopping

Our final day in Venice began, because we had a late night we didn't wake until 9:30!

I decided that I would get something for each of my friends. After much of a debate I got a family of cats for Patrick, Finlay and Lucy and a large dog for Oliver.

After doing this we wondered up to St Marco's square to feed the birds, but boy did we get a surprise. All the bird feeder stalls were closed!

Regretfully we left the pigeons behind, just as we left the square a pigeon flew into a pole! Then we walked around for a bit and retired to lunch.

After lunch we meandered around Venice's back streets, relaxing and licking the windows.

*

The whole of Venezia awoke slowly this gorgeous Sunday morning. Indigo and then George befriended two American sisters at breakfast who had arrived too late to see the fireworks. They were from Oregon and were spending three weeks travelling around Italy. Indigo told them about our adventures with George, Eliza and I interjecting with corrections and clarifications.

Today we would see no more sights, but just be a family and meander around the lanes and the squares of Venezia looking for small gifts for people back home. As soon as we had had breakfast it was almost time for lunch. It was quite late. Today, as we strolled towards San Marco no one seemed to be in a hurry. Under the *portici* of San Marco, we noticed that the cafes had little leather seats and sofas built into the marble. These looked like a terribly English place to have tea, but we resisted. The string quartets were already playing their music, but with slightly less gusto than yesterday. It was almost as if the whole city was suffering from post-Redentore blues: a sort of communal hangover

271

from all the festivities. Everyone looked as if they were walking around on eggshells.

The girls wanted to feed the pigeons in the square, but there was no one around today to sell us pigeon food. George spotted three or four birds who were lying dead. It looked as if the fireworks were just too much for them and that they had been frightened to death by the noise. The birds weren't starving though; the tourist had simply upgraded their diet to biscuits and croissants. Those that hadn't gone to pigeon heaven overnight must have thought that they had arrived this morning.

We thought that the bridge of boats might still be here this morning, but it was gone. We must have been some of the first people to have gone to bed as we had been whisked fairly sharpish off the water by our gondolier.

There were lots of streets to explore and a vast array of items to admire in shop windows: expensive (everything was expensive) shoes, designer clothes, bags, masks, and glassware. There was hardly anything a normal resident would buy. Practically every corner of the city was dedicated to the tourist, but I am sure there are some areas where the tourists do not venture in such droves – Murano back streets for one.

George wanted to buy her friends some glass animals for presents and we quite fancied buying some gaudy glass wine bottle stoppers for ours. We searched many shops looking at these and eventually bought some. We bought some postcards for Indigo's journal and went back to the hotel quite early to pack, snooze and drink a bottle of *prosecco* left over from last night.

Due Torri had been so good on Friday night, we wanted to repeat the experience. Just as we set off we bumped into the American girls Dejah and Jenna who joined us. We walked through Campo Santo Stephano and on to the Accadamia Bridge. The evening was warm and the evening sun played on the waters as we strolled. Ten minutes took us to Camp San Margherita and to the Due Torri, where we were aghast to see that the restaurant was closed. I had a quick wander around the square while I left them all watching an English youth orchestra busking. A nearby pizzeria fit the job but it looked as if we would have to sit inside. However, out the back, there was a hidden garden with loads of room. We spent a great evening talking about our pasts and the girls' background.

On the way home we stopped for our last Venetian *gelati*.

Day 90
Mileage 5999
Monday 22ⁿᵈ July 2002
Leaving Venezia

*

Indigo slumbered lazily in our bed after we had got up. At this age sleep takes them very solidly and they lie totally relaxed and innocent. She was thoroughly exhausted and it seemed such a shame to disturb her.

So another slow morning, but we were already mostly packed. We were ready to leave and said our goodbyes to the hotel staff and the American girls. We picked up our bags and wandered down to San Angelo water bus stop to wait for the number 1.

It was sad leaving, but if we had stayed longer it would have felt like an anticlimax after Saturday night. We were happy with what we had seen and content to know that there was more if and when we came back. The crowds had been overbearing, but we knew that at this time of year it was unavoidable. However, we all agreed that we had had some of the best times.

We passed under the Rialto Bridge and down the Canal Grande towards Piazza Roma. I was slightly anxious about the Galaxy but need not have worried. Everything was fine. The car park was full to bursting, more so than when we arrived. Our exit was blocked and we had to reverse and manoeuvre awkwardly to escape from the roof terrace. On our way down we passed the six thousand mile mark on our travels.

Soon we were on the road away from Venezia and on the autostrada leading up towards Padova.

Part 3: The Northern Borders

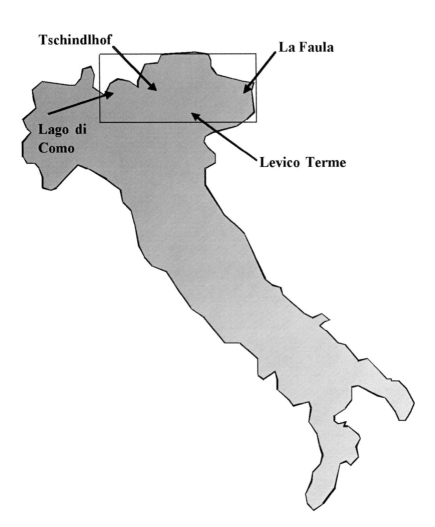

Levico Terme
Day 90
Mileage 5999
Monday 22nd July 2002
We Hate 4* Hotels

*

We had nowhere booked for tonight and were just heading north towards the northern mountains of Italy. Around Venezia it was very flat and dull. Vast swathes of land were given over to growing crops, but also there were plenty of small industrial plants around. Our first area was going to be around Trento so we headed for the Val Sugana valley from Padova via Bussano. Once past Bussano we were into the hills and immediately there were tracts of forest around with dramatic countryside. Plenty of pine and deciduous trees around.

On the map Levico Terme looked interesting at the end of a long valley where there were a couple of small lakes. When we arrived Levico Terme looked as deserted as an Eastbourne sea front on a wet and windy February weekday, but today was hot and sunny in the middle of July. This ought to be high season.

Down on the lakeside there were people swimming. It was sandy underfoot and unlike Lago Trasimeno did not reek of either sewage or escaping methane. This ought to be okay for a day or so while we oriented ourselves in the region. Back in town we saw a hotel with a swimming pool. We thought we would give it a try. Yes they had rooms available for a couple of days and they could arrange for us to have two interconnecting rooms. The receptionist gave us a price for both bed and breakfast and half-board. We went to have a look at the rooms, they were nothing special, but they would do. The swimming pool was supposedly heated but it was deserted when we went to have a look. When we had looked around the town there did not appear to be any restaurants, so we opted for half-board.

The children were happy that we had found somewhere and within half an hour they were settled by the pool. People were beginning to emerge from their siesta. There were quite a few families with small children so both ours soon integrated. There were a couple of teenagers who ran a kids club for the hotel around the pool. That afternoon they were making pancakes for the children around the pool. George and Indigo thought they were in heaven.

We got down to dinner late and immediately realised our mistake. The salad buffet had been already fully played out and there was nothing left that we could eat. We asked for some plain pasta for the children and ordered our food. The menu sounded interesting, but the food was dull, dull, dull. Yes it had sufficient calories in it, it was not burnt, but it lacked any degree of interest and we did not enjoy this at all.

The kids club took a small gang of children to play mini-golf near the lakeside. Much to Indigo's chagrin, they would not take her as she was too small, but George was very pleased to have this piece of freedom.

It was nearly eleven o'clock by the time they got back. They all appeared to have had a good time. George and I played cards in the bar afterwards with a bottle of water. George is suffering from a large number of bites.

Day 91
Mileage 6091
Tuesday 23rd July 2002
A Peek into Sud Tirol

*

The food was so disappointing that we decided to change to bed and breakfast if they would let us or else simply leave. At breakfast the head waiter was surprised that we would not be eating tonight, but passed no other comment. They agreed to let us change to bed and breakfast and I assumed that it would be at the price quoted to us yesterday.

Today the kids club were going down to the lake side at 3:15 and they said that they would take Indigo.

Yesterday, we had spent some time looking at places to go and see for our next stop. We knew there was a wine growing region between Trento and Bolzano, so we headed up there in the hope of finding somewhere more interesting planning to be back before the kids' club trip down to the lake.

About halfway between Trento and Bolzano we crossed the border into Sud Tyrol and suddenly everything was signed in German as the first language with Italian as the second language. This took us a bit by surprise until we realised that this part of the world had been part of the Austro-Hungarian Empire during the nineteenth century.

Here was a broad flat bottomed plain between two mountain ranges. It looked very much like a glacial valley. The plain was full of vines and orchards. Leaving the autostrada just south of Bolzano we quickly found the wine road and then almost immediately stopped at a tourist information point. The young girl here was very helpful and supplied us with lots of magazines showing guest houses and hotels in the immediate vicinity. She even supplied us with a list of vacancies as at yesterday afternoon. The place looked well organised and informed. She told us that there are lots of vacancies around at the moment. We decided to have a quick scout around Eppan to see if we could find one of these vacancies. The map of Eppan was not to scale and roadworks, diversion and one-way streets added to our confusion. As we headed up the mountain we both spotted an old building with a green roofed octagonal turret in the corner. The building was set in vineyards and orchards and was obviously old and full of character, this could be an interesting place to stay. We carried further on up the mountain road, but neither of us were convinced that the place we were looking for was actually on this road. Conscious of the time, we decided to abort and drive along the wine road to explore the area further.

We drove past Caltern and further. Everywhere was grapes. This area produces more wine than all of Tuscany. I was not surprised. Although Tuscany is famous for its Chianti, a lot of acreage is given over to wheat, olive, other crops and woodland. Here the vines are densely packed and have virtually no space between them. We take a road upward in search of a place to eat and find a deserted bar/restaurant who are pleased to see us and serve an adequate light lunch. Outside there is a small blue oasis of a swimming pool. We ask if they have any rooms, but they are complete. We come back down the valley and traverse the autostrada following the state route back to Trento and then back to Levico Terme in time to get George and Indigo ready for their adventures by the lake.

Now we have some quite time to look at all the literature that we have been given. There are two different maps of the area, but each has the same grid reference system. One version has a lot of numbers on it and the other version does not. The book of accommodation shows a grid reference and a number against each place, but its map does not have the numbering system. So, code breaking, we put the two together and find out where the places with vacancies are. All quite time consuming.

Nothing looks terribly interesting. There are also some places which advertise themselves as specialising in wine holidays, but the accommodation here looks terribly bland. We don't know what to do and decide to drive and see tomorrow.

The children come back and everyone is amazed at how adventurous our children are compared with all the rest. They have been in the playground and swimming in the lake and pretty well behaved. Up by the swimming pool it is a little boy's birthday and they all join in a small party with cake (full of cream and biscuit wafer which nobody likes including me).

This evening, as we are not having dinner, I take the girls down to the mini-golf as I had promised Indigo that she could have a go too. It is a long walk down and not where I thought it was. George was fine, but Indigo needed a shoulder ride.

After about two holes, Indigo gives up trying to play with a club and is content to roll the ball around the course. George's arithmetic seems very vague and she plays by her own rules. "Every time you start a hole again, you start counting the strokes again." I soon give up trying to make an honest player of her and just let us enjoy being together. There are two different courses here and we play the one she didn't play last night. "This one is much harder," she reveals quickly. The course is near some marsh-land and this is probably where the insects live that bit her so last night. Tonight, we are a lot earlier and so we are left alone.

The walk back up the hill was great: a view over the lake and through the park with George by my side and Indigo on my shoulders. The heat of the day had gone and the sun was drifting down to its bed.

Tschindlhof
Day 92
Mileage 6193
Wednesday 24th July 2002
To Eppan

*

Time to move on again today. We packed, had breakfast and went to check out only to find that the price for bed-and-breakfast was only €2 cheaper than half board. This was completely different from what we were offered when we booked in only two days ago. I was furious and had a stand up row with the manager, but Eliza, with a sound head diffused the situation and we came to a compromise. We had no proof of the terms we were offered and the staff member was not on duty that day and was not contactable. We left with a very sour taste in our mouths.

We followed the same road as yesterday driving to Caltern first. We tried to find the hotels which specialised in wine, but failed miserably. We drove onto Eppan where there were some residences available and decided to try the hotel with the green tower that we had seen yesterday. We found it with no problem and found its name – Ansitz Hotel Tschindlhof. We quickly looked it up in our magazine and found it was also one of the ones we had marked by its description and that we simply hadn't recognised the picture as it was taken from a completely different angle.

There would be no harm in asking about vacancies and drove in down the track in the vineyard and into the hotel.

There was no one around as we nosed indoors, but soon a lady speaking German arrived and when she realised we could not understand each other went in search of help. A young, tall and thin lady came to her rescue and helped us. We wanted either a single room where we could all stay together or two rooms next to each other, interconnecting if possible. She offered us a choice and showed us to two very different parts of the building. The first was an apartment for eight around the back with its own independent entrance, and the second was two rooms next to each other on the second floor. Although the big apartment suited our needs as we had told the receptionist the two rooms seemed much more cosy and close to the heart of the hotel. These rooms were bigger than those in Levico Terme, with much more individual character. Two rooms would be best for us, there seemed no point in looking around further and settled on a price. However, we did not want to commit too long in case our food experience was repeated.

We paused for a while and sat down in the sunshine near the vegetable garden hidden behind a waist level hedge. George sat down on the bench opposite us with her back to the hedge. I told her she would be surprised if she sat there too long. She looked at me with her right eyebrow raised and a smirk on her face saying "Why?" "You'll see," I said. The sprinkler in the garden started its downward path towards George. As a few drops fell on to her head she burst out laughing with delight. Luckily the sprinkler was set perfectly so that only George got wet.

After struggling with our luggage, still down to one bag and a couple of backpacks, thanks to Eliza ingenuity in packing, we decided to take a stroll down to the village centre. It was hot and humid, and ice cream was the order of the day, but the skies were grey and the clouds were threatening, so we did not want to venture too far. Muggins would end up carrying Indigo on my shoulders.

It was middle of siesta time and only the cafés and bars in the town were open. We chose one randomly and had drinks, ice cream and apple strudel. We toasted on our luck at finding such a good-looking spot and at our escape from Levico Terme. My anger from this morning had dissipated, but our dislike of large four-star hotel had been reinforced. The Tschindlhof was a small hotel run by the family von Mörl for about 25 years. It is set in the family grounds of orchards and vineyards – a bit like all rural buildings in this area.

Indeed we were very pleased by the food that evening. Eating under the shades of some large pine trees and amazingly, two small nespole trees – which "never grow north of Roma" – was a relaxing charm that was totally unexpected. There were only about eight tables in total, of either two, three or four people. There was another family with three children, but as we found out later, he was the son. Almost everyone except us was German, Swiss or Austrian. German was the first tongue of the hotel, with Italian a long way behind. We had not expected to be talking German in Italy.

The oldest part of the building was sixteenth century with various additions and refurbishments over time. I particular liked the green roofed turret and the internally arched ceilings.

Day 93
Mileage 6243
Thursday 25th July 2002
Up the Mandelpaß

Today we went up the top of the mountain by funicular. A small, single, red carriage. It can hold about 20 people. It is run by electricity, slowly chugging up the steep mountain track.

The funicular chugged steadily in to the mountain station and we jumped out on to the platform.

Thinking that we could see into Austria we clambered on to a road that lead into the forest. The path that we took didn't go into the forest really, but around the edge, but it still gave scary but tense atmosfear.

After ten minutes mum said, "Keep your eyes peeled for mushrooms, around here's the perfect place for porchinny mushrooms." Just as she had finished the sentence, she shouted in astonishment. "Dave, come and have a look at this mushroom. DAVE, COME BACK!" At last dad came trotting back, mum had taken a large pointed stick and touched the mushroom which immediately turned over.

We headed for the tourist information and asked if there were any major good viewpoints. The lady at the desk said the you would have to walk 1½ km to a chair-lift and then walk another 10 minutes for a good viewpoint.

After some refreshments we set off towards the chair-lift. We found the chair-lift was closed and opened again at 2.

Me and Indigo played in a small park near a shack. One time when I was going up the steps of a lime green slide when from behind the shack a great big St. Bernard dog came out scampering and barking as if we were about to kill someone! The dog had long shaggy hair, even though the dog was a St. Bernard it didn't have a bottle on his neck.

At last two o'clock came and the chair-lift started up and we were off up the mountain again. This time the chair-lift was very fast and we were near the top in next to no time.

We took the path that took us up to the view point. We came to the wizard's staircase – a little staircase made out of the tree roots.

We finally came to the view point and boy was it a good view or what, we could see about 100 miles or so!

After we had taken the whole view, I turned and saw a shrine for two men who had died up there and they were only in their 20's!

We walked back to the chair-lift and were down in no time. I walked over to dad and asked if he would take me on some walks with him. He answered by simply beaming at me.

I only have a rough idea of how we got back I only know that it was fast compared to the way there.

*

The Eppan Valley lies at the bottom of some mountains. There was a road and a funicular up to the top of the Mandelpaß. Today we wanted to go up on the train. The bottom was just up the road in Caldaro. We got on with a bunch of other tourists. The carriage itself – decorated outside in the local regional colours of red and white but without the eagle – was already tipped backwards facing up the mountain and the floor of the carriage was stepped and sloped away from us. It was going to be steep.

The bell rang and the door slid silently shut. "Mind the gap," I thought. Slowly, the carriage moved forward and we watched the track disappear up the mountainside. More orchards and vineyards slipped past the windows and then we were into rocks and woodlands with the occasional waterfall. The carriage gradually slipped backwards as the slope steepened. The railway went over a long viaduct and the track split in two to allow the descending car to pass us. And still the slope increased. We passed a corner of the road, which looked almost horizontal in comparison, with cars struggling up as we rose effortlessly. The up and down carriages were joined by a single cable and thus the weight in both carriages balanced each other out making the energy required less. At the top it felt as if the cars were leaning backwards.

The view from the station was very impressive, but the pass top itself was nothing special with a few bars and gift shops. There were lots of earnest walkers with backpacks, hiking boots and thick socks, shorts and walking sticks prowling around.

A path led us around the back of a hotel to find some wonderful woods. The dappled sunlight helped us find some mushrooms. There was a bright red one with brown spots and a large bolete. The bolete was not a porcini, it had the wrong colour to it and when it was broken the colour quickly changed from orange to yellow to blue as it oxidised.

Another path led to a chair-lift that would take us further up the mountain. The girls did very well walking most of the 1.5 kms without a fuss. Just our luck, when we got there the chair-lift was closed for lunch and we had to wait half an hour for it to re-open. Indigo discovered a swing and a slide to play on, but was scared away by a large St. Bernard who came out from hiding barking loudly. As soon as the chair lift opened a sudden queue materialised. As I had not seen anyone, either close or in the distance I was totally puzzled.

At the top, a signpost directed us towards a viewpoint ten minutes walk away. The path rose steeply through woodland and had us all stumbling over tree roots and through brambles. We could glimpse the valley below, but there was no clear viewpoint. I did not like leaving the path too much as there were some very severe and deep drops. The pine covered cliffs contrasted with the clear vertical stratified rock on which they grew. There were no visible paths downwards, but I assume that there must be some. The valley was a distant dream with its onion domed churches and vast acreage of next year's wine growing. In the distance was Bolzano, the regional capital.

Back down at the bottom of the chairlift we followed a different path to the top of the funicular. There were lots of cabins in the woods and the fields, some were occupied, but, even in late July, most were standing empty. The strains of someone desperately trying to play a tune on an accordion wafted over the fields. It took me a minute or so to recognise the tune then suddenly George and I were singing, "Oh when the saints, oh when the saints go marching in...".

Going down the funicular was just as spectacular as the ascent. At the bottom we decided to go to Caldaro for tea and cake. The market square was full of cafés and we were spoiled for choice. Indigo had ice cream and George had ice cream with a bowl of fruit. The apple strudel was in a crumbling biscuit cake form rather than the flaky pastry I was expecting. Very tasty, especially with cream and washed down with local red wine.

When we got back to the hotel, George and Indigo wanted the pool, except that it had turned a peculiar green colour and you could no longer see the bottom.

Day 94
Mileage 6255
Friday 26ᵗʰ July 2002
Outzi the Iceman

A late start meant late breakfast which meant we got out late.

Today we visited the Naturale History Museum, where Outzi the Iceman lives. Outzi is a 5,000 B.C. year old person, preserved perfectly up a mountain. Outzi was very important to his tribe, you can tell this because he was wearing a bear skin hat.

We actually saw Outzi's body in an ice room. You could see lots of muscles, which in a way look very dead indeed.

After 'bout two hours in the museum, we decided enough was enough.

I grabbed myself a pizza and started to eat ravenously. Indigo had a banana and mum and dad had sausages.

We were just about to turn off and go to the Hole of Ice when Indigo said she needed a wee so we went back to the apartment.

I was going to have a nice long swim in the lovely sky blue swimming pool, but I was completely put off when I saw the swimming pool had turned a light algae colour.

*

The road down to Bolzano was quite short. We went off in search of Outzi, the ice man, who was resident in a museum there. We did not know where we were going when we entered the town, but driving round we quickly found the archaeological museum with a big poster of Outzi outside. We found a parking space less than a hundred metres away.

The museum had evidently undergone transformation since Outzi arrived here. All the exhibits were displayed in an interesting and modern way. Although Outzi was the main exhibit here the museum tried hard at not concentrating on him and him alone but also showed the type of life he must have led. I was amazed at the muddle over who or what Outzi was when he was first discovered. There was a political wrangle over where the body should be stored for research (Italy or Austria), but for Bolzano, it was definitely a prestigious coup to keep the body.

His equipment had survived well and I was particularly impressed that they believed that he carried fire in the way of embers around with him and used dried mushrooms for kindling. We both hoped that these mushrooms were not porcini. All this interpretation and the way it changes over time (for it does, doesn't it?) brought to mind how future archaeologist would interpret our lives. Would they mistake cigarettes for kindling? Or think that razor blades were used in some bizarre male coming of age ritual?

We queued up to catch a glimpse of the man himself in his cold and lonely case. He was unexpectedly short. You could almost believe that he had fallen asleep in an awkward position and was surprised to be waking up in this room. It was hard to believe that he was over seven thousand years old and must have lived an active life for over forty years. Indigo didn't quite know what to make of him, but was very sad for him.

There were lots of videos to watch in the museum showing various aspects of the life and times of Outzi including how to make pottery and how to make flint knifes. There was one video showing the migration of sheep over the mountains during the winter which Indigo found really funny as one poor sheep was pushed off the track and went skidding down the snow. We watched this several times, but there was no clue as to whether the sheep was lost or rescued.

Time passed quickly and we made our way down the lane outside the museum towards a market. George and Indigo had a slice of pizza and we grabbed a würstel from a stand. Very Germanic, but unlike English hot dogs, extremely tasty with either *scenf* or horseradish. We would have liked to have stayed longer, but the children were complaining so we made our way back to the Galaxy and homeward.

The pool was back to an inviting blue and proved irresistible to all. There were some chairs and tables around the pool and a wonderful shaded seating area under a low set of growing vines. These were obviously the same vines that were used in the fields as even now they were heavy with bunches of green grapes. From the other side of the pool, the valley slowly slipped away to give gorgeous views across vineyards, Tyrolean chalets and churches. Beyond that lay the river and the autostrada south before the next range of mountains rose. To the left rose the small town of St. Paul and in the distance you could see Bolzano nestling at the confluence of three valleys. Behind us was the range of mountains with the Mandelpaß.

Day 95
Mileage 6275
Saturday 27th July 2002
Wet (Not White) Water Rafting

After breakfast I dashed to see what colour the pool was. When I got there, to my astonishment the pool was the colour of the sky above!

By the time I had raced round the pool and back to mum to tell her, she said something that made me punch a fist into the air. We were going rafting. Nothing could be better.

Even though we didn't start 'til one we left straight away. We wanted to find the place before we had lunch. Good thing too, there was a terrific jam 'bout an hour long. We finally pulled through and we arrived in next to no time. We only got there in time to.

Just as we hurtled open the door they were handing out the stuff we needed. After about half an hour of talking what to do, we set off.

After 10 minutes drive we got out. Getting to the raft was on thing but getting into it was another. When we were in we headed straight for some white water.

A huge dip was coming closer and closer. Suddenly out of no where came a stone, a large sharp stone. Cleverly the guide found his way round the rock and we were safe.

We had reached the rapids. There were huge stones and rapids that was going so fast we had to dodge them.

We turned sharply and went sideways into a big rapid and I was the only one who got wet by it! The rapid was huge rising higher and faster than the rest of them and it slammed into the side of the boat. The boat jerked slightly and I almost went overboard!

We bashed into the side and the guide leaped out and landed the raft against the side and told everyone to get out of the raft and go into the vans.

We arrived home in time for a swim and dinner.

*

After a leisurely breakfast, we took the road north beyond Bolzano heading towards Merano where we then turned west along the valley leading to passes into Austria, Switzerland and to Bormio. The pass to Bormio was over 2,700m and is the second highest in the Alps. We would have loved to have done this, but time was going to be against us. This was Saturday, a typical change-over day and one of the first of the summer school holidays, the traffic up and down this road was heavier than we had anticipated, but exacerbated by a 10km jam outside Naturno. We could see no reason for this jam except for weight of traffic. When we got to Naturno there were two sets of traffic lights letting the occasional car out into the main road in a very inefficient manner. This was the cause of the jam. If I lived near here, this would absolutely drive me crazy. We were heading for Laces, just a few kms east of Naturno where there was a rafting centre.

George was going crazy with delight ever since we had discussed the possibility of wild-water rafting at breakfast. They do a special children's version which caters for all ages from four upwards so this meant that both could go. I had never done this before either, so we didn't know quite what to expect. There was another large bunch of Germans also joining us, with several children too. We all had to get kitted out in wetsuits, helmets and life-jackets. This had the effect of making me very apprehensive rather than safe. There was a briefing in German, translated by Pascal, one of the members of *Acquaterra Rafting* in a very glib and general way. They showed us how to sit and paddle, how to fall in, how to pull others out from the river and how to swim in the river. "Everyone falls in. That is part of the fun!" said Pascal gleefully. "Oh no it certainly is not!" thought I.

We all packed up and went off in three battered minivans driven by spotty seventeen-year-old youths who didn't seem to understand what a clutch was for. All this gear we were wearing made us all very hot and sweaty. I found myself feeling very clumsy and unable to move. We arrived at the entrance point on the river and I thought, "Look at those rocks! They said that there would be no rocks. They're rocks down there the size of dustbins." The spotty youths started to prepare the rafts and fully inflated them. A small traffic jam formed around us. Eventually the rafts were shoved unceremoniously down the steep rocky bank into the water. I slithered along helplessly despite the fact I was helping. I was too far down the bank to help anyone else down, but they all managed it somehow. We came to rest in the raft and made ourselves comfortable. We were sharing our raft with one other family whose five-year-old was clearly petrified of the water and was howling and protesting loudly. I, at least, just kept stumm, and let my anxieties only show on my face. George and Indigo showed no fear at all and they were right not to. I was more concerned about getting wet "as part of the fun" than of being hurt. Rationally, I knew that their business could not survive if any children ever got hurt on this trip.

Suddenly, we were off. The second raft came over towards us and started shovelling paddlefuls of water in our faces. The other family were obviously expecting this and with great Germanic gerhawphs of laughter proceeded to retaliate. I sat there glumly, stoically ignoring all this.

The river was flowing fairly fast, but was very benign. There were occasional drops in the water and we were white water rafting. Everyone thought this was great fun. The third raft was way behind us and they looked intent on getting themselves wet. The second raft caught us up and one of our number was pulled into the water laughing and shrieking.

The look of shock on his face as he realised just how cold the water was knocked the merriment out of his soul. We pulled him back in and more paddlefuls of water were exchanged. Pascal, our guide, tied the two rafts together and waited for the third raft. He leapt into the third raft and immediately began to try and capsize it much to the delight of those on board. He eventually succeeded and then made his way back to our raft. We were set free from the second raft and headed off downstream.

We went under a bridge where we caught a large bag full of drinks. These were passed around as I sat there anxiously waiting for the next set of unnecessary pranks to make sure we enjoyed the experience to the full.

Then we were into the rapids, we all enjoyed the chaos and the thrill of this part – yes, even me! Yes, we all got wet from the water as we splashed though, but this was part of the fun and was not part of some orchestrated conspiracy to get us all wet. Suddenly, we were through it and we drifted for another few kms placidly enjoying the river and the passing scenery. We pulled over to the side and all got out back onto terra firma.

"Again, again" said George.

We all helped pack up the rafts and drove back to the centre in Laces.

The road back to Bolzano was a lot clearer around Naturno. We stopped for *würstel und frittes* – this could become a habit.

We managed a short swim in the pool before showering and dinner.

Day 96
Mileage 6346
Sunday 28ᵗʰ July 2002
At the Tschindlhof

*

Today both George and I tried to catch up with our journals.

The poolside was hot and we sat quietly playing cards and in the pool for a lot of the morning. George had become friends with Lino and for much of the time she was off with him. Lino had given George an old pen-knife and George had decided she would whittle a stick into a spear for a present for Lino.

Lino's mother was Austrian and she was the partner of Möhl's son. Lino himself was not related to Möhl, but his two younger siblings were grandchildren. The family used to spread out in the dappled shade by the apple and pear trees. The smallest baby boy was only five months old and was doted on by almost everyone. The sister – Elena, was about two and was walking around and would cheekily play with anyone who showed her any interest. Indigo enjoyed her company, especially as she was the elder for a change.

Mind you Indigo would go up to and talk to most adults in the place as well as the other children. She would be very charming and would show the adults something or pay them compliments on their clothes, jewellery or hairstyles. She would tell them about how much make up she had and that she could speak Italian and German, but when they asked her to say something, she would reply that it was a secret. Both George and Indigo would now say "*danke*" and "*bitter*" and were no longer bemused that not everyone understood what they said straight away.

George was continually refusing to do her journal. In the end I lost my rag with her and sent her upstairs to her bedroom to do some. Everyone got upset.

Indigo was getting stir crazy, so I decided to take her for a walk into the village. We followed the road down past the *Dracula Weinkellar* and past a whole series of quaint old Tyrolean buildings with alpine roofs and pretty turrets with coloured tiles, wooden windows and with shutters only opening at the lower half. The whole village was abloom with flowers in gardens. Window-boxes were full of pink, blue and purple flowers cascading over balconies.

One old building had its roof covered in cactus style house leeks, this was very reminiscent of home where we have a group of house leeks on a small tiled roof outside our upstairs garden. Two years ago this threw up a single flowering stem in a poor plant's attempt to emulate the century plants in Sicilia. On this roof, seemingly hundreds of these plants had thrown up their flowers sunward simultaneously.

Further round there was a playground. Indigo quickly impressed the other children with her dad's ability to spin a roundabout quickly. Several sickly and dizzy children scattered away later. Beyond the playground a large canvas roof was shading a large number of empty benches and tables. On closer inspection we discovered that we had stumbled upon a beer festival at one of those low periods between the lunch and evening sessions. I quickly bought a beer and Indigo an orange soda. Indigo kept insisting on tasting the beer and made lots of loud "aah" noises with great gusto and a broad toothy grin under her white foamy moustache.

After we went off in search of gelato and found something to satisfy George's cravings too: After Eight mint ice-cream. The dizzy Austrian children saw us coming and cowered behind their parents who were busy buying single-flavour cones for everyone: they all had vanilla which struck me as odd, but the whole group was physically pale too. Some of the women had the palest legs that I had ever seen. David in Frienze, made from the bright white Carrera marble, looked sun tanned in comparison to those almost blue legs showing between shorts and boots.

The hotel continued to operate smoothly in the evening. The receptionist, Francesca, wanted to know how long we would be staying, as we had first said that we would leave on Monday. We confirmed that we would stay until Wednesday, as beyond that we would need to change rooms. Francesca was very friendly and spoke all the languages that we needed as well as a few others. Her sister Eva also worked here, but we never saw them together. They were both in their late teens or early twenties, very tall and slender, with Eva maybe too much of a stick for her own good.

Day 97
Mileage 6346
Monday 29ᵗʰ July 2002
The Maso Corto Glacier

Today we went to the glacier. It took us a ling time to reach the Chocolate Box as dad called it. A chocolate box is a large red box which could easily lift 30 people up to 3,200 meters!

Up to the top we stepped and guess what was on the ground? SNOW! I know this sounds crazy snow in the last week in July! I mean it was as hot as England gets and there was snow on the ground, about 3 feet of it!

I went up and picked up a large chunk of ice and threw it on dad's back. SPLAT! The ice immediately turned to a wet slimy sludge and slowly slid down dad's back!

"Yuck! What in the world could that be!" dad yelled turning in my direction. It was very hard to contain myself from laughing out loud and doubled up with silent laughter!

We peered over the top of a large wooden barrier and saw a large sheet of ice. It was the glacier, I thought the glacier was large but I would never have guessed it would have been as large as this!

Dad looked up and saw that the clouds were closing in, he alerted mum immediately and we set off down the mountain in the chocolate box.

*

Today it was bright and hot first thing. We decided that this would be a good day to go glacier hunting. We followed the same route as on Saturday to Naturno, but today the traffic jam was not nearly so long although it was sufficiently long as to be irritating. Just past Naturno we took a right fork going up into the mountains. This road was narrow and steep from the outset. There were plenty of roadworks, as extra tunnels were being excavated to make the driving easier.

The woods and the fields were very much Heidi country. We half expected to see a group of nuns running across the fields, but we didn't.

Up further, there was a dam and behind it was a large green-coloured lake, down from its high water mark by about three or four metres. As the road rose, the outside temperature fell and settled at 18°C.

Further still, we came to Maso Corto at the end of the road. This was a small ski resort with only three or four hotels and bars. The big *funivia* was open – a typical red and white chocolate-box style. We watched the cable car rise up into the clouds and disappear and we thought it would be good to go up to the top. There was skiing at the top and I was interested to know how good it was. George berated us for not bringing all her skiing outfits with us on holiday for just such an occasion. We joined the short queue for the cable-car. There were mostly foot passengers, all dressed up for the cold and the mountains with serious hiking boots, jumpers, trousers and thick socks. We were just in open-toed sandals with no socks. George, Indigo and Eliza had all put on thick fleeces and trousers. I was carrying a sweatshirt just in case. A couple of keen youngsters were kitted out and carrying snowboards.

The *funivia* rose up stately over the rocks and steep slopes. There below us was a short ski jump with a very high ramp. On closer inspection this was actually a ramp for practising ski aerobatics. How people ever got round to jumping like this in the first place I just cannot fathom. At the top, 3200m, there were several ski runs and chair lifts open both down this side and to the far side of the mountain. It was very icy and you could see the clear icy blue of the glacier underneath the slopes and continuing down beyond the last chair. Luckily there was no snow in the immediate vicinity of the ski lift and we didn't have to suffer the indignity of walking in the snow in sandals. Now at the top it was clear and the view down the mountain was wonderful.

Across the valley from here was the Austrian border and the ski maps all marked the spot on the far side where Outzi was found. Were there any other people like Outzi still lying out there?

George and Indigo couldn't resist the opportunity to throw snowballs at me. What snow there was was quite hard, so I had to make the snowballs myself for them to throw at me.

The weather was beginning to close in and we'd noticed that the chair-lifts were going to close for lunch. This meant that there was going to be a rush to get the cable car down, so we went off to catch the next one. Our timing was not quite perfect as there was a large contingent of skiers coming down the mountain. It was not as bad a squeeze as it could have been, but it was quite unpleasant for Indigo.

Down the mountain we settled for pizza and würstel in one of the bars in the town before driving back down to the valley. The weather was closing in up top and the funivia was now longer visible up the top. As soon as we got back to the Galaxy, the rains started to come down. We drove down cautiously. Hikers and bikers were all taking shelter under the trees and at the mouths of tunnels, waiting for the storm to abate.

As we were down in the valley earlier than expected we decided to drive back to Eppan over the passes rather than round the valleys. We made for the Valley del Non. The road up to the Passo della Palade was long and windy, but not too high (1512m), but we had to take care that we didn't drive into the Val d'Ultimo as this only had one entrance and exit. As soon as we went over the pass we noticed that Italian was now the prime language again. The signs in German were now either subordinate or non-existent. The houses too had lost their Tyrolean feel and looked shabby on the outside. We had noticed this before on other occasions that the Italians were more concerned about interior comfort and fashionable furniture than exterior elegance. We drove down into the central town of the valley, Fondo, before taking the Passo di Mendola back across to Sud Tyrol. At the very top here, we slipped back into German-speaking Italy. We had been up this ridge on the railway. Although the road was steep it looked almost flat compared with the angle of the railway. The road was narrow and in parts there was only a two-foot wall between us and a descent of several hundred feet. This was a little unnerving.

Down at the Tschindlhof, there was great excitement as two boxes of ducks had arrived. We hadn't noticed, but a small duck pond had been dug in the vegetable garden. There was also a small hut now standing there too. All the children, and a good few of the parents too, had a look in the boxes and poked their fingers about. There were three females and one male. The family Möhl gathered around and watched as the boxes were emptied and the ducks coaxed into their new homes. There was lots of squealing and wailing from the birds, but eventually they were locked in and left for the night. They were to be released into their garden on Wednesday.

The ducks were a birthday present for Herr von Möhl. The lady who brought the ducks would be staying for a few days to make sure they were trained right.

Our waitress flowed through all the distractions. She was a very good looking woman in her mid-thirties with fiery (dyed) red hair and always seemed to have a dramatic, yet not too dramatic, pose as she swept around the tables carrying food and drinks. She always wore a long flowing yellow dress with a scarf tied around her waist. After a few days she knew what we liked and our table was always laid with water and Fanta.

In the background, the Möhl family celebrated father's birthday, with friends, cake and champagne.

Day 98
Mileage 6451
Tuesday 30ᵗʰ July 2002
Max's Room

After breakfast we moved rooms from a new made room to a lovely, old, original tower room. But the thing that was strange was that the room had a name – Max!

The tower was a tall, thin, elegant looking tower. On top were some bright, emerald green tiles for a roof.

Max was a lovely sized room. Above mine and Indigo's beds was a large, rose patterned canopy which hung in such a way that made it look like a huge spider's web.

After the chaos of moving we headed towards Lido Montiggl, a large green lake with large trees all round.

There was also a large pool with slides and all sorts, there was also a large jump into the lake, which is 6 –7 meters deep all the way round!

The longest slide was a long, winding slide which makes things very fast. To start with you went straight down, then suddenly you turn so sharply you almost get turned over onto your tummy!

The smaller slides were also very fast when you go down them you are shot down with the force of a bullet, then dropped into a small pool about 2 foot deep.

The jumps are definitely worth a visit. There was a 1 metre jump which was a very easy jump to dive from, but the bigger jump was more daring to jump from. You sort of hover for a moment and then you plummet like a stone.

A young boy about 3-4 years old jumped out of the 3m jump. He started to cry after a while. Launching myself forward, I went for him and took him back to the steps one hand round his tummy.

We retired at five o'clock to have a shower and the best dinner we had in a long time.

*

We had decided that we liked this spot so much that we would stay here if possible until Saturday morning before going off to Udine. Francesca thought she would be able to move people around so that we could stay put, but no, the people who were booked into our room had specifically asked for the room. Francesca went on a room hunt. I thought it was odd that in a hotel this small she would not know if any of the rooms were available or not. There were not two rooms next to each other, but she offered us a suite which we went to see. This was another lovely room but it only had a double sofa bed which George and Indigo would have to share. We went down gloomily to reception and thought that we would have to move on tomorrow.

Then suddenly Francesca's face brightened and she said there was another suite in the old tower with two single beds as well as a double. We went up into the old part of the house. Eliza had always wanted to have a nose around here. There was a staircase with some magical stained-glass windows out into the courtyard. The tower room upstairs was on the second floor. We had to climb up a narrow rickety staircase to get to the top floor. On the landing there were all sorts of old pieces of military paraphernalia together with an assortment of hunting trophies on the wall. There were a series of old photographs on the wall, but I could not tell if they were old family photographs or not.

The room itself was in the old green-tiled turret that had enticed us here on the day before we arrived. The double room overlooked the vineyards. The two single beds were in their own side room with a large canopy sweeping down on the ceiling. This would suit us perfectly for the next few days. Although the room had a number, it also had a name – Max, I wondered which member of the van Möhl family he was. We had to move either today or tomorrow, so we decided to pack and move now.

The climb upto the top of the tower was a killer, especially with the bags, but I thought it was definitely worthwhile. We dumped our things and then got ready to go down to the lakes. There were two lakes close to each other the other side of the wine road from Eppan. We took the road across the wine road, but hadn't realised there were two separate roads and ended heading in completely the wrong direction. It was becoming obvious that the map of the town that we had may have been topologically correct, but was certainly not to scale. According to the map there were some minor tracks leading back to the lake. We tried and eventually found one and followed it. The road quickly turned into dirt and narrowed into a tractor path. Suddenly we were around the back of a hotel car park. Quietly we drove into the car park and whistled innocently to ourselves as the guests around the pool looked around at us with grim and astonished faces wondering why we were disturbing their peace. The way out of the hotel led us to the right road at last.

Down by the lake the car park was full, so I left the family behind and went back up the road to find the car park in the woods. I walked down through the woods following a woman who I overtook quickly. Five minutes later I was suffering from déjà vu as I found myself following the same woman again. I had followed the path and I soon saw that she had followed a shortcut through the woods. One shortcut was enough for me today.

The lake side was well laid out and thoughtfully designed. There was a large swimming pool with two smaller children's pools with slides and many fountains. There was also a long slide from up the hill and swimming, jumping and diving access to the lake. We could sit and watch Indigo having fun in the smaller pools and let George have the freedom to explore the lake and overcome her fear of jumping in from 1 and then 3 metre boards.

Not only was the complex designed and run in a very organised, disciplined and Germanic way, but the customers behaved that way too.

Next to us there was a family of 2 adults and 2 children playing snap. I always thought that half of the fun of this game was its very riotous nature with screams and shouts all around. But not so for this family, they were fully equipped with a bell. The sort of bell you get at a hotel reception where it stands on the desk and invites you to tap it very gentle to attract attention. Well, this family used their bell instead of shouting, "SNAP". There never seemed to be any dispute about who rang first, nor were their any fights in trying to get to the bell first.

George and I swam out to a raft where there were twenty or so people sitting and sunning themselves. The raft was lopsided and different corners were going under the water in turns as the people shifted about trying to find some equilibrium. Everyone was enjoying this swinging party game, but after half the people left everything was back to normal.

Day 99
Mileage 6466
Wednesday 31ˢᵗ July 2002
Summer Freezer

For some time we have been keen trying to go to the ice hole or known as the Summer Freezer. Today we got our chance.

We drove on, eating up mile after mile. This was a very long journey for something that was meant to be a 20 minute journey!

We stopped at a hopeful looking place and asked a hopeful looking woman. We were on the right track it would be a lovely five minute walk. It might have been a nice walk but it will be more than that.

We walked for about 5 minutes and came out into a very shady path which as we came close was a T-junction path. We took the right path as the ice hole was directed there. A steep path awaited us with loose stones under our step and the small pinecones didn't help, but just acted as a load of marbles scattered all over the place.

We climbed over the loose rocks and somehow we managed to stumble over the pinecone marbles. I stumbled suddenly, a muscle pulled and I tried standing up and "Ow!" the muscle was strained

*

The view out of the tower was over the vineyards and up the mountains. The sky was crystal clear except for some slight mist at the top of the ridge. The last few days had been hot up here but the intense heat when we were in Tuscana was no longer present.

George and Indigo were getting used to the vast breakfasts that were available here. George has taken to eating soft boiled eggs by spreading the yolk on bread and ignoring the white. Indigo enjoys her croissants. Eliza is desperate for a decent cup of tea. Time is passing slowly here and breakfasts are getting later.

This morning the ducks' hut was opened and they had to be coaxed out. Once out, they stood up with their necks held high and strutted around the vegetable garden performing a synchronised quacking routine. Coincidently, duck was on the menu for tonight, but we didn't think it was these.

The ducks had been bought in order to control the snails in the vegetable patch. I had never heard of ducks being used in this way. They went around in a gang of four clucking to each other, but none of them seemed to be snail hunting. They were very shy to begin with and avoided the gaggle of little children trying to touch and play with them. Later I looked over the fence just in time to see them finishing off a nice juicy row of lettuces. They seemed to be doing more damage than the snails could have done in a much shorter period.

Up in the village, there was a spot in the wood called an ice hole. It was in the middle of the woods and according to Francesca about twenty minutes walk. We decided to drive to a spot nearby and walk from there. If the maps were to any sort of scale we parked right on top of the ice hole. The path through the woods was easy to follow but steep and the pinecones underfoot were like walking on ball bearings. The ice hole was down in a dip full of boulders all tumbled together. Between the gaps in the rocks a chill wind blew. "We've stepped into a freezer," said George.

I ended up carrying Indigo on my shoulders as we climbed back out of the ice hole. The path underfoot was a bit treachery and I stumbled on some pinecones and went a over t. I twisted my ankle a bit, but I was alright, more importantly I had managed to fall over without Indigo shifting from my shoulders.

Back in the town we wandered around looking at the old antiques shop windows and various other knick-knack shops. Not actually thinking of buying anything mind, but just being curious.

Day 100
Mileage 6476
Thursday 1ˢᵗ August 2002
The Fondo Gorge

*

The tower room is west facing so the early light does not wake me up. Although the tower itself is octagonal, it is only in the corner of the room. On the inside, three of the sides of the octagon have windows whereas looking from the outside there are four shutters. We find another false window between the tower and the children's bedroom, but cannot find any trace of it internally. The bathroom is most peculiar, and probably that's why we weren't offered it at first: there is no bidet. Any hot blooded Italian would have blanched as if drawn by Dracula himself with the prospect of spending days without a bidet.

Today the ridge was covered in cloud and we decided to venture back to the Valley de Non. George wasn't feeling 100%, but she needed to get out. Down in Fondo there was a flat walk in a gorge and further up there was a full blooded canyon with waterfalls and other such stuff.

George had taken to whittling a stick into a spear for Lino as a present. This had been going on for some days now and George had hoped to give it to Lino before they left for home today. Unfortunately she missed her own deadline, but now we were carrying the spear around with us as she continued working away at it.

Lino, his siblings and his parents said goodbye before we set off up the mountain. The gorge at Fondo started off gently like a school nature trail along side a gently bubbling stream. On both sides of the path there were very tall steep and narrow cliffs. Coming down one side was a cascade of water. It was very thin with water and you could practically stand underneath and only get the occasional splash. Individual drops dove out of the sky for three or four seconds before they hit.

Further up was an old water mill. It had three wheels, but only one was still operating. The stream had been split into two and the upper stream was fed to the mill. After this the gorge suddenly got very narrow and we could no longer walk alongside the stream, but had to follow artificial paths above the water. The stream had been dammed and some of the run off was diverted into a hydro electric plant.

At one point where the sides of the gorge almost met, a boulder was kept in place by the two sides. I didn't like to think when it would slip out of place, but I didn't think it would be today. The run off from the dam was thunderous from so close up and we could not hear each other talk as we climbed up the staircase in silence.

The Lago Smelderado was indeed very green. But it was a little too twee for my liking. We walked past the lake and followed the river upstream and into the woods. Although George and Indigo weren't enthusiastic to begin with, they were very chatty and happy as we ambled along. They were spotting butterflies and insects. We crossed the river twice over bridges made with wood, but if you looked closely the bridges were actually made with steel and just cladded with wood. It looked as if the local engineers no longer trusted themselves in the use of wood – very strange. We came across a very dark blue/black mushroom unlike any I have seen before. We all stood around in admiration before moving on.

Eventually we came across the confluence of two rivers and tried to work out which one to follow. One just continued along in the same manner, but the other would turn into waterfalls and the canyon but this was probably half an hour's walk away. However far we went we would also have to return. Although the children were happy at the moment they might not be still in half an hour. The sun had gone in and the wind had picked up. I thought it would be better if we turned for home. On the way back we marched rather than dawdled. We were quickly over the bridges and back to Lago Smelderado. Back down the gorge we found ourselves quickly back in Fondo. The rain had held off and by the time we found the car the sun was out again.

We wanted some refreshments and Eliza wanted some *sachetorte*. We knew we couldn't get this in Italian-speaking Italy, so we headed back up the mountain to the Madelpass where we knew we could get some. At the top the sun was strong and hot. We settled down for our cakes and drinks in the shade realising that this was day 100 of our trip and we were now in August. We ruminated on the trip so far. There was so much that we had seen and learnt about Italy and ourselves. We had met some very interesting people on our travels and had never really felt unsafe. Everyone's kindness had impressed us. Both George and Indigo missed their friends at home more than anything else. We too had missed our friends, but had not missed commuting and working. Neither Eliza nor I still had any clear idea of what we would do when we got back. We knew that immediate practical things would take over, but where and how we would earn a living remained a mystery. It seemed like an awfully long time ago since we were at home and we had managed to keep ourselves very busy on most days.

Day 101
Mileage 6511
Friday 2nd August 2002
Lago di Monticolo

*

This was our last full day here. We have been very pampered with company, food and wine and it was time to move on. Another morning where we all had a variety of things for breakfast.

Today would be a good day to spend by the lake. This time we were earlier and this time we drove the right way the first time. We all walked down through the woods and I told George that I had passed the same person twice on the way down last time and asked her how was this possible. It did not take her long to realised, she had taken a shortcut. We found the slip off the main path and took the shortcut ourselves, overtaking a great bunch of Germans.

The lake was splendid again. George and Indigo went back to playing the same games. We had promised George that we would hire a rowboat today, but they were shut. We enjoyed reading in the sun keeping one eye out for Indigo as she incessantly played in the fountains and slides. George was more adventurous as she used the large slide (Indigo would too, but she was too young), and jumped into the lake. The lake was about six or seven metres deep, so there was no chance of hitting the bottom.

Indigo and I went into the lake and found a shallow patch for small children. She was always wanting to go deeper, but, although she could swim a little, I always felt nervous being with her outside my own depth.

Nutella, jam and honey sandwiches were the order of the day for lunch followed by fruit.

Later we saw some rowing boats on the lake and we decided to explore again. Those for hire inside the complex were closed, those for hire outside were not. We eventually hired a small boat, but it wasn't a conventional rowing boat – more like a pedalo. It was very high in the water and with three passengers and an oarsman (me) it felt very unstable. I was afraid that if the girls rocked the boat everyone would go in as there were no sides. I rowed across the lake and we watched some boys climbing trees and then dropping off into the lake. I was surprised when George said that she would not like to do that. We were being blown ashore and I had to struggle quite hard to get back to the middle of the lake. Just as I was making progress a water snake, about a metre long, swam past us heading for the boys and their tree. It reminded us of the snake that George had caught when fishing in Lake Como two years ago, it had managed to get itself knotted in her net!

By now the wind was picking up and the clouds were joining together. We rowed back to shore and passed a couple who had hired a pair of inflatable skis designed to walk on water. George had seen these and was very keen to try them, but once she had seen these people struggle she recognised the errors of her ways.

We packed and I went to fetch the Galaxy.

That evening was our last here. The food was good as usual with do-it-yourself salad – I loved their apple vinegar which was slightly sweet – followed by "a taster from the chef" – this varied every night and was always splendidly arranged on the plate, tonight it was some smoked salmon – followed by a starter – normally some form of delightful pasta or light soup – followed by a main course and finally either a dessert or cheese or fruit. We had tried various local wines over the past few days including their own house wine. Tonight we had some Blaubergunder, the local name for Pinot Noir.

The children had much simpler fare, but were very happy and played with the other children. They liked to climb the nespole trees, but Indigo was forever getting stuck. Indigo used to charm the other adults and talk to them about goodness knows what – nobody seemed to mind. We had eaten outside every night bar one, a real delight.

La Faula
Day 102
Mileage 6521
Saturday 3rd August 2002
To La Faula

*

The early grey of dawn eased into my consciousness. It was not the light which had woken me, but a regular tapping noise. It sounded as though it was coming from inside the room, but I could not pinpoint it. I had memories of water dripping in Sciacca going through my head, but no, it was a dry knock. Yes it was coming from inside the beams and I wondered if this is what death watch beetle sounded like. After a few minutes it stopped and I did not think if it again.

We struggled to pack this morning as last night we were just not in the mood. Hauling our luggage down the stairs from Max's tower room, unloading and reloading stuff from the Galaxy until everything was in and we could shut the back doors.

We said our farewells and paid our bill. George left her spear behind for Lino who was returning in a couple of weeks.

We headed out of the village down through St Michael and towards Bolzano. We were going to go north and then east across the mountains. Another change-over day, so it was quite busy, but most of the traffic was southbound. After a short stretch on the motorway we turned east and drove towards Cortina (the ski area and not the car). Here the road was single carriageway and moved steadily enough if slowly. The last 20kms or so leading into Cortina were through a narrow ravine with very rugged mountains on both sides. Snow and ice were still on their peaks plus two glaciers. It looked far too steep though for skiing, but I sure some enterprising skiers tackle these mountains off piste. After the pass, the road down to Cortina remained as spectacular as ever, with the village nestling in the valley. We parked and found a small place for pizza. It felt good to be back in Italian speaking Italy. Even though we had enjoyed Eppan, we realised that 10 days was plenty. We had been very well looked after, cosseted and spoilt at the Tschindlhof and we were all very relaxed. The Sud Tyrol was very beautiful and just-so, with everything in it's place and a place for everything. Everyone, including the tourists, knew their place in the grand scheme of things and no one tried to break out of this straightjacket. The food was always well-cooked and presented, the streets were clean, all the building looked well looked after and the gardens were all immaculately tended and last, but by no means least, the state of their toilets really showed a cultural difference – there were no squatteroos and all toilets were sparkling clean. The haphazardness of the Italian organisational ability spoke volumes about the spontaneity of their lifestyle. Here was much more like the Italy we came to see, but Cortina itself was too full of designer shops selling winterwear already. There were not many people around. A few earnest hikers and day-trippers like ourselves. There were also some old lady residents whose youth had faded, but were still trying to dress the part with high heels, backcombed hair, wide and high sunglasses, gaudy jewellery and – the essential accessory – a small dog either clutched under the arm or tethered on a thin leather lead. They greeted each other with air kisses and (I guess) exchanged compliments and gossip.

From Cortina the road passed through various valleys and over lowering passes. The number plates reflected a change towards Udine registered cars. These cars somehow managed to be older and slower than everybody else's. We stopped for some water at the top of the last pass. Indigo wanted to go inside with me. We walked past a small pack of motorcyclists, they had all overtaken us in convey some miles back enjoying the pleasure of the open road, sipping beer (but only small ones). There were no customers. We were served by an old man with whiskers as wide as his ears. I asked for a bottle of water in Italian, he told me the cost in German, I replied, "Danke" and he said, "Thank you." I don't how he realised we were English, but there you go. On the wall, and for sale were a large variety of cuckoo clocks ticking away. These fascinated Indigo, but I thought that we had better leave before they all started chiming.

As we came off the mountain we were stopped by police at the side of the road. We had been caught at the end of a bicycle race. The whole place was buzzing with bikes and people and the other hangers-on, although not nearly as many as in Peccioli. Bicyclists were continuing to cross the finish line barely 10m in front of us. I could see the winners' podium further along and I wondered if we would be held up until after the presentation. We were there for half an hour, but it seemed a lot longer.

Down and down we went towards the plains and the motorway. Even though we had been stopped to allow the bicycle race to finish, there were still stragglers coming up the mountain as we went down. It was not long until we reached the autostrada for the last leg to Udine. We drove across some very wide and almost dry riverbeds. A look on the map later showed us that we crossed this river several times. They were very wide and the bridges were all long viaducts with several arches. This implied that they must have to cope with very severe runoffs either during spring melt times or in times of storms

At last, we found the autostrada, but were only on it for a few minutes before arriving at Udine Nord. The instructions we had for La Faula were somewhat vague and only Udine and Cividale were on our map.

"SS54 from Undine towards Cividale; 3km on, turn left for Salt, then Magredis and Ravosa. From Ravosa, direction Attimis then right, by shrine, La Faula is on other side of the bridge."

It was, however, straightforward to find and we pulled up in front of the farm house where we were greeted by Paul and three enormous soft white dogs called Mini, Barty (short for Bartholomew) and Spotty, and then from round the corner came a smaller black-and-white border collie called Nellie. This became George's favourite. The large white dogs were a special breed of Italian sheep dog. From a distance they really looked like large shaggy sheep, but would ferociously protect a flock from wolves and other predators.

George and Indigo were immediately in heaven with these creatures who were all bigger than both of them.

Paul showed us to our room and we unpacked a bit and unwound.

The room was on two levels with the children's beds upstairs. The staircase was steep and the room was split across the middle by an enormous wooden beam that acted as a barrier to stop anyone falling off the top floor. It also acted as a restraint for anyone getting into the top space as the beam was at a very painful height for me.

Downstairs Paul – a native New Zealander, was preparing a barbecue, which we immediately said we would participate in. The only trouble was he could not get the coals to light. Just like all the barbecues in the world. Greg, who was staying next door, came to Paul's rescue. Indigo had found the paddling pool with fountain and spent quite some time cooling off. A very comfortable evening sitting outside under the vine covered pergola, eating well and drinking more home produced red wine.

Day 103
Mileage 6711
Sunday 4ᵗʰ August 2002
Up To Slovenia

*

In the early morning there was a thunderstorm. It had been ominous as the dawn spread, and it got darker as the sun rose. I got great pleasure lying in bed listening to the rain falling onto the vines just outside our windows and when the thunder started we all got up to watch the lightning in the eastern skies. The storm was quite distant and the rain here was just a pleasant indication of what might have been. It rumbled on for some time, but it gained in strength and came down quite hard for just a short sharp snap.

We ventured downstairs to breakfast and join a throng of fellow travellers. Paul's partner Luca is there along with Sabrina – an Austrian help here just for the summer – and Tedjik – an Albanian refugee who Paul and Luca were training as an assistant. They were all making sure everyone's needs were satisfied. George and Indigo spend their time stroking the dogs rather than eating anything. Paul gives them a brush and they soon realise that the dogs love this more than anything. George quickly fills a bucket with moulting hair… and then a second.

Outside the front of the house people are standing around and discussing where they will go for the day. Several people head off for the beach, but the weather makes us think twice about this option. I notice that one of the plants has been stripped bare and Luca points to another plant in a tub and shows us their caterpillars. They have five of them but we can only find two and they are very large indeed, about as long and as fat as my middle finger. They are happily munching away at their fresh plant. Luca and Paul don't know what they are but think they are butterflies and are happy to keep feeding them to see what they do turn into.

As George and Indigo are happy with the dogs, and Paul and Luca are happy having them around, we decide to go for a short walk along the river. The path from La Faula has apple trees on either side. Fruit is hanging heavily on the trees and there are many windfalls. The gates are shut and do not look as if they have been used for some time. We turn right just before the bridge and follow a gravel track. This has lots of plum trees on it with fruit ripe and ready for picking. There are supposed to be swimming holes in the river, but we can't find any. The water is anyway very brown and not appealing.

We come back and decide to visit Trieste to see if we can find the Italians at play. We find the back way to the autostrada through a variety of other villages, all of which looked very Slavic in style to me, contrasting with both the style in Sud Tyrol and in the rest of Italy further south. The state road with the turning for the autostrada is a long strip of superstores most of which appear to be shut. As we get towards Trieste we take the coast road. It is good to see the sea for the first time since Toscana. This is our first view of the Adriatic. The coast road is very straight and all possible parking spaces have been taken. Judging by the number plates these are mostly local Italians come out so sun themselves on a hot Sunday August afternoon. We can't see down to the shore, but a lot of people are lying on the promenade itself.

We find ourselves on the portside of Trieste and park near the main city square. The square is paved in slightly off-white stone and surrounded by very grand buildings, but the square itself is deserted.

In the centre of an arch is a stone bearded face wearing a wolf mask over its hair and what looks like a pair of animal feet under his chin.

We follow the road around and my memory of the map tells us that there is an amphitheatre and a castle around the corner. We spot the amphitheatre and ask George what she thinks it might me. "It's an amphitheatre, Dad", she explains moaning. "Probably Greek or Roman."

Around the corner we come across an antique market, or rather a sign saying that an antique market is held here on the second Sunday of every month. Never mind, but we won't be back next week. We follow some small deserted streets and back alleys and find ourselves underneath the bearded face again. Back to the Galaxy and off up to Muggia – a fishing port close to the Slovene border.

It is still hot and sunny, but as we drive further east cloud start to gather and distant thunder can be heard. We drive through Muggia and start to look for somewhere to park. Everywhere is still very busy, but we don't have to go too far beyond the village centre. There are lots of people lying around on the promenade, but now we can see that just below the promenade are very large rocks. They look uncomfortable to walk on to get to the sea, but some determined youngsters have done so.

As we walk back into Muggia, the thunder rumbles some more and it starts spitting. It is still very hot and all the Italians do is squirm around and roll over, ignoring the threatening downpour. The town is quite picturesque, but looks run down, tatty and poor. We decide to take cover under the sunshades of a harbour side bar for nibbles, ice cream, wine and beer. The expected downpour refuses to come. The same bodies are still lying in the heat when we return to the Galaxy. They obviously can read the weather better than us. We are now so close to the Slovenian border that we carry on up the coast road until we find it, but we do not venture across the border. The way back to Trieste is very depressing as the area has been run down for so long and has not flourished with the new openness with the east.

Beyond Trieste the coast road leads to Gardo: a poor man's version of Venezia. Gardo is properly attached to the mainland, but the road does pass through a large open flat and unprotected plain. It seems quite benign at this time of year, but I am sure it is very susceptible to storm damage. We stop off at a fruit stall and buy some good-looking melon and amazingly sized yellow-fleshed peaches almost the size of Indigo's face. In Gardo itself there are islands, canals, bridges and lagoons. The pedestrianised area was full of seaside shops and cheap clothes shops – definitely no designer clothes shops here. The place appears to be full of Italians, with foreigners like us in a very small minority, the total antithesis of Venezia where the Italians were all part of the tourist service trade and very few of them tourists themselves. We couldn't see the beach itself, but could see rows of yellow, blue and red umbrellas, now all down for the evening, through the fencing. We found the old part of town and had dinner at a reasonably priced restaurant. Nothing special, but Eliza's mixed fish platter was really good looking and well priced.

In the deepening dusk we drove back through Aquileia. This is supposed to have been a second Roma which never fulfilled its potential. The state road up to Udine was easy to follow, but the road back to La Faula was more interesting. The dark was now complete and thunder and lightning were all around, but as yet no rain. We had some idea where we were going, but the roads on the ground and the roads on the map were very hard to marry up. La Faula was in darkness when we arrived and we went straight to bed.

The storm got worse overnight, with heavy rain thunder and lightning. Slowly the storm receded into the distance and quiet settled on the farm.

Day 104
Mileage 6862
Monday 5ᵗʰ August 2002
The Grotto Of Food

This morning after breakfast me, Indigo and Paul set off to make the dogs' breakfast. First we went and collected the dogs' food bowls from their houses, then we broke bread up into the bowl, then put on top boiled bone juices at last but not least two big handfuls of dog biscuits.

I took Nelly's bowl up to the cow sheds with Nelly close at my heels. The other three Spotty, Minny and Barty were led down to their homes down the path.

Nelly seemed to be enjoying every moment. She obviously wasn't used to having her lunch to herself!

Finally we were off going up the mountain road. Looking for a small lagoon in the river to swim in. Paul warned us that "the water is very cold".

313

We decided to go to the Grotta della Villanova.

When we arrived every thing looked shut. We went to look at the signs and the signs said that it opened again at two.

There was a little path – a footpath – that led to the grotto, a winding path that led round the mountain and led right down to the entrance.

We decided that we would go back after our lunch in the bar up the hill.

When we came back up to the bar, we walked in and was just about to sit down when they said – try not to smirk "chuisio" – closed. The woman who repeated this remark was old, her skin was wrinkly and had grey hair in a tight bun.

We walked out disappointed. Now where are we meant to have lunch? Then an idea popped into mum's head "We could have sandwiches down by the entrance, there was a bench down there right?" We all agreed heartily to this statement. So we (with great difficulty) grabbed the sandwich bag and trotted down to the bench at the bottom.

Indigo went to sit down and almost fell down the hill backwards! We figured that it would be safer for Indigo to sit on the steps. There we enjoyed our lunch munching happily on sandwiches and peaches.

At last, at long last, the guide for the caves arrived. We headed towards the ticket office eagerly, slowly we moved back to our seats me and Indigo felt very excited mum and dad also looked extremely excited.

We slowly entered the cave only to hear a creaking noise we all whipped around and to our complete astonishment we saw that the guides were locking us in! He turned around to see 8 amazed faces staring at him. Then he explained that it was to stop anyone but the staff could get in and out.

The cave was full of stalcatights (stalactites) and stalcamites (stalagmites). Stalcatights grow 1/10 of a millimetre every 4 – 5 years! Stalcamites grow faster they grow 1/10 of a millimetre every 2 – 3 years! These grow very slowly indeed!

At the bottom of the stairs there was a small natural pool with bubbles that popped suddenly and horribly. There was a dim but clear light in a tunnel which clearly showed a small stream which again like the pool was covered in the horrible bubbles, meaning that the water was not drinkable.

We continued into the magic corridor which we could not reach, but from the angle we were at it looked beautiful, with an orange stalcatight and stalcamite joined together, which looked just lovely in the light from the guide's torch.

We continued with a quick pace to the paradise room full of thousand year old stalcatights and stalcamites. A whole bunch of them were killed by flash. What we've got to realise is that they are alive; they are kept alive by dripping water, and a human touch is like deadly poison to these living rocks. Just because they don't move, just because they don't think doesn't mean it's not alive it still grows and it lives a very long life indeed, long, amazing to look at but dull.

When we were coming out of the cave we stopped in a dark, shadowy passage, where big, burly, bulky figure stood. The guide flicked the light on and where the figure stood was a bear like animal. He had a longer snout than a bear's and his teeth looked more dog like. His fur was slightly matted but he looked like a well groomed oversized dog!!!!!!

*

After last night's storm, another one greeted us in the morning. It soon abated, but the threat hung around for some time before clearing.

Paul recommended some itineraries close by where we could find some swimming spots in local rivers. We went off to see if we could find them. We start off in a very similar route to yesterday, but soon turn up towards the mountains. When we get to the village with the first swimming hole we cannot find it. We see a sign for a grotto and follow this instead. The river road has turned into a narrow ravine road with mixed forests on all sides, but then the grotto is signposted up the mountain and we turn off heading for Villanova. The road becomes very steep with plenty of crash barriers bent and rusty from years of abuse. Eliza drives with great caution using her horn as we climb. At Villanova we are sent further up the mountain and soon reach a parking spot for the grotto. The noticeboard tells us that they are closed for lunch. The number of times we have fallen foul of the long Italian lunch hours this trip and we still have not learnt. There is another couple on a motorbike who are also hanging about and trying to decide whether to wait or go.

315

We decide to walk down the stone path just to find out how far we have to go to get to the entrance. Into the woods we go following the steep path. It takes us about fifteen minutes to get to the ticket office and entrance. "Let's go and get some refreshments at the trattoria at the top," I suggest and we all hike back up the hill.

George and I venture into the trattoria where a family is comfortably sitting and eating. This looks ok I thought, but were then told by the lady at the table that they were *chuiso*. We walked out surprised and decided to double-check that the grotto was not closed in Mondays. The notice was quite explicit: it was open Mondays to Saturdays, we just had to wait until 2 o'clock.

There was some bread in the Galaxy. The children would eat this with jam, nuttela and honey. We would have some salami and tomatoes. We also had some wine and fruit. None of us were dressed for a trip underground with a temperature of 12°C. George had some long trousers to wear, but Indigo only had her shorts. Eliza slipped on some trousers, but I only had my shorts. George, Indigo and Eliza all had fleecies, but I had nothing. I wasn't worried, as I didn't feel the cold so much. Indigo we kitted out with George's red shorts. These were very baggy on her and came right down to her ankles. All we needed now was somewhere to have our picnic. There was nowhere to sit except in a shrine and that did not seem appropriate. On the path down there were some benches with a final bench down by the entrance. So, we went down the path again and settled down for our lunch just by the entrance.

At two, a young man turned up in his car, just as I was finishing my red wine. Another family also showed up, much more earnestly dressed for the occasion with hiking boots and rainproof coats and heavy jackets. Us English looked very amateurish, but I didn't care. We all set off together and entered Grotto Nouva del Villanova. There was a long staircase down into the mountain and a cold wind blew up the tunnel immediately chilling the air. At the bottom of the staircase there was a room with various exits and our guide began to talk to us in Italian as expected, my Italian wasn't up to understanding what was being said apart from the odd word or phrase. Eliza's Italian was better. The other family was French and again the woman spoke the best Italian. So we had this crazy scene where the guide would speak in Italian and then there would be two huddles as this got translated into both English and French with a few odd questions thrown back where things were not understood. After a while we even started cross translating from French into English and vice-versa.

The tour was quite long (exacerbated by the translation process), but much more intimate than that at Grotto de Vente in the Garfagnana Valley. There were also a larger number of chambers or rooms that we were taken to. The Italian speleologists seemed to be obsessed with food. A lot of the formation types were named after food. There were *spaghetti*, *macaroni*, *spaghettini*, and *salami* formations. There were thin slices of *pancetta* or streaky bacon where the different colours showed where different minerals had been laid down. There was even a *budino* or pudding that looked like a sticky toffee pudding. There was the paradise room, full of formations stretching from the ceiling to the floor. There was even a chamber where a stuffed bear had been placed, with a full opened mouth roar in progress, looking round as if taken by surprise. His skeleton had been found in the cave and he was thought to be about 15,000 years old.

After an hour and a half, we re-emerged at the surface and were hit by the rise in temperature. I hadn't realised just how cold it was until then. We bought a couple of posters of the formations including the famous *budino*.

I drove down the mountain and we went off in search of a bar and *gelateria*. We passed through a couple of villages where everything is boarded up. At another, larger, town we were more successful and the children went off to play in a nearby playground while we settled down for some wine and water. As we wandered back we found some ice cream and cakes to take home.

Although we had said we would have supper at La Faula, we had said we would feed George and Indigo, but as yet we had nothing to give them so we started looking for an *alimentari* or a *supermacato*, but everywhere appeared to be closed: Monday was early closing day. So we went looking further afield and drove down to the row of superstores near the autostrada. Even here, the food shops are closed. Then, towards Udine, we pass Carrefour on our right. Definitely open, definitely food.

The place was vast and heaving with mostly Italians. There were more people here than we had seen all week. There were a myriad of shops inside as well as the food market. We set ourselves the task of being in and out in 20 minutes. Some hope, but forcing the pace would help to stop us buying the shop out. Bread, breakfast cereal, milk, fruit, burgers... what could be easier? The choice was vast and the quality appeared excellent. In here we saw what must have been one of the world largest sausages being sliced on a deli counter. It was half a metre in diameter and over five metres long. The variety of pasta, fruit and bread was absolutely stunning. Everything was tempting, but we resisted fairly well and were out of the store in an hour. George and Indigo had take away pizza instead of burgers, but that would save us cooking!

We were soon back at La Faula and in need of wine and dinner. The children wanted to watch a film on the big TV and so we had time to ourselves and shared our table with Greg and his wife Carla. We started eating our dinner outside under the pergola, but the wind and the rain got the better of us and forced everyone to do a quick retreat indoors. Inside the evening just got was going well, I got out some of my Tuscan *limoncello* for everyone to sample. This made the evening go better and oiled the conversations and helped cement friendships with our hosts Paul and Luca.

Day 105
Mileage 6910
Tuesday 6th August 2002
Chocolate Bunny

*

Last night's storm was gone and I thought today would be fine. I was up early to empty the Galaxy. I piled up crates and boxes and our pieces of marble under some shelter near the cowsheds. Luca had helped me arrange for a service on the Galaxy. Tuesdays were their day off, but they were more than happy to escort me to the garage. It was a most dramatic drive, soon after we left, the rain started afresh and started coming down faster and heavier. I saw a woman cyclist desperately trying, but failing, to keep herself dry with an umbrella. The clouds were very low and seemed to be becoming lower by the mile. Everywhere we went there were drenched people looking around and disbelieving that this rain was real in August. Often, Paul and Luca go to the beach on their day off, but I did not think so today. I began to worry about our luggage lying out in the open albeit under some roofing.

Along the highway there were large numbers of garages, Citreön, Sabaru, BMW, Fiat, Renault, Audi, VW more Fiat, but still no Ford. The rain was very savage and there was no sign of a let up. We carried on driving north, rapidly approaching the mountain range. I thought we were going to end up in Austria until out of the gloom the Ford garage emerged. We left the Galaxy in their hands and went back to La Faula. Luca told me that there was an earthquake here in 1976. Pointing to a nearby hill he indicated the epicentre. The drive back was more of the same, but even in this weather, the Italians loved to drive at more than the speed limit and overtake dangerously. Paul told me that they had lots of accidents on this road and that every shrine marked a death, but that not every death was marked by a shrine.

The rain stopped by the time we reached La Faula, but underfoot it was very wet. Large puddles spread across the car park. Miraculously, our luggage was bone dry. The water marks from the storm were a good metre away.

Without the Galaxy we were marooned at the farm. When calm had descended onto the farm, Eliza and Greg decided to go blackberry picking. I stayed behind and they set off with the children and Nellie. Greg helped show George how to tell if an electric fence was on, but somehow the trick failed and George ended up getting a jolt. They climbed up the field quite happily until the heavens opened again. I got up and watched the rain from our balcony; this was very heavy and solid. I looked out of the door to see if I could see the pickers, but there was no sign.

Ten minutes later the cloudburst had stopped and the sodden party of blackberry pickers arrived back at the farmhouse. Drenched from head to toe and covered in mud, they offered me a meagre bowl of blackberries. "It was raining so hard, that we took shelter under a blackberry bush!"

said Eliza. Everyone was soon laughing at the experience and hot showers all round cheered them up.

Paul had told us that there were storms all over Italy. In Lake Garda he said that the Germans and Dutch were cutting their holidays short because of the bad weather. We caught some Italian news bulletins. There were some frightening pictures of storm damage in the lakes and in Tuscany. Pictures of car windscreens smashed by hailstones, the grape harvest in Tuscany was devastated by hail. There were no reports of anything in Lake Como. We rang up Cattia in Casanova to see if they were ok. Nicco told us that the storms were very localised along the coast and that they had suffered no damage.

Carla and Eliza decided that they would treat Paul and Luca to dinner tonight and they went off with Greg to do some food shopping. George and Indigo stayed and watched the same DVD as yesterday. The shoppers came back from the expedition to Carrefour laden down with so many goodies.

There are two ways to go shopping for a meal. The first is to be specific and know what you are going to cook and seek out those ingredients only. The second is have some ideas of what you are going to cook and to modify this by seeing what is good today. Then back home you use the ingredients that you have bought and your imagination to cook. Today, it seemed as if both happened. I must admit that the short trip to the supermercato yesterday should have pre-warned me, but it didn't. Greg described their shopping as a frenzy.

The menu was now looking like, salads for starters (emphasis on the plural), chocolate bunny (that is rabbit in a chocolate flavoured sauce) with *fagiolini* and boiled new potatoes smothered in butter and spring onions, apricots with *amerreto* biscuits, *masarla* and *mascapone*, six different types of cheeses, fruit.

Greg and I went off north to fetch our Galaxy. Although the rain had stopped now, it still seemed a long drive. The clouds were pouring over the mountains looking benignly white and soft, but full of promise of the thunderstorms to come. The Italian mechanic had been very efficient and was well pleased with the Galaxy.

Luca had to relinquish the use of his precious and very clean kitchen with reluctance, but with very good grace. George and Carla prepared salads and Eliza prepared the rabbit. Paul kept going round muttering thing like "I don't want chocolate bunny. I really would like some nice Provencal style rabbit with tomatoes and olives" and asking everyone else "wouldn't that be just great?"

I was sitting outside with Greg when we heard a scream from Indigo. I dashed round the corner and found her sitting on the floor crying loudly. She had fallen over one of the white dogs and bumped her head. I picked her up, but all she wanted was Mummy. The cooking stopped and we all sat down for a cuddle. She was growing a lump on her forehead. She told us that she had fallen over the dog and the dog had bit her, but this did not look like a bite. Then we saw her shoulder and her t-shirt. There were holes in her shirt and a bite mark on her shoulder. She was bleeding but only a small amount. Everyone started to get involved. I found Paul and he got quite worried. Greg went to get some special New Zealand honey that acted as a natural antiseptic, to cleanse the wound. We had visions of hospitals, doctor, and long queues into the night. Paul had visions of the authorities taking all the dogs away, destroying them and large fines. More calmly we worried about chocolate bunny. More calmly still we worked out that the dog had not actually bitten Indigo, but had been chewing a bone when she tripped over him. The dog had turned round in surprise and Indigo had grazed her shoulder on the dog's tooth before hitting her head on the ground. Who would believe such a story?

Paul called the local medical centre and explained what had happened. He made an appointment for us to go and see them. They were going to have to take all the dog's medical history and vaccination papers with them to prove that they were well looked after. We were just about to go when the Austrian family brought out their youngest daughter. She was very pale and covered in small spots. "Chickenpox" said Eliza immediately.

More trouble. Paul had visions of the whole farm becoming a quarantine area. Where were they going to send all their guests? How long would this go on? Eliza told Paul that it was too late and that once the spots were out in chickenpox, it was no longer contagious.

Everybody was standing and sitting around the front of the house. The two girls looked miserable. Paul and Luca rang the doctor again and now that we had two sick children, he would come to us. The smell of cooking rabbit wafted through the air.

We all tried to settle down and put life back to normal. I checked on the rabbit and tried to chivvy everyone along for dinner. George and Indigo were very helpful and soon the table was being laid and plates of salad arrived. We all settled down, including the dogs, who kept coming by begging and lying under the table around our feet.

The chocolate rabbit was a great success. It was cooked in a very slight chocolate sauce – not, as Paul was thinking, a thick chocolate sauce like profiteroles. Paul sung our praises over the chocolate rabbit and everyone was pleasantly surprised.

The Austrian woman borrowed our Calpol to help bring down the temperature of the girl. By now, Indigo was over her shock and was lively and alert. Her bump had not come up any further and the air was making her cut seem much better.

The doctor turned up eventually. He confirmed chickenpox and gently examined Indigo. We had to watch the bump on her head, but he thought nothing would come of it. He looked at the "bite", but again thought that nothing would come of it. If it started to heal normally in the next day or so we should just let nature take its course. He was more concerned about whether Indigo had had chickenpox and wanted to give her a course of treatment. This treatment not only helped those where the spots were out, but also helped those where the spots had not yet come out by reducing the illness' virulancy.

I liked him a lot. His English was quite good and he had a wicked sense of humour. He told us that on his surgery wall he had a picture of Harold Shipman looking like a saint with the words "Come to God with me" written underneath. He knew full well who Harold Shipman was, but none of his patients did! Because the tablets for the chickenpox were expensive, he decided not to write us a prescription, but would fetch the pills himself and bring them back this evening. We left him driving into the night to Cividale not quite sure when he would be back.

Meanwhile, the rabbit had been totally consumed, and Paul and Luca especially were now looking quite relaxed after a very fraught couple of hours where they could almost imagine their business going down the tubes. The apricots arrived on the table and more *limoncello* was consumed. The washing up was done and the kitchen was left spotless. Luca was definitely pleased.

Day 106
Mileage 6940
Wednesday 7th August 2002
Da Vinci's Palmanova

*

Everyone was late rising this morning except for Paul and Luca. The storms had all passed and it was hot again today. Paul could not believe how bad the weather had been for August. "It never rains in August at all," he said in a very uncanny recall of Salvatore in Sicily in May. We had heard all this before and no longer believed it.

The Austrian girl still looked extremely pale and lay limply in her father's arms. Indigo's bump had gone down and her cut was beginning to heal over.

We drove down to Palmanova between Udine and the coast. Here was a mediaeval town specifically designed and laid out for defensive purposes. It was designed by Leonardo da Vinci and had a wonderful threefold circular symmetry. The centre plaza was a hexagon laid to white stone. Of the six roads radiating from the middle, three went to the only gates; the other three were stopped by the walls. There were nine defensive earthwork mounds outside the walls with the latest techniques (at that time) used to house short and long range guns. Each of the gates had drawbridges, none of them worked any more. On one of the gates, the wooden wheels that controlled the lifting and lowering of the drawbridge were still in place.

What I did not understand was why this town was where it was? The interior of the town, apart from the central piazza did not appear to have any historical building of note at all. The size of the town was quite large for those days, but the place does not appear to have become a commercial centre at any time.

We stayed for ice cream and then drove on.

We went towards Gradova on the Slovene border. Here the iron curtain between east and west split the town into two before avoiding Trieste on the coast. The town was closed for siesta as we drove around it. Even though it was closed there were obviously enough here to make the town seem wealthy. We followed the signs for the wine road up into the hills north of Gradova overlooking Slovenia. It was difficult to tell where Italy ended and Slovenia begun, but we must have been very close. *Fattorias* were selling their wares on the roadside and we pulled up and sampled some. We bought a dozen mixed bottles and then we were on our way.

We drove on to Cividale, another old market town with a lot more character. The *Diavalo* Bridge over a ravine had been rebuilt after the First World War. Some houses were dug out of the cliff face and must have been a real pleasure to live in. Round the *pedioni* area were lots of cobbled back streets and small shops – all looked busy in the post siesta afternoon sun. George and Indigo were both getting very grumpy by now and we were all thirsty and starving. We found a café and sat seeking shade under some large umbrellas and watched the Italians go about their early evening *passagiata*. We had some cakes and *salatini* (savoury nibbles) as the world passed us by for a change.

Leaving Cividale we headed north towards Attimis on our way to La Faula. The weather was kind to us in the evening and we sat with Greg and Carla for dinner. Another English guest Paul, and his son James, also joined us.

Day 107
Mileage 7020
Thursday 8ᵗʰ August 2002
The Beach

*

The weather was hot and steamy this morning with unbroken blue skies. The children were all clamouring for the beach and the sea. The Austrians had been going to the same place for four days now and loved it. Greg and Carla had been there too and told us that is was empty. It was a good hour away, on the Adriatic, but this would be the last sea that we would see. We packed up a picnic and picked up some bits in the supermercato in Attimis and we were on our way.

We caught the autostrada south and took the Venezia branch. For a Thursday mid-morning it was very crowded. This made us think long and hard about the route we would take on Saturday. We finally decided to go over the mountains, it may take longer, but we didn't want to be caught in endless motorway jams.

Off the motorway, the area north of the beach was very flat and open. There were no signs to a beach but we knew we were heading in the right direction. The tarmac road gave way to a track running down along a broad flat desolated plain with little vegetation and the dust billowed round the wheels of the cars. There were woodlands ahead with a large mostly empty car park.

Through the woods there was a sandy path that took us down to the beach. There were no restaurants nor bars there and no umbrellas nor sun-bed ranks nor salesmen. The sand was a glorious yellow: just as you imagine it should be. The high water mark downward was covered in shells and the sea itself was very shallow and warm. Today it was very still and the sea looked as flat as smoothed out silver paper. Greg and Carla had already gone to the beach before us, but we did not know which way to go. The beach was not deserted, but was empty for an Italian beach and we settled down quite near the entrance. Some sailing boats were becalmed out near the horizon.

Before we had even sat down, George and Indigo were both itching to get into the water. Eliza had never really liked sand because of its ability to spread itself into every nook and cranny, even those that you didn't know you had. So, much to Eliza's annoyance, and despite all our pleadings to be careful, both Indigo and George managed to kick sand all over our towels within 30 seconds of them being laid on the ground. Without even waiting to get warm in the sun they were in sea with me very close behind. We all could go out quite a way without it getting too deep. They clambered all over me like a pair of irritating puppies: pulling me down and tickling me, using me as a jumping station and asking me to throw them. I soon needed to have a rest and managed to escape their clutches to join Eliza on the shore to get dry and hot.

George soon got bored with our company and went off in search of new friends. She found some Italian boys, all about her age, playing football and managed to join in. They played both on the beach and in the water. Indigo chased after them and rather than playing football chased all the boys to try and kiss them. This really flummoxed them, as they did not know how to react. They all ran away out of Indigo's reach, but still close enough to play football with George.

This was the first full week in August. Italian cities were now virtually shut down and families had mass migrated to the sea. The beach was full of white and red skinned people, some were braving the full force of the sun, but most spent a large amount of time huddling under sun umbrellas to stop themselves burning. We had been out and about in the sun for three months now, and were quite happy just sunning ourselves.

Last weekend had been one of the busiest of the year for the Italian motorways and next weekend was expected to be worse still. Most Italian families are creatures of habit and the vast majority all returning to the same place for their holidays year after year. It must be something in their psyche that makes them do this a little like salmon return from the sea or migratory birds returning to the same nesting site year after year. The unseasonably bad weather had only exacerbated the queues at the toll points, with two and three hour queues being reported near Venezia. Mind you, any hot weekend in August in England would have the same effect on the road network except in England you can queue for free.

Greg and Carla came walking out of the west towards us. Greg was looking a bit too red for comfort, but Carla looked as though she could spend another few days out here without burning. As we were talking we saw Indigo coming from the distance, when she saw Greg and Carla she started running flat out, flat footed, feet wide apart and arms swinging wildly. She was wearing only her black bikini bottom and a massive grin. She piled straight into Greg and gave them both very big hugs. She insisted on teaching Greg her favourite card game – Queens. She won one game and "let" Greg win one so honour was satisfied. Then she took Carla off for a swim in the sea. She had lost her plaster and the sea bathed her wound.

The whole beach area was set in a nature reserve with a wooded area immediately behind the beach. They were running a series of conservation and crop growing experiments in the area and seemed determined to extend the reserve further along the coast. Lots of wildlife, both birds and animals lived in the woods, but as one would expect, they were all fairly shy and none was on show. There were some straw huts erected between the woods and the car parks that turned out to be toilets. This disguise was very effective, but inside they were just bog standard portable loos. The whole area was a lovely place and it seemed to be a well kept secret.

Day 108
Mileage 7068
Friday 9th August 2002
Sweating Blackberries

The Austrian girl was crying during the night. Her crying was very plaintive and distressing for us, so it must have been absolutely dreadful for her parents. She had got chickenpox blisters on her tongue and was now refusing to take her medicine.

George wanted to get up early to help prepare breakfast. She had really taken a shine to Paul and wanted to come back here to work for a season when she was older like Sabrina. I woke her up as asked at 6:30 and then again at 7:00. She got up quite happily, but a bit groggy and went off to help.

At 8:30 she came back and complained that none of us were up yet. Okay, okay we said and got up and went downstairs.

Another hot day today. Greg and Carla were leaving en route to Edinburgh via Munich and Amsterdam. They were taking the train to Villbach in Austria and then changing there. Indigo in particular was very sad to see them go. Maybe, just maybe they would see us in England in September. James and his father Paul were still here and had extended their stay until Saturday.

We spent time quietly organising ourselves. Repacking crates and resorting boxes.

In the early afternoon, we decided to defy the weather and go blackberry picking again. It was just Nellie and us this time. I had to borrow a pair of Wellingtons that were not quite big enough and I went without socks. Although we did not go far it was so hot and humid out and so sticky underfoot that it was very uncomfortable. Paul saw us go up the hill and told us that all the electric fences were off. Flies the size of pennies kept landing on me to drink my sweat. Where it was especially sweaty, I was carrying Indigo on my shoulders making this very hard work indeed. Nellie was always in the lead, exploring the fields further ahead than us, but not always going where we wanted. George used to call her back and whistle for her to come. The blackberries were thinly spread on all the bushes and the best were always tantalisingly just beyond a normal reach and meant stretching into the brambles to get them. In one field there were three donkeys, two sheep and two lambs who all looked surprised at having company. If we were hot then the unsheared sheep must have just felt awful. The donkeys looked more content and were happy for us to approach them. They swished their tails over each other to shift the flies. Soon we had enough blackberries and we made our way downhill. On the way down George spotted two or three green praying Mantises. I was quite surprised at how small they were, but I suppose that pictures of them are always enlarged so you can see their detail. We did not look to see if there were any husbands about. I had a cold shower and I really revelled in it enjoying every moment and then lay on the bed recovering from the experience.

In the evening we made blackberry and apple crumble as our contribution towards dinner. George and Indigo watched more DVD.

Day 109
Mileage 7133
Saturday 10th August 2002
Over The Mountains

A six 30 start meant I was downstairs at seven to help prepare breakfast.

Nobody was around when I went down, so I decided to look for Nelly. So I went to search for her in her cubbyhole in the kitchen. Under the small green oven a small hole just big enough for the cheeky Border Collie. I flicked on the light had a look around, but no Nelly!

Going out again I met Paul. "Shall we go and let the dogs out?" Paul prompted. "Yes let's!" I said eagerly.

I saw Nelly standing on the top of her Nelly-sized kennel. When she caught sight of me her tail went bezerk, it went round and round in circles it looked like she could just fly over the fence to me.

We opened the gate and Nelly jumped up and licked my face, Spotty and Minny raced out, but Barty stayed in her kennel and Nelly turned over and got a good rub from me and Paul and Paul gave Barty her morning rub too.

We headed towards the kitchen and started work. Nelly was now back in her cubbyhole enjoying my company while me, Paul and Sabrina worked away.

James came down at 8:30 and we enjoyed a nice long breakfast together. After breakfast we went off and fed the dogs and then the time came to say goodbye to the dogs and Paul. I grabbed hold of his neck and gruffly I rubbed his head with my knuckles. This was a "hot" goodbye. Nelly came straight away when I whistled her. She went mad over me and went mad over her she licked me all over I cuddled her. I never wanted to let go.

We drove away me and Indigo felt very sad we never wanted to go but I said I would come back to La Faula again and I meant it.

We drove on endlessly over passes and more passes we stopped at the top of one of the passes and I had uno panni di marmalata di fragola – one strawberry jam sandwich. Before we left we bought a large slab of choclate.

Divided carefully, I gave Indigo a piece if chocolate and me a piece we sucked contently away all the way down the mountain until half had gone.

We stopped for dinner at 9:00 and came out again after dinner at 10:00.

We finally pulled up at last in the Brentano. I fell a sleep at once in the warmth of my sleeping bag.

*

George again got up early this morning to help in the kitchen. She was still enthusiastic and a little less groggy.

Big travelling day today. We were off to our flat in Lago di Como. Although we had done an initial pack yesterday there were all the odd bits and pieces to do today. The Residence Brentano is our second home, and we were very comfortable going there.

Paul gave us news that there were two hour traffic jams along the Slovene border and going into Venezia. This just reinforced our choice for going over the mountains. The day was overcast and we expected that the rain would come back with avengeance.

After breakfast we said our goodbyes to Paul and James – they were off to Venice for a night before returning to Milan and England. The Austrian family were also off back home.

Paul and Luca wished us well and hoped that we would be back. George can't wait to come back here. I told her she would need to write regularly.

It seemed to take forever to pack, but it was done soon enough. We set off north towards Attimis and the mountains. Steady going back up the hills we had driven down only last week using the map for names. Still fairly low down we saw mushrooms advertised at Funghi in Piazza in the local town, Villa Santina, and stopped to investigate. By the time we got there, there was some street theatre going on. None of which made any sense to me, except it was visually funny too. George got dragged in, much to her embarrassment and amusement and took part in the curtain calls at the end. Indigo laughed to see such sport.

I thought the mushroom shop would be simply a stall, but it was a permanent shop. I have never seen so many porcini mushrooms, both whole and dried in one place before. It was astounding. They had boxes and boxes of dried and fresh mushrooms of many varieties. The vast majority were porcinis: both dried and fresh and there were different quality categories within both groups. Eliza spent ages dithering on what to get. In the end we got a large bag of dried porcini to take home. This whole diversion took us over an hour.

The cloud base was very low and dampness turned into mist and cloud as we climbed. After a heavy cloudburst we rose through one layer of cloud, but were still not in the clear. We climbed Passo della Mauria, the first pass to 1298m. If we jumped it would take us to 1300m. It was damp and misty but lighter than before. Some motorcyclists were enjoying a beer outside, but today's selection were not the same as those we had seen last week and they also looked cold.

We drove onto Cortina, back-tracking the same journey still, but here we turned off to a different pass and found ourselves quickly climbing. Nearly at the top we stopped for some refreshments. It was too late for lunch as the kitchens were closed, but *panini* all round with drinks went down a treat. It was cold outside at only 6°C. as we were now well in the clouds. We wondered if it would get cold enough to snow. There had been 15cms of snow in Cormayeur earlier in the week. The top of Passo di Falzarego, the second pass was not far away but at 2105m the temperature did not drop any further.

The drop down the other side was steeper and more twisty with 33 *tornante* on the way down. This dropped us down into Sud Tyrol and we were back in German-speaking Italy. The towns were full. Everyone was walking around with heavy wet weather gear, looking bemused by all this rain in August. The drive along the valley was slow and tedious. We were suddenly in the valley between Trento and Bolzano where we had been staying. All the mountains were covered with low level cloud seemingly oozing out of the very rockface. We thought about the Tschindlhof and how sad and washed out it must be in weather like this. I hoped that their grape crop had not been damaged. We drove south looking for the road across the valley towards our next pass out of the Sud Tyrol. Here it was beginning to get drier, but still there was lots of traffic about proceeding in a very slow manner. We decided to get over this pass before stopping for dinner.

In front of us, leading the way up the mountain was a very slow coach. A stream of cars and another coach was between us. Gradually, the cars behind the first coach overtook the slowcoach where they could and then there was just a car and coach between us. A long straight appeared. The first car went, then the coach and then us. All overtaking the slowcoach at once. Eliza kept her foot down and when the coach had passed the other coach we passed our second in the same manoeuvre. I was very impressed with Eliza's nerve. At the top of the third pass, Passo del Tonale at 1883m, there was a large ski resort. It looked big, brash and un-appetising. We were out of Sud Tyrol again and headed down the mountain towards Sondrio. Now we started to look for a restaurant in the dark. After some while we found one that was still open and settled in for pizza and pasta. Not only were we delighted to have anything at all but were delighted by its quality.

The cloud base was like a black blanket in the darkness. The only lights were from other cars and the occasional house. Fed and watered I was refreshed for the final leg to Lago di Como and Mezzegra. The road started rising again and we found ourselves in a fourth pass that I hadn't noticed on the map before. Now there was no traffic, but this made things harder as there was no one to watch to guide us forward. Suddenly in the valley you could see the stream of sodium lamps illuminating the main state road. We turned at the top of the Passo dell'Aprica at 1181m and headed downwards into the valley for the last time.

The road along the valley was monotonously straight and I had lost track in my mind on how much further we had to go. Sondrio went past and the signs started showing Milan and Lecco. At Colico we found the signs to Menaggio and crossed the tip of the lake to drive down its west side. We were now in familiar territory as we drove through the plains of Dongo and Gavedona. There were few people about at this time of night. Down into Menaggio and onto Caddenabia and Tremezzo. Bellagio was lit up across the water in the centre of the lake as beautiful as ever. We arrived at Mezzegra and turned up the hill to the Brentano. We stopped just after midnight – over thirteen hours on the road. This was the longest day's drive of the entire holiday. I was exhausted, but so pleased that we had come over the mountains. I really loved the experience and the stunning scenery. If it had been all dry and sunny, somehow it would not have given me the same satisfaction and joy as the mists, cloud, cold and rain.

Lago di Como
Day 110
Mileage 7451
Sunday 11ᵗʰ August 2002
Mezzegra and Malpensa

*(**Note:** George stopped writing her journal here. She had had enough and for her the Brentano was like a second home so she felt that there was nothing new here to comment on – Dave.)*

Peace and tranquillity reign after our long drive. It is overcast yet warm, but for the moment the rain has stopped and we feel at home.

The view from the balcony is as dramatic as ever. The noise of rushing water can be heard flowing in the mountain torrents, normally barren at this time of year.

Sunday is quiet and we are all tired and relaxed. It is traditional to go and fetch fresh croissants and bread from the bakers down the hill. This morning Indigo and George come with me. George has promised to go on her own while we are here. The walk down is only five minutes, but it is steep. The olive trees that were planted last year in the field just outside our gates look established, but I wonder how many years before they fruit.

The road comes to the torrent and we can see the extent of the water caused by the recent rains. The road down to the village covers this storm drain, and a tap and drinking fountain at the top are dated 1978. This road is still not wide enough for two cars to park, but is considerably wider than the old cobbled road that still runs parallel. We take a footpath off to the right and follow its cobbles down the hill crossing one road before emerging on the lakeside state road – Via Regina. Here the baker's shop is hidden in a little niche behind some large red gates. The sign reads *"Domenica aperto"* – luckily for us. Inside is the produce of last nights work with over a dozen varieties of bread. A lot of the bread is very aerated and here it is sold by weight rather than by piece. The Italians are buying large bagfuls of individual sized *ciabattini* and *forcaccini*. We settle for our normal *croissant con marmalate*.

Only one other shop is open this morning – apart from the bars of course – and we get our supplies of *latte fresco* and some *fromaggio*. We meet the man who used to run the Ristarante Bisbino – after all our years coming here we never found out his name. We loved his restaurant, but it is now closed. His first wife used to do the cooking and his second wife used to help with the money, but eventually she refused to spend any more. The Bisbino is now a Chinese restaurant.

The lady in the shop makes a face about the weather, but says that the sun will be back on Wednesday and will be very strong. We resign ourselves to three more days of rain.

Outside the shop we met a Belgium family who were staying at the Brentano two years ago. The family has three boys, Coons, Peter and Ben: all older than our children, but George and Indigo would have some friends to play with. We arranged to have pizza together tonight.

We go to the Tre Arci for a coffee. Here the television is on, showing news of floods throughout Italy, Europe and beyond. The Czech Republic is devastated. There are floods mentioned in Britain and in Japan. It has been snowing in Courmayeur with over 40 cms settled. There are pictures of hail stones in the other lakes. It seems that we were let off lightly on our drive yesterday and that Lake Como has only avoided the deluge that other parts of the mountains have suffered. A bad weather alert has been declared in Italy. We cannot tell about elsewhere.

Going up the hill back to the Brentano is always harder on the legs. But everyone is in good humour this morning and makes it without whingeing.

We settle down for breakfast on our balcony. I love these croissants, they are different from French ones which often have too much butter and are far too flaky for my taste. These are more sponge like and have a secret jam middle. Orange juice and tea make this perfect.

In the early afternoon, George and I set off for Malpensa airport to pick up Jan who is coming to stay for a week. The rain has now come back and makes the whole landscape look miserable. George plays the paymaster at the autostrada toll booth and gives a surprise to the man who definitely wasn't expecting a ten year old on that side of the car. The airport run is straightforward, but I have not been to Malpensa for many a year. Last time I was here, it was a local Italian airport with most flights internal to Roma, Napoli or Sicilia etc. The flight I was on was the only international flight of the day. Now, this airport seemed vast and busy. We got stuck in a long tailback just to get into the airport and park. I guessed that we would need terminal one. The car park was more Italian chaos, with small parking spots, badly parked cars and anarchic placement of portable concrete pillars to contend with.

George and I wander inside the vast arrivals hall. Because of all the queues we get here only a few minutes before Jan's plane is due. The arrivals board is full. There are fifty-four flights showing and they are all international. What a change from my last visit. We wait patiently for Jan to emerge. George can't remember what she looks like even though she has visited us and even house-sat for us in the past. I can hear George thinking about how she may recognise her and she starts asking a series of questions. Some I can answer. How tall is Jan? Does she have frizzy hair? What colour is it? Is she travelling alone? Some I can't. How much luggage has she got? Is she wearing trainers? A hat?

George has a detective game where faces are eliminated by asking these types of question and I thought she might be playing this in her mind as other passengers came past. I was waiting for "Does she have a moustache?" but it never came.

You could immediately eliminate a lot of travellers. Those who were brown and wearing shorts had not come from London. The London arrivals did look amazingly pale and wan. Jan did arrive eventually. Her backpack had got delayed in the special luggage container. It was really nice to see her. We hugged. George jumped up and down with glee and then we headed out to the Galaxy.

The rain was miserable and I apologised for bringing Jan out on holiday from rainy London to rainy Italy. Jan was quite relaxed about it and was happy just to be away from work. George spoke incessantly on the way back about all sorts of subjects. Jan was allowed to interject from time to time, but I found it difficult to hear what she was saying and impossible to slip a sliver of a word between two of hers before being drowned out.

By the time we got back to the Brentano, the rain had stopped. Eliza and Indigo had already gone off to the Balognet. George saw the Belgiums who were just leaving and went off with them. I showed Jan around and then we drove off to the Balognet. We overtook George and the Belgiums just as we arrived.

It was very pleasant eating out albeit under cover. Carmello's pizzas are as good as ever. George says they are the best in the world. We like Carmello and his wife Franca, and we have always eaten well when we come here. Halfway through our meal, the cloud cover was lifting and the sun broke through and shone a vivid pink onto the mountain peaks opposite. As the sun set the cloud formations picked up the light from underneath. They were the most peculiar smooth wisps of clouds, looking as benign as whipped egg whites.

Home again, with long chats on the balcony with Jan before bed.

Day 111
Mileage 7558
Monday 12th August 2002
Climb To The Sanctuary

Amazingly, despite all the predictions, the sun is back this morning. The storm has cleared the air fantastically. We can see all the distant peaks with a clarity that is normally reserved only for those quiet still cold spring mornings.

George and Jan and I go down to the bakers while Indigo and Eliza sleep. George amazes everyone by having the courage to ask for croissants in Italian. We go on down to the harbour and show Jan around. The central square had one of my most favourite trees in it. It is an enormous evergreen *floribundi magnolia*. It must stand at least fifteen metres high and has a grand classic symmetric shape. It blooms are a beautiful white and are the size of my pair of hands. Today there are only a few blossoms on the tree, but they are magnificent. I have noticed how prevalent this type of tree is in Italy and I'm always pleased to see specimens of it. But to me this is the best.

Down by the water front the motor boat yard of Tuille Abbate is open for business. The view across the water is simply perfect with the mountain backdrop. Behind us and behind the Brentano rises Mount Crocione. Not a particularly tall mountain at 1700 m, but magnificent nevertheless. Its crown is treeless and there is, of course, a cross glinting on the top.

As we walk along the old via Regina, a large truck carrying a large motorboat is making its way to the boatyard. This is the only way in and out apart from the lake. The public park on the lakeside is a small strip of land that appears to have been "donated" from one of the villas on the front. It seems very peculiar to walk around the front of this house with its own garden fenced off from the park. The stonework on the lakeside is of the decaying elegance variety with pillars and masonry flowerpots. A stone staircase takes us up for a grand view of the lake. The peninsular beyond Lenno with the Villa Ballestaios dominates the view on the right and the ridge on the middle of the lake lowers gently towards Bellaggio. Along our side of the lake Tremezzo church stands proudly chiming his bells. The platform we are on forms the roof of a private boathouse, but this year, despite all the rain, the lake is low – a good metre lower than last year.

Further along is the Mezzegra Parco Publico. Although this is a small park there is a short avenue of very tall pines. I love their magnificence as they stretch skywards. I do not have any idea how old these trees are but I imagine that they were planted in the mid nineteenth century. Three trees are sadly missing from one side of the avenue and have been replaced by much shorter pines of a different variety.

Retracing our steps along via Regina, we find that the large truck has still not reached the boatyard. It has been inching along making sure that walls and windows are not scrapped and the cars are not scratched. Carefully, the boat is manoeuvred around a last corner and suddenly it is passed the narrow point.

We go back up to the flat and sit on the balcony and stare at the view.

Later, we take a walk on to the fish farm above Ossuccio via the back roads and paths up at the Brentano level. We go out of the back gates of the Brentano and walk up to the church of S. Abbondio built in the fifteenth century on the site of an older church. The view from in front of the church by the war memorial is stunning: both of the lake and mountains in front, the mountains behind and the clear blue sky above. It always amazes me, but it is obvious that it should be so, that all the very best views are owned by the church and their cemeteries. At this level the view changes continuously almost by the minute as we stroll along. There is a staircase down at Pola marked for pedestrians only, but a few metres down the staircase there is a car parked. If there is a chance of being able to drive somewhere, then the Italians will have done it. The narrow lanes are no problem to the normally thin Italian cars and especially not a problem to all the motorbikes, apes and scooters. The path leads past the Lenno cooperative with its boules bowling lanes and then across a broad valley with a mountain stream. The stream has come down from the fish farm, but unfortunately the fish farm is closed on Mondays as well as the Tuesdays which we expected.

At the entrance of the fish farm is the first shrine in a series of fifteen leading up the Sacuary di Madonna della Soccorso. The climb is stiff, Indigo does some of it on my shoulders, but everyone else manages it to the top where the small trattoria is actually open!

After plates of salami and pasta we make our way down. This time we follow the stream down where we can hear the noise of a waterfall. Some of the river is captured in a run off to an old mill and we sit and cool our feet off in it. I am trying desperately not to worry about the children falling in and getting soaked or falling out and tumbling down the mountain. As we come to the lakeside we come across a magnificent villa whose name I do not know and then we get to the lake at Campo. A few Italians are lying on the stony beach or are swimming in the Lago itself.

We have come down from the mountain on the wrong side of the Lenno penisular which now means an extra long walk than I was expecting to take us to Lenno and refreshments. It is now very hot and steamy, but the thought of ice creams speeds the children along although gentle whingeing has now settled in. The old road crisscrosses the new road: once by going over a stone footbridge.

The back streets of Lenno get nearer and we slip into their shadows for the last ten minutes before coming out into the main square. This afternoon the town is empty. Tomorrow, for market day, it will be full. We stop for gelato and drinks on the front. Before going back up the hill to Mezzegra.

We take Jan past the spot where Mussolini was shot in 1945 after his capture by partisan forces near Dongo. His mistress desperately jumped in front of him in a vain attempt to save his life. There are different versions of his final moments, but the one I like best describes him as pulling open his coat and saying "Shoot me in the chest, here!" The execution is botched once as the rifle jams, but there is no second error. The pair are then taken to Milan where there bodies are put on public display hanging upside down. Postcards of the spot, the room and the house that they spent their last night are still on sale down at the bars in the town. Clearly, this event makes Mezzegra famous.

Monday afternoon is early closing day, but we have already sufficient in the house for our evening meal. After our long walk no one has any enthusiasm for eating out.

As we sit on the balcony late into the evening watching and listening to the very distant flashes of lightning and rumbles of thunder, we gradually realise that this is not thunder, but the flashes and noises of a distant firework display. Then we see a meteor, with its bright streak covering over a quarter of the sky. It is very bright and it is there long enough for me to point it out to Eliza and for her and Jan to actually see it.

In the middle of the night Indigo starts crying with pain and complains about her feet. It is neither cramp nor any other injury that we can see, but it may be tiredness induced by today's long walk. She has complained about her feet periodically before.

Day 112
Mileage 7558
Tuesday 13th August 2002
Lenno Market

Tuesdays are market days in Lenno. After yesterday's long walk and Indigo's crying overnight, we think it is prudent to drive rather than walk.

The town square is full of stalls and these stretch along the waterfront to Albergo Lenno. The market has not changed much in the years we have been coming here, and it is much more of a locals market than a tourist market with fresh fruit and vegetables, cheeses, cold meats and salamis. There are the usual selection of clothes, household linens, tools, shoes and plants and sweets. This year the two very black Africans who sell African tourist produce have at last got their own stall instead of selling straight off the floor. The lakefront has been refurbished since last year. The paving has been relaid and there are new benches and flowerbeds. It makes the whole town look wealthier.

We have croissants and drinks at the café on the front and enjoy the heat of the day and the view across to Bellagio. Some teenagers are jumping off one of the jetties into the lake. George watches enviously as they jump and twist and dive until one misjudges his jump and it looks as if he had cracked his skull on the jetty. There was an anxious few seconds waiting for him to surface, but he comes up totally oblivious to how close he came to disaster. After that the youths are a bit more subdued for a while, but their enthusiasm returned quickly.

We buy some fresh fruit, cheese and meat, a spit roasted chicken and a piece of pork. We are, however, too late for bread. The chicken is still hot by the time we get home and goes down very well with some cold white wine on the balcony. A couple of wasps start to investigate us. George fetches the swatter and the large blue spray of wasp killer. One whiff of this is enough to deter them and we are left in peace. Two large humming bird moths come and drink from our geraniums. Their wings a blur as they hover by each flower in turn unreeling their tongues for a drink.

Back at the Brentano are Rafaele and Patrizia with their 10-month-old baby boy Francesco, plus granddad Alberto and two cousins. We all coo and smile. They are living in Lenno, but we have known them for many years through the Brentano. The grandparents live below us so we see a lot of them later in the week.

The pool is inviting and we all spend the afternoon down there, enjoying the sun and the water. George and Indigo spend time with Peter. He and his brothers later take them off to play tennis and football. George is very happy and wears the biggest grins that she can fit onto her face, her eyes screwed up with delight and her hair standing erect with gel and sometimes her right eyebrow raised quizzically. Indigo's laugh is very loud and distinctive and I just love to hear it.

In the evening Jan and I walk to the Darsena at Tremezzo while the others drive. Up on the first floor we have some typical fish risotto made with local perch. None of us are hungry for anything else. We take a *passegiata* along the front and watch the lights across in Bellagio sparkle in the water. Under the porticos we treat the children to ice cream.

Day 113
Mileage 7563
Wednesday 14th August 2002
On Lago di Como

Indigo wakes us up when she crawls into our bed this morning. She goes downstairs and wakes up Jan as well. We don't know how long the good weather is going to last so we decide that today is a good day to spend on the lake. We have learnt from past experience that it best to drive to Caddenabia where the car ferries run frequently all day rather than walk to Tremezzo and rely solely on the passenger ferries.

There is a ferry waiting when we are parking. I thought we would miss it so I take my time buying tickets, but Eliza and the others have run ahead and are holding the ferry up waiting for me. A quick dash and a *mille grazcie* to the ferryman and we are off. I always love the way the landscape drops away as the ferry pulls out into the centre of the lake. Cadenabbia comes into view, and then the Villa Carlotta. The San Martino church hangs majestically on the rockface half way up the mountain. The northern part of the lake comes into view with the true foothills of the alps on the horizon. All too quickly, the boat is nearing Bellagio with its clutch of lakefront hotels rearing upwards. The boatman nonchalantly tosses the rope around the moorings and we are docked. Cars come off first and then the passengers. I study the opposite shore and the grey barren strata of rock that slashes Mount Crocione and Griante.

Bellagio is known as the jewel of the lake and for me is the prime tourist trap in the area. This is the peak week of the season so it is busy, but nowhere near as busy as any coastal resort or Venezia. We are horrified at the latest piece of tourist buffoonery as a train drives past pulling three carriages. It is a complete fraud, as there are no rails and the train is electrically operated, but it is disguised to look like what the Italians imagine a steam train from the wild west would look like complete with funnel and whistle. The driver looks exceedingly bored and I really cannot understand why anyone would want to ride in this.

From the car ferry dock we walk north to the passenger ferry area where there are some cafés and we have croissants, drinks and a *mataloc* cake – this is a speciality of the area and is a bit like a small individual light Christmas cake. This is all very civilised. There are lots of English, German and Dutch voices around. I buy an English newspaper. It is full of news of floods in Europe with today's focus on Prague.

A long stone stairway leads to the upper road. Just looking in the windows is an entertainment: expensive silk ties and scarves, alligator skin style handbags, maps, postcards and newspapers, ceramic plates and chicken jugs, wooden toys and Pinocchios of all sizes but always dressed in red, prints of watercolours of the lake and marquetry pictures. At the top of the stairs is an olive wood shop full of expensive pieces. There are jewellery and glassware shops already selling expensive hand blown baubles for Christmas trees. And yes, there are some *maceleria*, *alimentari*, *otofruta* and *tabacchi* shops for the inhabitants.

We stroll away from the crowds and down to the point. Here you get a grand view of the northern part of the lake and the western leg down to the Lenno peninsular, but only a partial view of the eastern leg. The small harbour looks as if it has been refurbished and Indigo makes a dash for the very end of the wall. Here there are no guard rails but she is quite sensible. There are people sunbathing here including a potential winner of the glamorous grandma competition and I bet they get really fed up with people walking over them just to get to the end. Even today, this place is empty and exudes tranquillity.

It is time to go to our next point of call and we head off to the ferry point to catch the boat to Varenna. The boat travels across the lake to Menaggio on the western side before traversing back across to Varenna on the eastern side. This is the real centre of the lake and the view down each limb is perfect.

Varenna is one of the most unspoilt towns on the lake and it retains a lot of its original character. The promenade along the coast from the ferry point clings to the rock face. The stairways up are steep and are good for the legs. The children want pasta, but the cafés by the harbour either sell pre-prepared pasta or none at all so we climb up to the town square and sit at an outside table. When the waitress realises we want to eat we are invited to the garden at the back. This is much more delightful. Indigo finds out that they make pizzas here and insists on watching them being made. The pizza ovens are wood fired and making them is hot work.

Varenna has two wonderful gardens and we went off to see the Monasteri. I had forgotten how desperately beautiful the gardens were with their statuary, follies, tall pointed Cyprus trees and simply breathtaking views of the lake. The colours of the flowers are today very vivid. The variety of greens that can be seen always astounds me. Every time we visit the lake my love for it grows stronger. I have never felt tired or bored with its beauty and magnificence.

There is a cosmology conference taking place in the Monasteri and judging by the posted programme its scope covers everything from photons to neutron stars with cosmologists from all around the globe. I have always had an amateur interest in astronomy and my second choice of university was to study astronomy at Edinburgh. I often thought about how different my life would have been. Here was a glimpse of what might have been. Coincidentally, the newspaper reports that it is also the twenty-fifth anniversary of the Voyager spacecraft.

Somewhere near here is the *fiumelatte*, the shortest river in the world. I have never found it, but it is supposed to run milky white at certain times of the year. We would have to wait for another year to find it.

As the day progresses the haze over the lake increases. The Lenno peninsular starts to fade and the mountains behind it almost thin out into nothingness. The ferry takes us back to Cadennabia and we drive home stopping at the Tre Archi for ice creams.

The children are tired and we get them to bed quite early. George is soon asleep, but Indigo is suffering from the no-sleep blues and keeps coming downstairs to see what we are up to and just to be cheeky. Eventually she manages to talk herself to sleep, apparently stopping in mid-sentence.

I'm tired too and go to bed leaving Eliza and Jan to talk until the early morning.

Day 114
Mileage 7572
Thursday 15th August 2002
Ferragosto

The sun seemed to burn my eyes it was so very bright this morning. Jan and Eliza were not stirring so I went off down to the shops to buy supplies. The car park, roundabout and shops at the bottom of the hill are little islands of Italian chaos at any time of the day, but first thing this the morning they are more chaotic than usual.

Today is *ferragosto* – the principal Italian bank holiday of the summer and marks the climax of the season. It is the day when Mary was told who she was carrying by the archangel Gabrial.

I do not normally drive just to buy some small items, but nine litres of water is pretty heavy on its own. This morning a member of the Cabinieri was there to help direct traffic and thus slow everything down. In his crisp uniform and wearing a smile, a cap and designer sunglasses, he was waving his little red paddle, telling drivers where they couldn't go and when they weren't allowed to. The car park was full and cars were just parked wherever – blocking those who wanted from getting out. Although it was chaos, everyone seemed remarkably placid about this and happily waited until it sorted itself out. No one hooted, nobody swore (out loud anyway), no one gesticulated and everyone was calm. The lake side road is well known for the sudden build up of traffic either at busy times or simply when wide vehicles or inexperienced (lake side) drivers have problems passing each other on the narrow roads. I have never seen an Italian driver get angry at this chaos and I expect it is just part of the natural way of life here. They all seem to take the delays in a very stoical fashion.

In the shop, the queue at the meat and cheese counter was also quickly building up. The woman at the front was ordering enough food for the whole village with a half kilo of this and half kilo of that. She was also talking with great speed. A couple of metres away was another woman who looked like her daughter who was busy interlacing words into her mother's speech. Her mother was standing still, but the daughter held her thumb and first two fingers together and her arm was rapidly moving at the elbow seemingly pulling the words out of her mouth like some conjuring trick. "Ooh and half a kilo of this and half a kilo of that" said the mother. I could not understand a single word of the conversation between mother and daughter nor from their body language or the tone of their voices could I tell if this was a very public stand up row or simply a very loud conversation about the day's preparations. Neither looked agitated, but both continued to rant vociferously and without the slightest pause until their business was done. Eventually, they moved away from the counter, amid lots of smiles, "*Ciao*"s and "*Aguri*"s. The queue and the couple behind the counter all looked around and seemed to give a collective sigh of relief. After the slightest pause normal conversation and service resumed.

Both Eliza and Jan were suffering the consequences of too much red wine and too little sleep. Although consciousness prevailed, their eyes had that opaque sheen which read, "do not disturb" and "keep the noise down". I evacuated the children to the poolside and spent the morning playing with them. The Belgium boys enjoyed the children's company as they got fed up with each other's. George is at the age where she is really beginning to enjoy board games and has the mental stamina to think beyond the immediate roll of the dice and to develop strategies.

We play Tabula – an old variation of backgammon where both players go round the board the same way, and Othello.

At lunchtime Jan has revived, but Eliza elects to stay in bed.

In the afternoon we are back at the poolside again.

George and Indigo are with the Belgiums for most of the afternoon, in the tennis court and down in the fields. They are enjoying having a little piece of freedom away from us.

There are fireworks tonight at Lenno and as the evening darkens we prepare to walk there. Eliza is not coming, but we are going en masse with the Belgium family. I take the pushchair for Indigo who is insisting on wearing some dark glasses which immediately become known as moonglasses. We walk up along the road to the church and I marvel as ever at the view. The lights are coming out all along the lakeside. Down slopes and up stairs we carry the pushchair. At the market square there is a large crush. Hundreds of people are sat down on rows of benches, eating and drinking. The kitchen is turning out large quantities of grilled meat and polenta. There is a dance floor set up and music playing. The art of ballroom dancing under the moonlight lives on. Couples whirl together to the rhythm of foxtrots, rumbas, tangos and waltzes.

We find the bar and get drinks all round. This is a money-free bar, but it is not free drinks. You have to pay for your drinks (or food) at one counter where you are given tickets. These tickets you can then exchange for the real thing at the bar itself.

We have to weave our way slowly down to the front past the dance floor. Tonight is perfect for fireworks as it is clear and there is no wind. Almost all the voices are Italian. It is almost as though we were intruding on a private party. The atmosphere is friendly and I think that most of the Italian adults have been grazing and sipping drinks all day long. The whole front is full and we are lucky to find a spot where we can see. There are boats in the bay crowding round for a better view.

We have to wait until about 10:30 and Indigo has now fallen asleep. The display starts with a couple of loud bangs. I try and wake Indigo up, but she seems happy to carry on sleeping. After a few moments she does come round and sits up eagerly. The fireworks are good. A lot of effort has been put into to the choreography of the display and it focuses nicely on different styles of fireworks. One effect that is stunning is their golden rain. Here, not only have they used rockets to allow rain to stream down from the sky, but also they are launching golden rain directly from the water. The proportion of the sky covered is awesome. Individual tableaus are applauded by the crowd.

The rockets are loud and the noise echoes off the surrounding mountains. The climax pitches a rich tapestry of colours and incessant booms into the sky. Then there is a sudden quiet, a round of applause and cheers, the music from the band starts again and everyone carries on with the party. We go off for ice-cream, surprised that the queue is not too long. I take the girls to the toilet, where the queue is not too bad. One man is trying to pick up the women in the queue by suggesting that they share the toilet to speed up the queue. I'm not sure if he meant with each other or with him, but neither go down well as pick up lines.

The children are really enjoying the atmosphere but it is soon time to walk back up the hill and home.

Day 115
Mileage 7573
Friday 16th August 2002
A Brush With The Pigs

The mountains across the lake have settled under haze today even though it is clear and sunny.

Eliza is still not feeling well and now she suspects that a bug has got the better of her. We decide to take Jan up to the refuge above Pigra to see a different side of lake life and set off leaving Eliza in peace. The drive along the lake is a complete contrast to last Sunday in the rain. As we turn off the lake at Argegno, the road rapidly rises through a series of bends, the lake drops away and our view expands. Again there is a lot of development work going on here with new houses and apartments advertised for sale everywhere. At San Fidele we take the road off to Pigra. The white lines disappear from the middle of the road as it narrows. I love this drive. Although it is narrow I have never found it dangerous. The hill side is mostly wooded so the road goes through small villages and dabbled woodlands. Occasionally, you can catch a glimpse of the lake now looking magnificent in its smooth silkiness occasionally rent with the white wake of the *alifasco*. At Pigra there are a clump of houses holding onto the very cliff face. The road up to the refuge bears off and now becomes a single track as it winds its way behind the houses and into the mountain park. The views from these houses are staggeringly beautiful, but I do not think I could live with the isolation.

It is five kms up to the refuge. We meet no traffic coming down, but do see some nuns in white habits. The track carries on now entirely in woodland with a vertical drop on our right and the mountain on our left. I am reassured by the presence of new crash barriers since last year. And then suddenly we see a parked car and we are signalled to stop. In front of the car is a pick up truck trying to manoeuvre in front of the parked car. I wonder how long they have waited to be rescued and whether the pick up driver has ever been up this road before. With a few more skilful manoeuvres, he manages to get the car off the road. I've been worried about how he will stop the car rolling back down on us, but it is well secured.

By now there are some cars wanting to come down the track. The cars coming down pull so far over that they are half hidden by the rocks. The pick up truck goes on to the verge and goes forward gingerly. Suddenly he is past and free.

We come above the tree line as we approach the first refuge and decide to drive on. It is distinctly cooler up here and we see a small herd of cows bathing in the little lakes. The next stop is the Buffallo Ranch where we park. Indigo is too tired to walk and takes to her pushchair as we stroll on further up the mountain. A group of cows lazily watch us walk past, their bells rattling with different tones as they sit and stand flicking their tails and twitching their ears. The footpath signs give walking times and not distances and indicate that the mountain path is 5hr 40 mins to Grandola ed Uniti up above Menaggio. George doesn't want to go any further so we turn around and leave Jan to go on for a while. She will meet us back at the refuge.

We sit and wait at the refuge. Other groups of people are happily tucking into plates of *proscuttio* and *salami*, but we decide to wait for Jan. She is not gone that long and says that she got a view of Lago di Lugano on the other side of the mountain. We try to attract the attention of the waitress. When this does not work we go and sit at a table that is laid. This catches her attention alright. She asks if we have reserved and I say no. This table is reserved. We ask if we can eat, not if we have not reserved. We ask if we can have a drink, not if we have not reserved. Not even water, not even water. It is not worth arguing and now sour grapes has set in as all the food begins to look quite unappetising. We decide to go back to the first refuge and hope we are not too late for lunch.

There we are made most welcome, and even though it is late, there is plenty for us to eat and drink. I think we are the only non-Italians here. George suffers from not liking anything whereas Indigo tucks into spare ribs ravenously. Jan enjoys her *polentia ucia*, but I stick to some *maiale* and, of course, water and wine.

Much refreshed, we walk out along the ridge to get a view of the lake. It is very stony and the ground is covered with a maze of cowpats. Down below us we can see Pigra and buried in the haze is the lake. Up here is a very different country from the lake level. It is still wild and virtually uninhabited.

We were visited by some wild – yet friendly – pigs. They were much amused by our Galaxy and after it had been inspected by them, just like some Italian youths admiring it, the pigs decided to brush themselves. Our car was now a grey dusty mess, but unscratched. The pigs went away snorting with contentment.

Day 116
Mileage 7608
Saturday 17th August 2002
Jan Leaves

Jan goes home today. Eliza is still in her sick-bed and now we definitely think that it is not a hangover. She is feeling queasy, nothing too serious, but enough to think twice about moving around.

Poolside is busy today. Even so only about a third of the flats are occupied. The sun is hot and Jan and I sit and read. Sometimes I'm in the pool with the children. It is traditional for Indigo to push me in, but she is not strong enough to do so if I resist, so this becomes a prolonged game. When I go, she lets out a roaring laugh.

The Belgium boys and George seem to spend most of the time on the diving board trying out twists and jumps so as to make as much noise and the biggest splashes possible. Francesco – looking very pale but with a good sized baby belly – is taken for a swim by Rafaele and absolutely loves it. His parents and grandparents all are doting on him.

I leave the children in Eliza's care: she is almost better now, and take Jan off to the airport. Today's drive is a real pleasure in the sun and light. Jan watches the lake disappears. Whether she will be back I don't know. The traffic is quite intense going north into Switzerland. No queues anywhere, and so we managed to drive straight in to the airport. I took Jan inside saw her safely checked in then left to go back to the Brentano.

The pool side had thinned out a piece by the time I got there and we stayed until the sun had dipped below the mountain round the back of the palace. Nobody believed me when I said so but within ten minutes it was raining, and then quite heavily. The rain looked white and at first we thought it was snow or hail, but it was just very large drops of rain. We just stood on the balcony and stared. Somehow, watching the rain here is interesting and a treat – unlike back in England. The atmosphere freshens and the scent of the trees and flowers intensify. The noise can be quite dramatic too, but today there was neither lightning nor thunder.

Day 117
Mileage 7713
Sunday 18ᵗʰ August 2002
Parco Pubblico

All quiet outside this morning after last night's storm. The only problem was that the swimming pool had gone green. Although it is hot, sitting by the pool today will be no fun. We arrange with the Belgiums to take a picnic and go to the public park in Tremezzo. Here there is lots of sun and shade and access to swimming in the lake.

Although this is the peak weekend in the season, the park is not too crowded and we spread ourselves out over quite a large area – partly in sun and partly in shade. The Belgium boys and our children are desperate to go in the lake and I accompany them. There are two sets of steps down to the lake one of which leads to a small sandy beach and we all go down here.

George and Indigo have brought their fishing nets with some expectation of catching something. The lake level is down from last year so this gives us more beach, but still only a couple of metres. Here we can walk into the water which deepens quite rapidly. We stand around knee deep waiting, but of course the fish are far quicker than we are. If you stand still long enough, the smaller fish do come up to your feet and some nibbled away at my toes. It tickled.

George takes the Belgiums around to the other steps and shows them the wall where all the Italian children jump and dive from. Its at least three metres high but Koons is soon diving from this height much to the annoyance and fear of Mie anticipating disaster. I don't blame her one bit – this looks too dangerous to me. Koons however is confident and does not hurt himself. He has set a precedence for the rest of the day.

Meanwhile up on shore us adults relax, play cards and Othello and avoid worry about our children. Really they are all well behaved, but we are too conditioned as parents.

The fountain in the centre of the park, with its coy naked lady and two cherubs squirting at her, contains some large fish and its yellow and pink water lilies are in flower. Indigo is eyeing up the fish with her net and Peter is encouraging her. Fishing in the lake is one thing but the fountain is just not right.

In the middle of the afternoon a boat race takes place – the 5th Regatta of Mezzegra. Some traditional fishing boats with wooden hoops to hold canvas covers overnight are lined up. There are two rowers in each boat and they stand facing forward with a pair of oars each. We are at the starting line. The finishing line is somewhere near the harbour in Mezzegra. The starter has to make sure the boats all line up before he sets them off. He keeps guiding some backwards and some forwards as it is evidently tricky to keep them all still. Then they are off with a great shout of "Via!" The four boats row off into the distance and the sun. From where we are it is very difficult to tell who is winning. There are more motor boats following. There are two races.

The starting line is marked with a large red inflatable buoy about

200m out. Naturally George and the Belgium boys swim out to it. It's the farthest George has swam out into the lake and it makes her realise just how wide it is.

Indigo is lonesome when they have all swam out so I take for a swim in her pink rubber ring. She too wants to go out there, but although I could swim it I feel very nervous if any thing happened to Indigo's ring so I insist we stay close to shore. We swim around the steps and beyond the diving wall. Further around there is an avenue of trees whose roots are in the water. Their trunks are swollen at their bases as if compensating for the lack of earth. They are still very high going up about fifteen metres and thier foliage dominates that end of the park. We land here and no one else is around. Indigo calls this her secret port. There is no sand only stones and it is a very tranquil sunny spot. She sorts out stones and asks me whether I find them interesting.

Up above Indigo's secret dock is a snack bar. The adults decide to have some refreshments. I love the view of the lake and mountains from here. Sitting in the sunshine is sheer bliss. We have some beer, coffee and *salatini*. We chat about lifestyles and whether we could live in Italy and how we could earn money, but come to no conclusion except that it would be good to spend more time here and less time in the grey of England and Belgium.

Day 118
Mileage 7715
Monday 19th August 2002
Menaggio

This morning the pool has again turned green. There is obviously something strange going on for in the all the years we have been coming to the Brentano only once before has the pool been green. This happened when the condominium had run out of money.

We stayed in the apartment and played games and cards with the children most of the morning. Afterwards, the children found the Belgiums and teamed up with them for games. Nobody is by the pool. All the Italians have disappeared, they have either gone away to the sea-side or gone home.

In the afternoon we went down to the bar Cicolo, down in the harbour. This bar was done up last season, but now has lost all its character. There is no ice cream for the children so they play on the children's roundabout as I act as engine: both clockwise and anti-clockwise. The Tre Archi has our custom again for ice creams.

Later we head off north on the lake road in search of a different restaurant. We have seen one we have never been to before and decide to stop and have a look. Eliza goes to have a look at the menu and decides that it is too posh with the children. On we go to Menaggio with trepidation, we have yet to find anywhere decent to eat in Menaggio but we do keep on trying. The restaurants on the front are all attached to hotels. We have been told there is a good pizza restaurant around the back which we have never found and start to hunt for it. We find one, but doubt if it is the right one. Nevertheless, we go in only to find that the waiting time is too long for us tonight. We end up going to a hotel restaurant. The menu is very bland and short. We should have been warned. The service is slow, the food is dull and cold. George's food was ordered plain without anything. It doesn't arrive, we have to chase it up and when it does come it is covered in flour and breadcrumbs. George's face looks like she is sucking a mouldy lemon. It goes back and the waitress protests that you cannot have *scalopine* with nothing on it, it is impossible. We have all lost our appetites by now and just wait for a new version of George's *scalopine* to arrive. Nothing happens. We ask for the bill and pay. They have not included the original *scalopine* on the bill.

Menaggio continues to be our bug bear. This is where the bogey men of restaurants are all established. Menaggio is often one of the first ports of call for visitors and it is here that the first impressions of the lake are formed. Here is the reason why the guidebooks always seem to give Lake Como a bad press, but at least there is no tourist train as yet.

In the centre of the town is a carousel roundabout. There are no children around, but Indigo still wants a go. She looks very happy going around in majestic silence waving at her subjects (us) as she goes.

The night sky is streaked with clouds and a veiled almost full moon appears. Above the moon on the other side of the sky is the illuminated San Martino church seemingly hanging there in its own majestic piety. The moon drifts free of the clouds entangling it and shines strongly. The two heavenly bodies are about the same size and it feels very strange to appear to have something above the moon.

The ice cream parlour on the main square is full of happy smiling people. The mini-golf course up by the campsite is surprisingly busy. The main promenade is nearly empty and the town already has a faded end-of-season feeling about it.

As we are sitting out on the balcony later there is more thunder and lightning, but tonight there is no rain. George comes down as the thunder is scaring her. This time Indigo sleeps peacefully through it all.

Day 119
Mileage 7724
Tuesday 20th August 2002
Lenno (twice)

The sun shines as thinly as the moon last night. It is overcast and cool and the sounds of distant rolling thunder echo around the mountains. The lake lies tranquil with mist entwined in the lower hills. Soon it begins to burn off and the day turns hot, humid and sweaty. No one wants to get up this morning, but eventually everyone surfaces. The pool looks much better this morning but there are hazard strips around it. We later find out that it is too acidic. Extra chemicals have been added after the pool turned green, but these have over compensated.

No one wants to go to Lenno market again so I set off walking on my own. The market is again busy, but today I buy bread first. More chicken, salami, cheese, fruit and vegetables. It starts to drip and then to rain slightly, but people scatter for shelter. I make my way back up the hill and along the back road to Pola and the church. I am wet, but it is a horrible mix of sweat and rain. The sun is still out, but neither the sun nor the rain are strong enough to produce a rainbow.

The lakes, and especially Lago di Como, all seem to have a microclimate where the weather is more unpredictable than most places on the continent. In fact this area seems more like England, where we have weather and not climate. This year, however, the weather here is less reliable than usual. Still, there is an underlying seasonal climate that is milder in the winter and hotter in the summer than England.

I dry off and show my wares, but apathy has taken hold. The children want to do painting and are very good at keeping the mess to a minimum. We get out the body boggle for them to play with, and have much laughter at their attempts to twist around spelling words without falling over. Outside the rain has stopped and Indigo spies Peter by the pool and wants to go and see him. We all go down as we are a bit stir crazy and take the body boggle with us. The Belgium boys soon get the hang of this and everyone joins in.

Eliza and I set to work to make some more *limoncello* before getting ready for dinner. Skinning the zest of the lemons does not take long. We leave it to soak in the wardrobe upstairs and I hope we don't forget about it.

Mei and Hans ask us to join then for dinner at the Plinio in Lenno tonight and we agree. They have booked a table for five for them. There is an outdoor cinema in Lenno main square tonight so there is likely to be crowds and nowhere to park. We go down early to make sure we can get a table, but there is no cinema: the threatening weather has cancelled it. We get a table for four outside under the shelter with a grand view across the lake to Bellagio. It is dark early tonight as the weather again threatens with thunder and wind, but no rain yet. We have to struggle to hold the tablecloths down but then calm arrives. Mei, Hans and family arrive and we put all the children together on one table and have an adult table to ourselves. It is Mei and Hans twentieth wedding anniversary. I asked whether they had enjoyed their day twenty years ago and whether it was the right decision. Mei was emphatic that it was definitely the right decision. Sometimes they wondered about what they had started when they had three boys. We wondered the same about our children. All our lives would be so different without them. Certainly less stressful and we would all be richer, but our lives would be comparatively empty without them.

The youngsters get restless and wander off into the gloom to get ice cream from down the road. Indigo insists on carrying her umbrella despite the fact that it is no longer raining.

When we get back all the youngsters want to watch a DVD, so we set one up for them while we go to the Belgiums' flat for more drinks and to taste our *limoncello*. The evening is very late before everyone settles into bed.

Day 120
Mileage 7726
Wednesday 21st August 2002
At Rest

The sun was out today, but the pool was still not right. George and Indigo spent most of the day with the Belgium boys. Playing around the pool, but not in it, playing football and tennis.

The Belgiums were going home tomorrow and we would be sad to see them go.

The day slipped away quietly. Eliza spent time putting the flat in order. I tried to help, but I only seem to get in the way.

The Belgiums and us go off to have our last supper together at the Balognet. We enjoy each other's company and hoped to see each other again next year.

Day 121
Mileage 7726
Thursday 22nd August 2002
Vilia at Chiavenna

The sunshine is back and the swimming pool is better, but today, we're off to see Vilia at Chiavenna. Vilia used to work with Eliza's mum in London doing market research and we first met her one year when Eliza's mum came out to stay in the flat. Vilia has been very good to us over the years and helpful in sorting out Italian administrative problems for us. We had hoped that Vilia would spend some time with us during our travels in the south and particularly in Sicilia, but it was not to be. Vilia's mother has had cancer and has suffered several relapses over the past eighteen months. Only now is Vilia's mother better enough to be at home, but she is housebound. Vilia has had to spend almost every day with her mum and has not been able to get away.

Trying to get everyone out of the house this morning is tiresome, but we manage it and we pick up some croissants and some juice to eat as we go. The variety of juices that the Italians have put the English to shame. George loves her pear juice, but is very conservative and does not like to try anything else. I pick up some mango and apricot to try and Indigo simply adores it. The croissants are straight out of the oven this morning – we are late and this must be a second batch – and need to be left to cool down.

The lake road is quiet today and we get the feeling that it is becoming very end-of-seasonish. The Brentano is empty. Tremezzo, Cadennabia and Menaggio are beginning to take on the appearance of empty towns. As the Italians have mostly now fled there are plenty of places to park and the percentage of German, Dutch and English number plates have increased. I do not feel this is a bad thing as we feel more comfortable with the extra space, but it is quite surprising that the turn has been so sudden and dramatic this year.

North of Menaggio, the road drifts into a series of tunnels taking the pressure of the small coastal villages. Some of these tunnels are only partially complete and are in the same state of construction as they were five years ago. In one sense these tunnels are a shame as you can no longer get the feel of every town along the coast, but these by-passed towns then wrest their own privacy, quietness and sense of solitude back from the car.

For the houses alongside the main road, life must be pretty noisy and harrowing. Buses and lorries have difficulty passing each other. Today we see a new challenge that we have not seen before: a double truck. We pass on a very narrow point and have to reverse into someone's drive to let it through. The driver looks very nervous and ashen faced, but this cannot be a one-off as it is a Chiarella water lorry.

Chiarella is the local mineral water from up the Menaggio Valley. The bottles carry a label with a glorious picture from up in the mountains of the two southern legs of the lake with Bellagio – the jewel right in the middle. They have altered the label from time to time in the past, but this view is a classic. The still mineral water is always labelled red, the sparkling mineral water is always labelled blue. Occasionally when we have ordered half a litre of still (*naturale*) and half a litre of sparkling (*frizzante*) we have been given a green variety which is "both sparkling and still". I have never quite got my head around the green bottles. All I can assume is that it is naturally fizzy. To avoid any such problems Eliza now always asks for *naturalle senza gas*. We drove up the mountain once and found the bottling plant itself. Amazingly enough the view in the picture was genuinely the view from the gates. The drive was pretty stiff, but how on earth they managed to get double truck up and down there and along the lakes amazes me. I have much admiration for these types of drivers.

Once we get past the Chiarella lorry we fall behind another queue going our way. This time we are sitting behind a C10 bus. No wonder the Chiarella lorry driver looked anxious, even we find it hard to pass a bus at this point in the lake road!

At the high lake in the north, the bottom of the valley spreads much wider to give a plain. Then as the lake ends, suddenly the mountains appear with avengeance and squeeze the valley from both sides. Chiavenna lies in the confluence of two valleys, one leading up to the Spulgen pass and the other heading off towards San Moritz.

Vilia's apartment is a couple of kilometres out of the town centre on the San Moritz road. Much time is spent in general greetings with "*Ciao*"s and hugs and kisses and we talk about her life and her mother. We drive up to the mountains towards the Swiss border for lunch and find a very nice spot to eat. On the way there are some very long and stunning waterfalls in full gush from the recent rains. At the restaurant, there are quite a number of old privately owned *crottos* where Italian families store wine and cheese. Some of these *crottos* are very small and have low roofs. The old stonework and often the roof tiles have a good covering of moss.

The restaurant does typical local mountain dishes with grilled meats and *polenta* being the main offering. They also do a form of pasta called *pizzocherri*, but here this is *pizzocheri de Chiavenna* which has onions, cheese and potatoes in the dish. And of course, dishes of *porcini*.

There is a children's playground and George and Indigo can go and let off steam. George and I play table football and then we play several ends of boule before George gets tired of the game. She finds some boys to play football with and is much happier playing real football rather than table football. Indigo finds some girls and starts talking to them. We all enjoy this place and manage to have some adult time together.

Vilia has to go off and see her mother. She has employed a Ukrainian woman to help look after her, but Vilia has to relieve her. We will try and meet up again next week and go for a trip up to San Moritz. Our time together is over far too quickly, we drop her back home and go to Chiavenna town itself for a stroll and maybe some ice cream.

I like the town very much. Its historical centre is quite small, but it feels like a real town with few tourists, the roads are not perfect, the cobbled streets have tarmaced areas in them where they have been replaced. The railway looks like the very end of the line as the weeds spring up between the rusty rails and through the gaps between sleepers. People are out for their late afternoon stroll and the shops and cafés look busy. The old bridge across the river gives us a good view of the great rocks below and water cascading down the mountain. Just next to the bridge is a wonderful gelateria which used to be run by a friend of Vilia. It seems that most of Chiavenna is a friend or an acquaintance of Vilia's.

On the way down we digress and go off in search of an Iperal hypermarket which is supposed to sell furniture, not that we need any now, nor because we intend to buy any now, but just to see what is available and for ideas. We follow the signs to Sondrio, but this takes us along a white, but pretty road unfortunately by-passing the road where the hypermarket is. By the time we have realised our mistake and turned back we are caught in the middle of the Sondrio rush hour with continuous, but moving queues of traffic. The hypermarket was a complete let down, with very little furniture and most of that of such cheap quality.

Day 122
Mileage 7827
Friday 23rd August 2002
Como

Now the clouds are back and we are fearful that the weather has well and truly broken. We get up early, picking up croissants again, but today although these are fresh they are not hot. We head off south to spend the day in Como. We are already thinking about going home and today we need to buy some shoes for Indigo and maybe some for George. The cloud coverage is low as we drive along and snickets of cloud drift around the hillside villages and sometimes even down to the lakeside niches.

George is planning who she is going to see when we get home. Indigo is excited by the prospect of going to school with her friends and wants to start as soon as she can.

We have a bank account that is set up solely for the purpose of paying direct debits for our electricity bills. The problem is we need to feed it money every year. So today is the day. In the centre of Como is Piazza Volta, named after Alexander Volta the scientist son of Como. Here we can park, but as usual there is a queue. So Eliza queues for the car park, while I queue in the bank. Quite a reasonably equitable division of labour.

We go off in search of shoes and boots for the children. The local department store has been taken over and refurbished, no longer Standa, but now Coin. We hunt out some bits and pieces for the flat, for presents and for home. The Duomo square looks as elegant as ever, but is looking sadly empty. We go to the Belli Deli which has some wonderful cakes and sweets in the window and buy some of their lifelike, if slightly garishly coloured, marzipan vegetables. Eventually we find some shoes for Indigo, and George is mightily pleased when we buy her some DMs.

We have lunch at a quiet hotel. The food was good, but the atmosphere was more like a funeral parlour. Three dour waitresses hung around dressed in black uniforms with starched white shirts. They did not raise any eyebrows at either George or Indigo's antics, but eventually one cracked a smile at Indigo. The restaurant had old photographs of Como with views of Piazza Cavour with trams and horse-drawn carriages and of the Piazza Duomo flooded under several feet of water full of boats and people amazed at finding themselves in this position.

Down at the water front in Como is the harbour where all the boats come and go. There is also a seaplane based here and you frequently see him flying up and down the lake. I believe that this is the last seaport for flying based in Europe and therefore probably the last seaplane based in Europe. It will be very sad day when the plane is no longer viable. Above Como on the eastern side there is a funicular railway to the top of the hill with a spectacular view over the area. One of the main town squares

Piazza Cavour stands next to the harbour. The whole centre of Como has been pedestrianised for many years, but this year in particular it at last seems to have become more formalised. Special paving has been laid and roads are properly blocked. Piazza Cavour itself has gained an array of extra flower-beds and looks good.

After we bribed the children with ice cream, we make our way back to Piazza Volta and head off home along the lower lake road. This is much thinner, more interesting and a lot slower road than the main lake road. The houses and town are cramped together and it feels altogether very claustrophobic for a tourist area. As we rejoin the higher road, more space appears. The sun is beginning to come back out and the lake views just raise my spirit.

Back home, we take advantage of the sun and go pool side.

Both George and Indigo had been going on about the Chinese restaurant at the bottom of the hill for some days now and now it was time for us to take them there. It feels very strange going into a Chinese restaurant in Italy. Although the food is much the same, the menu is definitely bent to the Italian palate with "spaghetti" instead of chow mein and sweet and sour ravioli. The children really wanted Peking duck with pancakes, but they were out of luck. They had their duck though, and lots of egg fried rice, so they were happy. Both Eliza and I begrudgingly enjoyed the meal, but I would not come back here out of choice.

Day 123
Mileage 7862
Saturday 24th August 2002
Last Saturday Night

I am much in demand in the pool and both George and Indigo use me as a climbing frame. George has climbed on my shoulders to jump and dive for many years, but now Indigo has discovered this trick. She's still a little apprehensive and has to hold my thumbs when she jumps. Next year there will be no stopping her. Although she has been swimming further and further all holiday she has never liked to swim whole widths, but this afternoon she swam one without me tricking her into doing one. Well done, Indigo. Normally she will happily swim to me in the middle of the pool, but sometimes I used to walk backwards after she has started to force her to swim further, but she really hated it when I did this so I had stopped.

As this is our last Saturday in Italy we go and have lunch at one of our favourite restaurants, the Fagurida. The restaurant itself is up in the hills above Tremezzo and you wouldn't come across it by accident. Although it is only just off the road the drive is quite narrow and awkward. By the small car park is the chicken run. There used to be rabbits here too, but not this year. The rooster struts around with confidence while the chickens all look hen pecked by each other. Over the chicken coop, a large kiwi vine grows with plenty of fruit hanging down. The front of the restaurant is decked out in flowers and looks at its best. Unfortunately we were too late to get an outside table with a lake view, but inside suits us nicely. The rustic furniture is still there and on the wall is a picture of the two men and one woman who were the founders some – I guess – twenty or thirty years ago. Here the English view of Italian cuisine does not exist. There is no pasta and no pizza, but there is an apology on the menu. The anti pastas are simply wonderful, with many varieties of cold meat, beans, onions, Russian salad, *nervetti* (brawn). Wine is served unpretentiously in clay mugs. The main dishes are all straight meat: either rabbit cooked slowly in garlic or rosemary, or very large steaks priced by the 100grams.

After a slow meal we drive down to Menaggio via the back route through the mountains. The view of the lake mysteriously disappears for a short while as we pass through a hidden valley. After a stroll and ice cream in Menaggio it is back to the flat and the pool for the children. Still later, Indigo and George help me add the water and sugar to our *limoncello*. All it takes now is stirring, draining and bottling. Somewhat nervously, but not as excitedly as the last batch, we taste and give it our seal of approval. We use a small bottle to give to Carmello and Franca at the Balognet.

Indigo and George start talking about wanting to be at home **now** and the fact that they can't wait any longer, and that they want to see their friends, and that they want to be at school.

We also are starting to think about coming home and all the practical things we need to do once we get home.

Day 124
Mileage 7872
Sunday 25th August 2002
Mount Bisbino

This morning we decide to drive up to the top of the mountain, not to Pigra, but closer to Como. The road up Mount Bisbino rises from Cernobbio up to about 1300m. Once we find the right road from Cernobbio the road up is narrow with loads of hair pin bends. We are early enough to avoid all the Italians driving up or down the mountain: today all the good Italians are either at church or visiting their families or some shrine or other. However, the road is full of cyclists. Not hundreds, but we pass at least a dozen going up and more coming down. Apart from us going uphill, the cyclists freewheeling at breathtaking speeds have other obstacles to avoid including potholes, children, dogs and cobbles. Some of the hairpins still have old mountain boulders as their surface and not tarmac, we have to take great care on these corners, but not as much as the cyclists.

The top of this mountain is pine wooded. The last kilometre or so has been properly tarmaced and is smooth, allowing the cyclist to concentrate on just the climb. There is a view point up top, but today we are in the clouds and can only see a small way. A great shame and disappointment as from here we should be able to see the alps over in Switzerland. There is also a refuge bar/restaurant at the top, but it looks very inhospitable unless you were actually seeking refuge.

Coming down is also tricky, but now we are faced with the post-church parade Italian family traffic on picnic duty. We pass at least two dozen cars coming up. Most are sensible and pull over in the passing places or wait dutifully for us to do the same, but there are a couple who feel that this is their road and will not try and use only half of it. This breed of Italian also have never discovered reverse and plough onwards regardless of the consequences. Still, we come through unscathed, though I am now suffering from "hairpin shoulder" and have stabbing pains in my right arm.

Down the mountain we head off towards Lenno in search of lunch. A lot of places are too posh or inappropriate for today and we end up at

Lenno for a Sunday pizza, spaghetti, large prawns and wine.

Today there are two more families at the pool, one French and another Belgium. George spends her time playing merry pranks and tries to get us to guess what animal she is imitating as she flings herself unceremoniously off the diving board. Indigo has taken to diving through a hoop that I hold at the side of the pool, plunging straight down. She is very excited and pleased with herself and laughs every time she surfaces, her great big grin showing off her teeth below a pair of black goggles and crowned with a blue and orange swim hat.

Eliza and I (but mostly Eliza) start to organise how we are going to pack up the Galaxy for the last leg home. Eliza is worried that the amount of stuff we have seems to have diminished, but we have been drinking some of our wine and other items seem to have compacted themselves more. I think it is down to Eliza becoming even more effective as a packer over the past few months.

The children are getting fractious again and rows ensue over baths and supper.

It starts raining and thundering again overnight.

Day 125
Mileage 7924
Monday 26th August 2002
Chi vidiamo

The rain continues to come down and you can hear the storm torrents running again. We speak to Vilia and decide that today is not a good day to travel up to Chiavenna and San Moritz. The weather feels very unseasonal but does remind us that today is a bank holiday Monday in the UK.

The children start talking about being at home again and we also realise that it would now be better to go home sooner rather than later. With some sadness we decided that we must pack today and travel tomorrow provided it was not gloriously sunny. Suddenly we were suffering from ground rush.

We spent the morning packing. It was not as bad as we thought it would be. We saw Franco, the caretaker, and his wife Lanita to arrange for cleaning and laundry and to ensure that they would have enough money for the refuse collection bill in September. Franco said we could park inside the condominium today as it was almost empty.

In the afternoon, the weather improved and I tried to persuade the children to go into the pool, but no one was interested.

We telephoned Pauline, who was living in our house, and left a message on the answerphone warning her that we were coming home early.

In reality, we had done remarkably well with the weather considering that we had missed storms in July in Tuscany and all the storms in northern Europe and the Alps. We had had some rain in Sicilia, Frienza, La Faula and some here. We had had a heatwave in June and July. And we certainly had missed a very poor summer in England.

In the evening we once again went to the Balognet and managed to eat outside for probably the last time this year. The children were lively and excited and full of expectation of going home. They knew the journey was long and tiresome for them but were fully reconciled to it. While Indigo was playing, she managed to pull half a brick off the top of a flowerbed onto her head ending up with gushing tears and a lump the size of a pigeon's egg for her trouble. Everyone was apologetic, but no real harm was done. We gave Carmello his bottle of homemade *limoncello*. He politely thanked us and put it to one side saying that he now only drank on holidays. They go away in the winter and travel south to Sicilia for some winter sun. they showed us some pictures of them swimming in a small outdoor hot thermal spring in Toscana surrounded by snow. Carmello told us that he used to be a cocktail waiter for ten years at the lido discotheque in Cadennabia and showed off his skills by preparing up a pair of daiquiris. Very nice indeed and totally unexpected.

All too soon it was time to go and we bade them farewell and that we would see them again next year. *Chi vidiamo prossimo anni!*

Journey's End
Tuesday   Day 126
Mileage 7929
27th August 2002
Out Of Italy

I was up early and made tea for Eliza. I brought the Galaxy up to the front door and packed the last of the bags. We woke the children and got them dressed. There was the usual scrum, stripping beds, emptying the fridge, sweeping the floor and disposing of rubbish. We had one more look at the view from the balcony. A thick layer of cloud wrapped the mountains, the sun was up and out, but looked a pale replica of its normal self. We shut the shutter and the doors, switched off the electrics and went.

We started driving at eight stopping at the baker's shop to pick up some croissants and rolls for the journey. We went alongside the lake to Argegno and then took the road up Val d'Intelvi. At the top we took the pass to the Swiss border. The sleepy Italian guards waved us through and we all shouted goodbye Italy as we drove through no man's land. The road here is very steep and windy even compared with all the other passes we have been across. Once past the boundary stone, the road becomes exceptionally narrow and is not recommended for the fainthearted and is impassable for buses, trucks and caravans. At the Swiss border we sop to buy a vignette for the motorway. I pay in Swiss francs and go back to the Galaxy, this has taken the border guard by surprise as he rushes back and asks for more money as he expected me to pay in Euros.

We slip off into Switzerland, down the road and onto the motorway near Campione d'Italia, a small enclave of Italy entirely surrounded by Switzerland. Everything is just so in Switzerland after chaotic Italy, the landscapes are perfect and even the grass looks like it has been cropped with nail clippers. The route up to the San Gottard tunnel is uneventful, but there is a queue for the tunnel. Last year there had been a minor fire in the tunnel near the southern end, but no one was hurt. Taking this into account and compounding it with the fire in the Mont Blanc tunnel two years ago, the whole method of passing through the tunnel has changed.

Previously the entrance to the tunnel was continuous unless the weight of traffic demanded that spacing was introduced into the traffic in which case traffic lights at the entrance were used. Lorries are now segregated off into their own queue and both cars and lorries let through in convoys. This seemed a big operation, with lots of police about. I hated to think how long we would have to queue when it was busy. As it was we were only queuing for about twenty minutes. Throughout the tunnel, all the exit points were more obviously marked and were never far apart. Extra signs were on the road encouraging people to space out while in the tunnel.

In the middle of the tunnel our phone rang. It was Pauline, she was upset that we had not given her much notice of our early return. She had been using our bedroom and that she had already made arrangements to move out on Friday morning and did not want to change them. I told her that we would be happy to stay in the spare room downstairs until then.

Out of the tunnel the weather was still grey and it remained that way for the rest of the day. The queue for the tunnel going south was much more extensive and went on for about three miles. Managing the flow through the tunnel had obviously become a major issue with the Swiss as there were new lane separators along this stretch to segregate the queues. It looked as though the number of lanes in any one direction could be easily changed according to the relative flow. Further along we have also been keeping an interested eye on some more major roadworks. They are building some extensive tunnels and it has seemed to be going on forever. This year some of the tunnels are now operative and we see a sign saying that the roadworks are planned from 1998 – 2004. So only a couple of more years to go then.

The Swiss-German border at Basel arrives soon enough. We drive along here for a short while before turning off to Mulhouse and France. Once in France I manage to take the wrong turning at a roundabout and find myself driving toward Basel again, but this time on the French side. Despite having driven this route back from Italy many times, there is always one point where an error or a lapse in concentration means I go wrong. One year I missed the turning for the M25 and ended up going into central London. I soon managed to turnabout at the next exit and head on up to Strasbourg, Metz and then Reims. Between Metz and Reims the rain comes at last in really heavy, but short and intermittent cloudbursts. Visibility varies down to fifty metres in the heaviest parts and we have to slow right down.

It is damp and miserable but we had decided to stop here rather than try and go all the way. We follow the signs to the Cathedral and the Tourist office. These seem to take us round the city twice in a spiral and then I lose the signs and have to start again. Eventually we find the office and they help book a hotel. We find an underground carpark almost right by the hotel, get our rooms and flop quietly for a while. The children are thirsty and near to eat. Both Eliza and I are all in a dither and cannot make our minds up as to where to eat. There are too many places for steak and chips or crepes or pizza, but we would like a reasonable French meal. These places look too expensive and do not serve anything that the children will like. We find one with a children's menu and settle for that. We are all quite tired and not really in the mood for relaxing over a nice meal. Once we start though our mood is lifted and we do unwind. Not perfect, but okay.

Day 127
Mileage 8424
Wednesday 28th August 2002
Home At Last

Grey light wakes me up. Outside, from our balcony, I can see that everywhere is grey. Grey pavements, grey buildings and grey skies. I think it is a very sad way to end our journey on such a grey day. It is still early and only a very few people are about, but gradually the town begins to waken up.

We get up and are ready to go quite soon. We skip breakfast here, check out and take our bags down to the Galaxy. George was not interested in going to a champagne cave, so I decide that I would like to go and see the Museum of Surrender where the Germans unconditionally signed their surrender at the end of the Second World War. It is a good twenty minute stroll from the hotel, but the grey sky holds the rain back.

The museum is in an unpretentious building. It was Eisenhower's HQ during the last year or so of the war. There was a brief synopsis of the allied advance from the D-day landings in June 1944 to the end of the war and photographs of some of the action. The German Air force, Navy and Army all surrendered unconditionally at 2:16am on May 7th 1945 in this very building. The announcement of the surrender was made in each of the allied capitals the following day at 15:00 hours. The table where they signed was still in place and each chair had the name of the person who sat in it marked. The war maps in the room were as they were in 1945. You could easily recall the daily activity that must have gone on here for those last remaining months.

In the photographs the Germans looked extremely exhausted and tired. Eisenhower had an enormous grin on his face. It must have been a very very emotional time.

The exhibition did not stop here, but finished with a picture of De Gaulle and Ardenhaur in 1962, working towards a Europe where Europeans would not fight another war. Despite all the rhetoric about the Common Market, the EEC, the EU and the Euro, this has been a very successful policy and it is one that our generation of western Europeans fail to realise.

I was moved by it all and it reminded me how lucky we were to be alive now, I was white, male, well educated and healthy. Unlike my parents' generation, I never had had to face war, pestilence, famine or death.

I could earn a very good living. I had a good life. I was happy, with a wonderful family. I had a beautiful home in Essex and another in Italy and I had managed to find the time to spend these last four months away from home with my family. I had a life full of all the riches that society could provide. I was surrounded by an amazingly good quality and variety of foods. I had an abundance of entertainment to choose from. I owned things that my parents could not even dream about.

I owed a large debt to all the people who gave their lives in the Second World War to give us this freedom. I owed a lot to my parents who brought me up and who were now sadly dead. I wondered what they would have made of this trip. The great stirring of peoples that Hitler induced also, in a perverse way, led to my very being. My mother was a Jew, born in Vienna, and her escape with her family to England was a small miracle. It was in London that my parents met by chance during the war.

From the museum we wandered back into the centre of Reims passed the Roman gate of Mars which was supposed to be the largest surviving Roman triumphal gate. A little bit of Italy here in the middle of France. We all had crepes for a late breakfast and early lunch. We bought a box of champagne and then we headed off for Calais.

Grey remained the natural order of the day until we were nearly at Calais. The sky lightened and the sun broke through at about the same time as we saw the sea.

The crossing was calm and clear. George and Indigo both watched Dover approach with joy. They were so pleased to be back in England.

As we came off the boat I became nervous as ever approaching British Customs. I always feel guilty going through Customs, even though I was totally innocent. I was just very worried that we were going to be searched and the Galaxy was going to be stripped. There was, of course, no need to worry, it was just my innate sense of paranoia.

The sun was shining in Dover, making the Kent countryside very welcoming. We had forgotten the congestion around the south east and the efforts being made to widen the motorways up to London. George wanted to know what congestion was and I said wait until we hit the M25. Timing could have been better and we got to the M25 at five o'clock. There was a queue for the Dartford tunnel. I told George that this was congestion. After the tunnel the queue coming southbound was something else. This was congestion. I was so very glad that I didn't have to do this every day. Luckily our way was relatively clear. The M11 was also clear until we approached J8 where roadworks were in progress upgrading the link to Standsted Airport.

George and Indigo finally recognised where we were and there was much excitement. We went through Stansted Mountfitchet, Ugley and turned into Rickling Green. We passed the green and we were at our house. Journey's end after 8690 miles, that's more than both our original estimates together. We were all in one piece and very glad to be here. Lindsey's car drove past on the road. I waved and two minutes later she drove up. Her children, Tom and Daniel spilled out and came to welcome us home.

Soon Lindsey's husband David turned up and we all celebrated our homecoming with a bottle of champagne.

George was so pleased to be with Tom that she went to spend the night at their house. "I love you very much, Mum and Dad" she said, "but I've seen enough of you right now."

We were all pleased to be home.

We round off the evening with a take-away curry from the Sonagow in Stansted. Our first meal back home just like our last meal before we started.

Epilogue

Back home the time away suddenly feels like nothing…

All we are left with are the memories and the experiences. But these are the things that count more than we possibly imagined. To have seen and done the things we did may not have been terribly adventurous or unique, but as a family they will always remain unique and will be with us all for the rest of our lives. If we had not gone then I know with absolute certainty that I would have always regretted letting the missed opportunity drain away like sand through my fingers.

As with all travellers, the question remains open as to when we will go again. Not if, but when. Alas, sadly, I cannot see this happening until our children pass out of secondary education. And the other question is where….

It may not be Travels in the Galaxy, but I promise it will be travels.

Dave Horth
1st November 2004

Travels In The Galaxy

Dave Horth